DAR AL-KALIMA
UNIVERSITY PRESS

Rooted in Palestine

Palestinian Christians and the Struggle for National Liberation 1917-2004

Xavier Abu Eid

First Edition

Rooted in Palestine
Palestinian Christians and the Struggle for National
Liberation 1917-2004

Author: Xavier Abu Eid

Copy right © 2022 Dar al-Kalima University Press
ISBN : 978-9950-376-49-6

Art direction : Dar al-Kalima University Press
Designer : Ingrid Anwar Khoury
Printing Press: Latin Patriarchate, Beit Jala

Book cover photo: Demonstration in Beit Sahour during the First Intifada – Copyrights WAFA.

Abu Eid, Xavier
Rooted in Palestine: Palestinian Christians and the Struggle for national Liberation 1917 – 2004 / Xavier Abu Eid Foreword by Feda Abdelhady
p.143 cm.
ISBN: 9789950376403
1. Christianity - Palestine - History   2. Christians - Palestine   3. Christians - Palestine - Political activity   4. Arab Christians - Palestine I. Title

BR 1110.E52 2022

w w w . d a r a l k a l i m a . e d u . p s

Contents

Acknowledgments

This book is the product of more than five years of research under a variety of circumstances and could not have been realised without the support of many people. In particular, I would like to mention those who took the time to read the book and provide valuable comments, including Alaa Tartir, Fatima Abdulkarim, Majdi Khaldi, Rania Zabaneh, Husam Zomlot, Dalia Qumsieh, Aboud Hamayel, Nadya Rashed, Ghassan Khatib, Amira Hass, Nasser Al Qudwa, Varsen Aghabekian, Meir Margalit, Dalal Iriqat, Nabil Shaath, Ines Abdelrazek, Jalal Abukhter, Feda Abdelhady, Asem Khalil, Nathan Thrall, Hunaida Ghanem, Jack Khoury, Kholoud Badawi, Yousef Taha, Johnny Mansour, Sami Abu Shehadeh, Afif Safieh, Ibrahim Khreisheh, Raphael Duizend, Rana Arrabi, Diego Khamis, Shireen Salti, Nidal Rafa, Jonathan Conlon, Noor Bimbashi, Bassim Khoury, Aoyfe Lyons, Husni Abdelwahed, Hassan Faraj, Christian Hodges, Enas Al-Muthaffar, Gabriel Abdallah, Tomasz Gryza and Miguel Moratinos. A special mention goes to Saeb Erekat, Suha Jarrar and Shireen Abu Akleh, may they rest in peace.

I am also grateful to Mahmoud Muna from the Educational Bookstore in Jerusalem and the personnel of Sharbain's Bookshop in Ramallah. Other friends deserving of mention for a variety of reasons include Issa Totah, Hanna Rabah, and the late Jamil Rabah, may he rest in peace.

If this book was inspired by any figure in Palestinian history it would be Patriarch Michael Sabbah who accepted to sit with me for hours. Claudette Habash was also an important source of information and inspiration. I am grateful to the following people for their willingness to share their experiences with me: Bishop Jamal Daibes (Khader); Bishop Atallah Hanna, Rev. Dr Munther Isaac; Fr. Adeeb Zumot; Rev. Fadi Diab; Rev. Kamal Farah; Fr. Rifa'at Bader; Fr. Talaat Awwad; Soeur Frida Totah; Fr. Hanna Salem; Fr. Remon Haddad; Soeur Mary Yousef; Soeur Lora Salibi, Fr. Abdallah Julious; and Fr. Akhtam Hijazeen. I would like to add a special note for two priests who have left this world but who are part of this book: Fr. Peter Madros and Fr. Faysal Hijazeen.

I am grateful to Rev. Dr. Mitri Raheb and the board of Diyar for their confidence in immediately agreeing to publish this work.

My uncle Nakhleh and his wife Ilham were particularly helpful in describing the details of their lives in Palestine between 1948 and the first years of after 1967. Ilham's passion and exceptional memory were invaluable. Likewise, I would like to thank my dear friends Awad Khader (Abu George), Henry Khoury, and Joe Moghannam for their patience and support.

I would like to thank my grandfather Judeh who was unable to return to Palestine and left this world 12,000 kilometres away from our homeland. I like to believe that this book would have made him proud of his spoiled grandson. This sentiment is extended to my grandmother Nameh, who also contributed to indulging me, and acted as a master of Palestinian public diplomacy in introducing our culture to my classmates. May the memories of my grandparents be blessed.

Foreword

From the very start of reading *"Rooted in Palestine: Palestinian Christians and the Struggle for National Liberation 1917-2004"*, I was reminded of an adage I have consistently shared with all junior diplomats and students I have trained: not a day does not go by that I don't learn something new, every day brings with it an opportunity to read, to engage, to expand my understanding of issues concerning not only Palestine and the Middle East, but the world as a whole.

In this way, I have tried to encourage them to pursue life-long learning as a service to themselves and to the noble, just cause of Palestine we are privileged to represent. I was fortunate to have been taught to do so early in my career by a wise mentor who insisted that we diplomats did not rest on our laurels, foolishly believing that we "knew it all" by virtue of a college degree and a few years of work, and urged us to read and learn at every opportunity both to better inform ourselves and better serve our people.

Xavier's *"Rooted in Palestine"* will now surely be added to my list of recommended readings for the junior diplomats and university interns I supervise, as well as my colleagues, among them the diplomats of other countries, legal experts and academic scholars engaged on the Palestine question.

From the introductory pages, Xavier presents a factual and illuminating perspective on the history of Palestinian Christians in the Palestinian national movement, highlighting their diversity and the dynamic roles played. From this unique angle we are shown how they, whether as clergy, writers and journalists, political activists resisting the British mandate, Zionist colonization of Palestine and Israeli occupation, or diplomats advocating for Palestinian rights and national aspirations, have been a vibrant part of Palestinian socio-political life.

This perspective is rarely considered within our prevailing narrative that - while acknowledging Palestinian Christians as part of the Palestinian populace and as a reflection of the plurality of our people and their centuries long presence and ancient heritage in this land, the land where Jesus was born and preached - is a more defensive narrative, often simply trying to remind the outside world of the basic existence of our Christian community in our attempts to foster solidarity and mobilize support aimed at bringing an end to the cruel, illegal Israeli occupation of our land and its long-running attempts to erase our people and achieving a just solution to the Palestine question.

That defensive approach has been provoked by the false narrative promoted by Israel and extremist Jewish settlers, along with Zionist sympathizers (including Christian Zionists), that this is a "religious conflict between Muslims and Jews", rather than the political, territorial and human rights injustice that it is. This distorted narrative practically ignores the Palestinian Christian presence to advance a toxic "us vs them" agenda. Where Christians are occasionally invoked by this narrative is in cynical attempts to pit Muslims and Christians against one another, falsely portraying Palestinian Christians as a persecuted "religious minority" in Palestine, rather than as among the Palestinians being driven out of their land by the ruthless Israeli occupation, as we witness today in Jerusalem, Bethlehem and elsewhere; or as the Palestinian community favored and privileged by Israel, including in repeated boasts about so-called shared "Judeo-Christian" values, attempting to polarize and divide us.

But the reality, as reflected in this book, is that Palestinian Christians are part, not distinct from, the Palestinian people and equally part of the Palestinian struggle for justice and liberation, including even priests, pastors and patriarchs. They have suffered the same human rights abuses, indignities, aggressions and painful losses and traumas in the ongoing *Nakba* being endured by our people at the hands of a ruthless colonial occupier and apartheid regime, while also maintaining the same resilience and *sumoud*, same pride in their Palestinian identity, history and heritage, and same attachment and commitment to their just cause as any other Palestinian.

Their presence, contributions and sacrifices woven into fabric of Palestinian society and the history of our people, national struggle and achievements. On a personal level, aside from the Palestinian Christian colleagues I have long worked with in nearly 30 years of diplomacy and the friends I have made, I became cognizant of this fact at a young age as my mother, a Palestinian Muslim, attended a Catholic girl's school in Ramallah, where Christian and Muslim girls studied and lived side by side, and my family's circle of friends and acquaintances, including many of the shopkeepers my grandfather routinely visited and patronized, were Palestinian Christians.

"Rooted in Palestine" thankfully rectifies the distorted narrative peddled by others about Palestinian Christians and does so with clarity and strength. Throughout the book, I found myself highlighting facts that I was reading for the very first time and passages significant to Palestine's history and our ongoing national project.

In writing this book, Xavier helps us to better understand and appreciate the role of Palestinian Christians in our just cause and to see them, not as a separate group, but rather as one of the vital components of our people, all sharing one national aspiration: the liberation of the Palestinian people and realization of their inalienable human rights, including the right to return to their ancestral homeland and to self-determination, finally allowing them to live in the freedom, dignity and peace they have been so long denied.

In this struggle, all Palestinians are equal, old and young, woman and man, Muslim and Christian, urban and rural, occupied and refugees, rich and poor. *"Rooted in Palestine"* helps fill in the gaps, revealing and weaving together the facts in a compelling presentation of the history of Palestinian Christian contributions, efforts and milestones from the time of the cursed Balfour Declaration until the passing of President of Yasser Arafat in 2004. While the book ends there, it crucially gives hope in the ongoing journey for Palestinian liberation and justice.

This book is even more important in today's polarized world, where religious narratives are too often aimed at glorifying one over the other and inciting one against the other. Instead it offers a story of genuine coexistence and national struggle among compatriots of differing religions for one just cause.

Xavier's writing of this book reflects that collective attachment to Palestine, an attachment that cannot be broken despite the brutality colonization, occupation and apartheid meted out against our people and years of exile. Although born and raised in Chile, where his Palestinian Christian grandfather emigrated to in 1951 and where his parents were also born, Xavier has been inspired by the same love of homeland borne by millions of Palestinians, even across thousands of miles and decades in the diaspora. That love and attachment compelled him to return to Palestine, to serve the cause, to tell the Palestinian story in his own unique way, to make his contribution to Palestine.

There are countless of Palestinians like him, in occupied Palestine, across the 1967 Green Line in Israel, in the refugee camps throughout the region and in countries all over the globe. As the late Palestinian author Ghassan Kanafani long ago wrote: *"Everything in this world can be robbed or stolen, except one thing; this one thing is the love that emanates from a human being towards a solid commitment to a conviction or cause."*

This book is a reflection of that everlasting commitment and should be included among the principal accounts about the Palestinian national movement, offering both knowledge of and pride in the history of our movement, helping us stand taller and firmer against those who seek to erase our history and the Palestinian presence on our land, to divide us and defeat us. They never will.

Feda Abdelhady
Ambassador - Deputy Permanent Representative
of the State of Palestine to the United Nations
27 January 2022

Introduction

Born in the village of Beit Sahour, Ibrahim Ayyad (1910-2005) was sent to the seminary of the Latin Patriarchate at a very young age. He was a devoted priest who is remembered within his community for his hard work, including the building of the Al Ahliyya School in Ramallah. However, growing up in Palestine in the wake of the Balfour Declaration marked Fr. Ayyad's formation as a priest. Just like other Catholic priests of his generation such as Zachariah Shomali and Louis Dibsi, Fr. Ayyad became active in the national movement of Palestine. By May 1948, this young priest was dodging bullets in Jerusalem, and opening church properties to facilitate the work of the resistance to Zionist groups. While hundreds of Palestinian villages were ethnically cleansed between 1947 and 1949, Fr. Ayyad remained committed to the cause of his people, and paid the price with his own exile. He would only return to Palestine in 1995 after the signing of the Oslo Agreement and passed away 10 years later in the same place where his patriotic awakening had begun: the Latin Patriarchate Seminary of Beit Jala.

Fr. Ayyad's story, although largely unknown to Western audiences, is remembered clearly by PLO officials as Yasser Arafat appointed him as his personal envoy. But were Fr. Ayyad's actions the exception or norm for the clergy in Palestine? The Balfour Declaration of 1917 forced churches in the Holy Land to confront a new reality. The national aspirations of their congregations conflicted with the commitment of the new rulers, the British Mandate authorities, who had promised Palestine to the Zionist movement.

Palestinian Christians proudly state that they have an uninterrupted presence in Palestine since the Pentecost. Despite several challenges, from the catastrophic effects of the Crusades to the imposition of the *Jezia* under the Ottomans, Palestine maintained a well-documented Christian presence. The diaries of several European travellers between the 17th and 19th centuries noted that from Jaffa to Jerusalem, and from Bethlehem to Nazareth and Acre (Akka), the main holy sites of Christianity (including the churches of the Annunciation, Nativity and the Holy Sepulchre) were protected and included institutions such as schools to serve their communities. The Franciscan School in Bethlehem, today known as Terra Sancta School, was founded in 1598 and is the oldest school still functioning in Palestine.

Jerusalem has always remained the centre of Christian life. By 1917 there were several recognized churches operating from Jerusalem. Historically, the Greek Orthodox Patriarchate had been the most relevant church for Christian life in Jerusalem, sharing control of the most important holy sites mainly with the Armenian Orthodox Patriarchate and the Franciscans.[1] Numerically speaking, the Greek Catholic Church (Melkite) was large in comparison with other communities (mainly in the Galilee). The Coptic community had grown over the centuries thanks to pilgrimage from Egypt to the biblical cities of Jaffa, Nazareth, Jericho, Jerusalem, and Bethlehem. The Maronites, Syriacs (Orthodox and Catholic) and Armenian Catholics also had a presence in Jerusalem. Some Palestinian families converted to Protestant churches, giving a presence to Lutherans and Anglicans in the country.[2]

For the churches, the most important challenge was to stay on the land and retain the benefits enjoyed from the Status Quo Agreement that had prevailed since the Ottoman period. For church communities, the aim was to achieve national independence. All of the churches opposed the Zionist plans, although some heads of churches were particularly careful in dealing with the British Mandate. The presence of the Status Quo Agreement for the Holy Sites, with the involvement of other foreign powers such as France, Italy, Belgium, and Spain, was reassuring for the most traditional churches, although some such as the Latin Patriarch Luigi Barlassina were known as fervent opponents of British rule. Barlassina's opposition had little to do with the stance adopted by of his Arab Palestinian congregation but was in line with his own national loyalty as an Italian national.[3]

The arrival of 1948 and the Nakba introduced a different scenario for all Palestinians, including Christians and their churches. This book explains that it is impossible to analyse the current situation of Palestinian Christians without looking at the Nakba. Although it does not reference all relevant names or events of history, the book aims to present a coherent analysis of the processes, context, and contributions in which Palestinians of Christian religion took part, from the Balfour Declaration of 1917 to the death of Yasser Arafat in 2004. The book focuses on diplomatic processes and as such, has certainly omitted other aspects that are relevant to understanding this historic process.

Palestinians Christians have participated in all aspects of the national movement, from diplomacy to armed struggle, and their presence challenges the narrative that this is a religious conflict between Muslims and Jews. They have participated in the national struggle as Palestinians rather than as a "religious minority", despite attempts by several Western leaders, including some heads of churches, to portray it as such. This book also attempts to portray the organic relationships with the rest of the region, including the historic relevance of pilgrimages and how the national movement, mainly under Yasser Arafat, turned this diversity, including Coptic and Armenian components, into an asset for the national cause as a whole.

1.

From Balfour to the Nakba 1917-1948

The Balfour Declaration was made on November 2, 1917, more than a month before British troops entered Jerusalem. The colonialist British policy had decided the fate of Palestine: it was to become the "Jewish homeland". Many Christians worldwide, including some in Palestine, saw the British victory over the Ottoman army as a "victory for Christianity", but for those who believed that the entrance of the armies of His Majesty would benefit the future of Christianity in Palestine, the reality turned out to be very different.

When the Ottomans left Palestine, the population was made up of about 618,000 Muslims, 70,000 Christians, and close to 59,000 Jews.[4] The Jews were divided between the local population and the Zionist immigrants who arrived in Palestine as part of plans to turn Palestine into a Jewish state, between Ashkenazim and Sephardim, between Jews from Aleppo, Kurdistan, and Istanbul, and those from Russia or the rest of Europe. When the British troops entered Palestine, Christians represented about 9% of the population, a sizeable number distributed over almost all of Palestine. For many of them, Great Britain represented a positive development at a moment when the country was suffering economically and many Christians were emigrating to the West. In this context, British troops were received "with flowers in the streets".

Palestinians fought against the Ottoman Empire as part of a major Arab revolt in which it was believed that the British were committed to freedom for the Arabs once the war ended, in accordance with the

Hussein-McMahhon correspondence of 1915. Yet, the British promise to the people of Palestine was broken by the Balfour Declaration. What was supposed to be a "victory for Christianity" became a symbol of the differences between Christians in the West and those in the East.

According to Stephen Sizer, Balfour was raised in an evangelical house sympathetic to Zionism. He was *"committed to the Zionist programme out of theological conviction and had no intention of consulting with the indigenous Arab population."*[5] Balfour would state: *"Zionism, be it right or wrong, good or bad, is rooted in age-long traditions, in present needs, in future hopes, of far profounder import than the desires or prejudices of the 700,000 Arabs who now inhabit this ancient land."*[6]

It is estimated that around 93% of the population of Palestine in 1917 were Arabs. Among the "non-Jewish population", using Balfour's terminology to refer to the vast majority of the population, were Christians divided in churches from three main groups:

- The Eastern Churches (Greek Orthodox, Armenian Orthodox, Syriac Orthodox, Coptic Orthodox, Ethiopian Orthodox).
- The Western Churches (Latin, Greek Catholic, Maronite, Armenian Catholic, Syriac Catholic, Chaldean Church).
- The Protestant Churches (Episcopal and Lutherans).

While some churches enjoyed only a symbolic religious presence (Ethiopian Orthodox, Chaldeans), others represented large segments of Palestinian society, mainly the Greek Orthodox Church, the Roman Catholics (Latin) and the Greek Catholics (Melkites), although this last group had a much larger presence in the Galilee than in Jerusalem. The Armenian Church also had important numbers in Jerusalem (as well as in Jaffa and Haifa). The Protestant churches were the newest addition to the Jerusalem environment as a result of European missionary activity during the 19th century.

The Status Quo of the Holy Sites

Clashes over the status of the holy sites in Palestine led to the need to regulate their use and access, including the performance of religious rituals. Beginning with the "Status Quo of Faith" of 1517, several arrangements were made to regulate the "well management" of the Christian sites, with most of the arrangements lasting until today.[7] Eventually, the Status Quo became a practice respected for centuries under Islamic rule and throughout different periods, including the Turkish-European Wars (such as the Crimean War between the Russian Empire against an alliance of French, British, Ottoman Empire, and the Kingdom of Sardinia[8]), and other diplomatic ruptures where control over holy sites would be used as a tool for political bargaining. By 1852 the Status Quo had become a written document sponsored by the Ottoman authorities and confirmed by the Treaty of Belin in 1878.

Article 13 of the British Mandate of Palestine stated that the authorities would be responsible for *"preserving existing rights and securing free access to the Holy Places, religious buildings and sites, and the free exercise of worship, while ensuring the requirements of public order and decorum".[9]* Article 14 proposed that in cases of disputes over Holy Sites, a special international committee would examine the case.[10]

The Status Quo developed under Ottoman rule to include some important diplomatic components, particularly with a number of countries that were to act as guarantors of the rights of the Christian communities, including countries such as France Italy, Spain and Belgium. Foreign involvement in local churches was not always received with enthusiasm by the local Christian population that viewed protection of their religious rights as a positive aspect, but at odds with the rise of Palestinian nationalism, especially in the Greek Orthodox Church.

Churches during the British Mandate:
Between the Status Quo and the Palestinian National Movement

In 1847 the Latin Patriarchate of Jerusalem was reinstated. While the Franciscans had assumed the task of taking care of Catholic rights over holy sites since 1217, the Latin Patriarchate was created with the main goal of taking care of the communities. The Franciscans did not favor the presence of a Catholic Bishop in Jerusalem, and France initially opposed the establishment of a Catholic Patriarchate for the local population. Nevertheless, the Holy See proceeded because priests were needed to care for local Christians as *"the Franciscans do not know Arabic or the customs of the country, which constitutes an impediment in the way of the pastoral work"*.[11]

The first Patriarch was Joseph Valerga (1847-1872) who had two doctorate degrees in theology and law. In addition to Italian, he knew several other languages including French, Latin, Greek, Hebrew, Arabic, Chaldean, Turkish, and Kurdish.[12] Valerga was keen to promote the church via local clergy, stating that *"a Patriarchate without national clergy is a mockery and is something like a ghost"*.[13] This move brought criticism from the Franciscans, as well as consternation from the Greek Orthodox Patriarchate, which had constantly discriminated against the Palestinian Christian population. Eventually, Patriarch Valerga succeeded in creating a local seminary in 1852 and even appointed as the second director of the seminary, the first Palestinian priest of the Patriarchate, Fr. Abdallah Comandari from Bethlehem.[14] This added to the work of the Greek Catholic (Melkite) Church based in the Galilee that had mainly Arab priests.

The Latin Patriarch during most of the British Mandate of Palestine was Louis Barlassina (1920-1947). He was a native of Turin and led an Arab congregation that, a century after the reinstallation of the

Latin Patriarchate in Jerusalem, had dozens of Arab Palestinian priests and a number of new communities. According to an agreement, the Latin Patriarchate left the Greek Catholic Church to be responsible for most of the communities in the Galilee, but kept a strong presence in the communities around Jerusalem. Barlassina was described as "anti-Zionist", maintained a difficult relationship with the British authorities, and lobbied for French control over Palestine,[15] although according to a number of Palestinian priests who served with him, his deep desire was for Italian control over Jerusalem.[16]

The nationalistic view of members of the church was evident in the *Raqib Sahyoun* magazine edited by Fr. Ibrahim Ayyad. The official voices of the Patriarchate, for example in the *Moniteur Diocesan*, expressed the position of Patriarch Barlassina, but were void of political content, as seen in the pastoral letters and weekly homilies. Even during the period of strongest Palestinian resistance to the Zionist project, there were virtually no references to the situation on the ground.[17] Patriarch Barlassina represented a strong voice, but not of support for the Palestinian national movement. He did care about safeguarding the rights of his community as Catholics rather than just as Christians in national institutions and went as far as asking for seats for the Latin community in the elections of the Jerusalem Municipality.

According to Fr. Peter Madros, Patriarch Barlassina presented a real problem for the British occupiers despite not necessarily supporting the cause of the Arab community or even the Arab clergy: *"He founded the shrine, Our Lady of Palestine, at Rafat. He was very devoted to Our Lady, and he was really feared by the British authorities because he wouldn't hold his tongue, wouldn't keep silent, and would defend our people. At the same time, internally speaking, he would not promote the Arab clergy (...) For example, there was a very gifted priest called Issa Bandak. If he had been Italian, he would have become the Patriarch and even more. But he was sent 'temporarily' to Artas (south of Bethlehem) and stayed there for fifty years."[18]* For the Italians in charge of the Latin Patriarchate, Arabs were probably not "mature enough" to assume a senior position in the church. In fact, the first Arab Bishop in the Latin Patriarchate was Monsignor Mansour Jallad, a priest from Jaffa appointed in 1950.

While Catholics were opening up to the Arab community, recruiting seminarians, and investing in institutions, the Greek hierarchy of the Orthodox Patriarchate closed ranks as much as possible around their Hellenic identity. Patriarch Damianos I would not take into consideration the national aspirations of his community, nor the political situation. The struggles between the Greek clergy and the Arab Orthodox congregations grew under the British Mandate and an organized movement came into being with its own agenda.[19] In the context of a national struggle for independence, Orthodox Palestinians also had to face an internal struggle within their own patriarchate. In 1922 the Greek Patriarchate sold a piece of land to the Zionist Palestine Land Development Company despite calls from the community not to sell it.[20] The issue became a scandal that even reached the discussions that were taking place in the British Parliament over the Mandate in Palestine. Lord Sydenham, who had been briefed by Christian representatives from Palestine, said: *"Recently, I alluded, in this House, to the sale of the lands of the Greek Church. That sale was so arranged, and the plots were so large, that the Palestinians could not purchase them, and I believe that they all went to a Jewish syndicate for the sum of £320,000. Nobody knows who the real owners of these valuable suburban plots are."[21]*

The sale of Orthodox land to a Zionist enterprise demonstrated the disregard of the Greek hierarchy for the local congregation. The most significant response from the Arab laity was the first Arab Orthodox Congress that took place in Haifa a few weeks later.[22] The Arab

Orthodox organization had a nationalistic approach to obtain the rights of Arab Palestinians over the Greek hierarchy in the same way that the Syrians had done with the Patriarchate on Antioch, Arab since 1899. The Greek heirarchy of the Patriarchate were not sympathetic to the Arab nationalist movement and even ex-communicated some prominent Orthodox members such as Khalil Sakakini from the church.[23]

Clearly the Greek hierarchy of the Patriarchate were not comfortable with statements made by Sakakini referring to Saint Jacob's Church in Jerusalem, the place where the Arab faithful pray on the sides of the Church of the Holy Sepulcher, as "a national church illegally occupied by the Greeks". One of the symbols of this struggle was when the Arab faithful took over the church and handled the keys to Khalil Sakakini for "safekeeping". This eventually determined the Patriarchate's refusal to allow Sakakini to get married in the church. Negotiations took place with the Greeks by, among others, Issa al Issa, the prominent editor of *Filastin*, and the Greeks agreed to allow the marriage only if Sakakini returned the keys of the church.[24]

At this time, the Palestinian national movement sparked a flourishing number of media outlets, with the most significant of them owned by Palestinian Christians. Among them was *Filastin* (Palestine), created in 1911 and owned by the al-Issa family. Its famous editor, Issa al-Issa, had received a Catholic and Orthodox education (in Palestine and Lebanon respectively, later becoming a graduate of the American University of Beirut) and became one of the most prominent anti-Zionist exponents in Palestine, while also making use of the newspaper to address the problems of the Orthodox Church. Issa al-Issa made clear what his goals were, in addition to the struggle for national independence: *"My purpose in producing the paper was to serve the Orthodox cause above everything else (...) Anybody who reviews the successive issues of Filastin from that date until the present will note that the Orthodox movement predominates on its pages."*[25]

Filastin was the most prominent Arab Palestinian newspaper during the British Mandate, but there was a tendency for the leading newspapers in Palestine, other than *Filastin*, to belong to Palestinian Christians, particularly from the Orthodox community. Salim Tamari's research lists: *"Jurgi Habib Hanania (publisher of Al Quds); Bandali Elias Mushahwar and Iskandar al-Khoury (owner and chief editor respectively of Al-Insaf, launched in 1908); Khalil Beidas (Al Nafa'is political weekly published in Haifa, 1908); Wahbeh Tamari (publisher of Abu Shaduf, a satirical weekly in Jaffa, 1912); Emile Alonzo (publisher of Al-Taraqqi (...) with Adel Jaber in Jaffa, 1909."*[26] Also, Issa Bandak, the son of an Orthodox priest, started a monthly review in 1919 under the name of his hometown, *Bethlehem*.[27] This magazine emphasized nationalist Palestinian discourse and was distributed to 2500 subscribers from the Bethlehemite diaspora in South America. Bandak was one of the founders of the Reform Party (alongside the mayors of Jerusalem, Acre, Gaza, Ramallah and Beit Jala)[28] and was one of the few people on this list to retain a prominent role after the Nakba, becoming the mayor of Bethlehem.

One of the main problems faced by Palestinian media outlets during the British Mandate, and particularly during the first period when Herbert Samuel, a fervent Zionist Jew, was Britain's High Commissioner, was censorship. *Filastin*, for example, was threatened on several occasions, and was even closed for some time. Issa al-Issa tried to balance his opposition to the Balfour Declaration with tolerance of the British presence in Palestine, describing his dialogue with Herbert Samuel as follows:

> *"The High Commissioner rose to greet me, shook my hand, and then said, 'I read your paper with a lot of interest but without pleasure. Won't you make a truce with me, and end your campaign? (...) Is Sir Herbert Samuel speaking to me as a Zionist leader*

> *or as the High Commissioner?' I asked. 'As High Commissioner and as leader,' he replied. I then asked, 'Are you asking for a truce from a defender or an attacker?' 'From an attacker, of course,' he replied. I answered, 'I am only defending the rights of my country in the face of a Zionist attack, so how can you ask me to be silent? (...) You are indiscriminately spreading around any and all kinds of Zionist pronouncements.' 'If you weren't publishing these things, we wouldn't have the tension that exists in the country,' he said."[29]*

During the British Mandate, Palestine had only one Arab head of church: the Greek Catholics (Melkites) had an enthusiastic and active Lebanese Bishop called Gregorios Hajjar. As a young priest, he was exiled to Egypt by the Ottomans for his pro-Arab independence activities, returning only after the end of Ottoman control. Bishop Hajjar became a key voice against European colonialism and in favor of Arab unity. He joined the Palestinian delegation sent to London in 1921 to present the British government with a list of requirements from the people of Palestine, including a national government, democratic parliamentary elections, and the nullification of the Balfour Declaration.[30]

A census conducted by the Greek Catholic Church during the first decade of the 20th century showed that numbers were few in areas in and around Jerusalem. Between Jerusalem, Jaffa, Bethlehem, Beit Sahour, Ramallah, Ramleh, and Taybeh, the total number of Melkite churches was eight, with 1,105 faithful and one seminary, tiny numbers compared to the Greek Orthodox or Roman Catholic Communities, or even the Armenians. Nevertheless, the nationalist work of Bishop Hajjar would bring him often from the Galilee to Jerusalem, where despite the fact that he did not have a large congregation, he enjoyed significant respect from other national leaders, and particularly Islamic leaders as part of the promotion of inter-religious dialogue that he had initiated and encouraged. This was in the context of several initiatives undertaken by the national movement and most of its parties to highlight the Christian component of the Palestinian identity, not only to promote national unity against Zionist plans but also in an attempt to influence European powers.

The Muslim-Christian Associations created in several cities during demonstrations marking the first anniversary of the Balfour Declaration[31] became the main bodies of representation for local Arab Palestinians during the early part of the Mandate. The Jerusalem branch had 38 representatives (28 Muslims and 10 Christians: five followers of Eastern rites and five followers of Western rites). One of the main points of consensus within the Palestinian movement was the rejection of the Balfour Declaration. Demonstrations took place on the occasion of the first anniversary of the Balfour Declaration and the British authorities reported to their capital: *"The sequel of yesterday's events occurred this morning when a deputation of all Christian and Muslim sects headed by the Mayor (of Jerusalem) marched singing to these Headquarters... the Mayor... informed me that he had come to protest against the assumption that Palestine was to be handed over to any of the three religions practiced by its inhabitants..."[32]*

The significant Christian presence in the demonstrations against the Balfour Declaration was a wake-up call for the British Mandate. From Balfour to Herbert Samuel, colonialist British policies had refused to consider the indigenous population of Palestine as a nation with the right to self-determination. They were now confronted with the fact that the vast majority of the population saw themselves as part of the same national group and were demanding the right to be free. Several Zionists perceived Palestinian Christians, such as Issa al Issa, as more of a "driving force" of the Palestinian national movement than Muslim leaders[33].

One of the first Palestinians to write about the Zionist project was Najib Nassar, a Palestinian Christian from Haifa and editor of the nationalistic magazine *Al Karmel*. In 1913 he wrote: *"Should we allow the Zionists to revive their nationalism at the expense of our nationalism? Have we agreed upon selling them our land piece by piece until they expel us from our land in groups and on an individual basis?"[34]* A few years after the Balfour Declaration, the British Foreign Office received the following message from William Stanley Edmons, one of its officials: *"The petitions are identical. They protest against Palestine being 'appropriated' by the Jews. They are signed by both Moslems and Christians."[35]*

The Holy See understood that the Zionist project represented a threat to the rights of the Christian population in Palestine. Despite efforts by the Zionist movement to gain the Holy See's support, Pope Benedict XV (1914-1922) had a clear opinion on Zionism and stated: *"Zionist aims to oust Christians in the Holy Land from their previous position and put Jews in their place."[36]* This view would certainly have been emphasized in the reports by the local churches, particularly from Latin Patriarch Barlassina. The Christian presence in most Arab Palestinian diplomatic missions to Europe also aimed to sensitize Christian audiences about the fate of their "Christian brothers" in case of a Zionist success. On May 15, 1922, the Holy See's Secretary of State, Cardinal Pietro Gasparri, presented the official Vatican position on the Zionist plans for Palestine:

> *"The Holy See does not oppose the principle that Jews should have the same civil rights as other nationalities and religious confessions in Palestine,*

> *but cannot accept that Jews be given a privileged and predominant position vis-à-vis other nationalities and religions; that the rights of Christian confession be insufficiently guaranteed.* "[37]

The third church with a prominent role in the Status Quo of the Holy Sites was the Armenian Apostolic Orthodox Church, known also as the Armenian Patriarchate of Jerusalem.[38] While Armenians have had an uninterrupted presence in Palestine since the fourth century, there was a sudden transformation when thousands of Armenian refugees arrived in Palestine. According to Armenian sources, numbers grew from around 2,000 Armenians before World War I to some 15,000 Armenians,[39] mainly concentrated in Jerusalem but also distributed in other places such as Jaffa, Haifa, Nazareth, Ramleh, Bethlehem, and Jericho.

While Palestinian Armenians identified with the national dynamics (from cultural aspects to their position against the implementation of the Balfour Declaration), the new refugees knew no Arabic and had different traditions.[40] Eventually, Armenians integrated within Palestinian society, distributing themselves in the Armenian Quarter and in neighborhoods outside the Old City.[41] Despite their sizable population, they were still largely outsiders when it came to Palestinian politics and their Patriarchate focused on issues of the Status Quo and the reception of refugees. A similar process also took place with the Syriac community in Palestine, also victims of persecution.

In 1842 the Bishopric of Jerusalem was established as the first official Protestant presence in Palestine. The Episcopal (Anglican) Bishop in Jerusalem at the time of the Balfour Declaration, Rt. Rev. Rennie Miles MacInnes, opposed Zionism and supported the national aspirations of his congregation who were Arab Palestinians.[42] Episcopal/Anglican churches had been set up during the XIX century in Palestine and several communities were either established or expanded during the British Mandate, including in Acre, Shafa Amr, Nazareth, Zababdeh, Nablus, Ramallah, and Jerusalem.

During the debates that took place in the British Parliament for approval of the Mandate over Palestine, some representatives quoted the concerns of the Anglican Bishop of Jerusalem as reasons to reject the Mandate, mainly because it included implementation of the Balfour Declaration as part of its goal. In 1922 the British Mandate was rejected by 60 votes to 29. During the debate, Lord Sydenham said: *"Two years ago, I quoted in this House the opinion of the Anglican bishop of Jerusalem upon those immigrants (Zionists), based upon what he had himself seen. I am sorry that the noble Earl (Balfour) did not see the opinion of the Anglican bishop, but the Latin bishop, who has been in this country, has confirmed in every way the statement of the Anglican bishop, and has told us of the moral injury which some of these people who have congregated in Palestine have inflicted upon the people of the country."*[43]

In the same debate, Lord Islington made reference to the discriminatory policies that were being adopted by the British authorities in favor of Zionist immigration, making the case of two Palestinian Christians from Bethlehem: *"I am further told that the Deputy Governor of Bethlehem forwarded to the Palestine Administration a proposition on the part of two wealthy Bethlehem Christians, who were able to put a considerable sum of money into a scheme to operate the electric power and agricultural development. The answer was, "No concessions can be given at present"—I think until the Mandate is ratified. Yet within the last few months we see, that a gentleman—I think he is a Russian Jew—has made his application, and has been accepted."*[44]

While it would be difficult to argue that the Anglican Church had a prominent political role during the British Mandate, there are a few elements that can be deduced from the literature. First, the church served the British authorities in Palestine while they were making political advocacy for a Jewish homeland in Palestine, including the Balfour Declaration; second, they learned about the local communities through their growing Palestinian congregations; and third, they were confronted by their own Arab community. For example, the local community rejected a proposal in 1947 granting Palestinian Anglicans (Episcopals) full recognition within their church, calling instead for full recognition as an indigenous Arab organization.[45]

Even though Protestants were a minority within the Christians, they still managed to have members in the national movement, including Shibly Jamal. Arab society, though, was still unfamiliar with Protestantism and they were not accepted by other Christian religious groups. Another prominent Palestinian Episcopal, Edward Said, a child during the British Mandate, recalled that his identity as a Palestinian Protestant was seen as a contradiction in itself while living in exile in Cairo. As a Palestinian Christian born in Jerusalem, not a Catholic and nor an Orthodox, he would be asked: *"You're an Arab after all, but what kind are you? A Protestant?"*[46]

Educational Institutions

Christian schools served all the population of Palestine and were a traditional part of the landscape of the country during the British Mandate. In fact, they played a determining role in the making of the Palestinian leadership. While schools were one of the means used by Western missionaries, mainly from the Roman Catholic Church, to expand congregations, Muslim students were also accepted alongside Orthodox students whose Patriarchate seemed reluctant to engage in the education of their community.[47]

The first coeducational school in Jerusalem was opened within the premises of the Armenian Orthodox Patriarchate and Convent in 1869 (the Sourp Tarchmentchate Armenian School). It was erected on the site of the Sourp Guyane School which was established in 1862 for girls but which was expanded later to include both boys and girls at all educational levels. The school focused on the education of Armenians but eventually opened up to Arab students.[48]

At the end of the 19th century, there was a proliferation of foreign-funded schools, including the Saint Joseph School for Girls or the Beit Jala School for Girls, known as *Al Moscowiye,* inaugurated in 1882 by Russia's Imperial Orthodox Palestine Society. In Jerusalem, a German Catholic congregation inaugurated the Schmidt School for Girls outside Damascus Gate in 1886.

In 1928 the Freres School published a leaflet to mark the occasion of its 50th anniversary in Jerusalem. Adorned with an image of the large school building by New Gate in Jerusalem's Old City, the leaflet was in French and reflected some of the contradictions between foreign clergy and Palestinian communities in that almost no mention was made of Palestine or Arab students, instead focusing on the founders of De La Salle schools and their institutions worldwide.[49]

Local churches also ran a number of schools from the 19th century onwards, including the Sisters of the Rosary, the first Arab order of Catholic nuns in Palestine initiated by Soeur Marie Alphonsine Ghattas[50] with the support of Fr. Joseph Tannous, chancellor of the Latin Patriarchate of Jerusalem. These developments ensured that the Christian population enjoyed high levels of education, an element that determined the prominence of Christian names in the Palestinian national movement.

According to Rashid Khalidi, Palestinian Christians contributed significantly to raising literacy rates in Palestine; by 1931 only 3.3% of Muslim women in Palestine were literate. The situation was similar in Egypt. The literacy rate of Palestinian males, both Christian and Muslim, was comparable to that in Turkey and Egypt at that time.[51] Christian schools were open to all Palestinians, including a large number of Muslims. Therefore it would be fair to believe that Christian schools positively influenced literacy rates in Palestine, particularly in their locations in and around Jerusalem, rather than just those of Palestinian Christians.

Areas in and around Jerusalem also benefited from educational institutions founded by the Protestant missions in Palestine, namely the Saint George School (Anglican, attended by the renowned intellectual Edward Said), the Lutheran Talitha Kumi School (today in Beit Jala after Israel took over their building in West Jerusalem during the Nakba of 1948), and the Syrian Orphanage (Schneller School). Another important institution was the Scottish Tabeetha Mission in Jaffa.[52] In his unpublished memoirs, Lutheran pastor Ibrahim Mattar referred to his experience at the Schneller School: *"Schneller's school was noted to be a factory for turning out Protestants. They never imposed on the students their dogma or obliged them to follow their creed, but through living a true Christian life they set before their students what true Christianity means...*[53]*"*

It is important to mention Khalil Sakakini's efforts to establish secular education in Palestine. Despite Sakakini being one of the leaders of the Palestinian Arab Orthodox Movement to reform the church and provide rights to the Arab community, he believed in the idea of secular education as seen in Europe. He founded *Al Dusturiyyah* School in Jerusalem while the city was still under Turkish rule. Though Khalil Sakakini's name is still remembered as one of the most talented and dedicated educators in Palestine, his school did not survive for long.

Christians in the Palestinian National Movement

The Palestinian national movement underwent significant fractions around the 1930s. This caused divisions among Christians who acted as Palestinian citizens rather than as a religious group. Hajj Amin Al Husseini was the main leader and was close to several traditional Palestinian Christian families. This was an element used against Husseini by his main rival, Fakhri Al Nashashibi, who also associated with several Christians but still tried to exploit the presence of Palestinian Palestinians in important positions around Amin Al Husseini to his advantage.[54]

The divisions in the national movement were detrimental to a coherent strategy of national resistance. Nevertheless, the revolt initiated in 1936 with a general strike of six months, forced Palestinian forces to unite. They created the Arab Higher Committee (AHC) in which a number of Christians were appointed to key positions, including Yacoub Farraj, a prominent Palestinian Christian leader from the time of the Muslim-Christian Committees and the Arab Orthodox struggle. He was a member of the Jerusalem municipality and a member of the Ad Difa Party of Ragheb Nashashibi. The AHC also included Alfred Rock, a lawyer.[55]

In this context, divisions between the foreign religious leaders of most Palestinian Christians and their communities tended to grow. A Franciscan monk, Albert Rock, who was later put in charge of the Status Quo of the Holy Sites as a representative of the Catholics, was one of the Palestinian Catholics who adopted a stronger line than that of their foreign superiors, stating: *"In this country there is not Muslim and not Catholic and nor Orthodox and not Protestant."* This may be seen as a response to the "Catholic identity" emphasized by Patriarch Barlassina. In any case, the Latin Patriarchate had a strong card to play to its community: it had never sold a piece of land to non-Arabs[56] and had even bought land, such as that in Al Tayyasir near to Toubas, an area with almost no Christian presence, to prevent it from being taken by Zionist settlers.[57]

According to Rashid Khalidi, the national conscience of Palestinian Christians was influenced directly by their differences with foreign heads of churches. In particular, the Greek Orthodox Church continued to prevent the Arab faithful from exercising their rights within the Patriarchate.[58] If Palestinian Catholics were not being supported by their heads of churches, at least they were not being blocked and could also benefit from the services provided, including schools and clinics. The Greek Orthodox Patriarchate was criticized for its weak support for the sustainability of their communities, including selling/ leasing land to Zionist enterprises.

By the middle of the British Mandate of Palestine, it had become clear that the issue of the Greek Orthodox Patriarchate had gone beyond Orthodox circles to become a national issue. In 1909 Muslims had joined Christians in their demonstrations against the appointment of Damianos I as Patriarch,[59] but by the 1930s the issue had bigger dimensions. As Arab Orthodox organizations became increasingly prominent in Palestinian society, intellectuals such as Khalil Sakakini adopted stronger positions:

> *"If the community is now seeking to demand its rights from the Brotherhood of the Holy Sepulcher, I will try, from this very minute, to reach a farther goal, namely, to expel this Brotherhood from the country and to purge the Jerusalem See from their corruption and wrongdoing. The goal I am seeking to achieve is to remove the yoke of the Greeks, because they have no right to the presidency, whether ecclesiastically, politically or morally.*

> *Had they done their duties properly by loving and caring for us, or had they displayed a good attitude towards us, we would have accepted their leading role. However, they have despised us and sunk deep into their lust. Therefore we are not to blame for discarding them or working for their expulsion."* These words eventually got him excommunicated by the Greek hierarchy.[60]

Patriarch Damianos died in August 1931, leaving a bitter legacy of controversies regarding the rights of the Arab Palestinian community. What could have been an opportunity to change the course of relations between Greeks and Arabs became a new source of problems when Greek monks elected a new Patriarch in the absence of any laity representative, and the British High Commissioner Sir Arthur Wauchope allowed this to take place. A meeting was held between Palestinian laity community leaders (led by Yacoub Farraj, Nakhleh Kattan, and Shukri Dib) and Arab Orthodox priests, together around 400 people, at Saint Jacob's Church in Jerusalem. The meeting decided that the Arab congregation would not recognize the Patriarch. Immediately, Hajj Amin Al Husseini saluted the meeting and its conclusions, stating that the Arab Orthodox cause was "part of the broader Arab nationalist movement".[61]

In the pages of *Filastin,* Issa al Issa called upon Muslim and Christian Palestinians to stand against the three "Western occupiers": the British, Zionists, and Greeks.[62] (Issa had been considered as an anti-Zionist and anti-Greek activist, but not anti-British.) Soon a new Arab Orthodox Congress was held (this time in Jaffa) and more pressure was mounted. Joint efforts by the Orthodox Clubs all over Palestine prevented the British Mandate from recognizing Thimotheos as the new Patriarch (elected by the Greeks in 1931), but recognition finally took place in June 1935, provoking divisions among the Arab communities of the Patriarchate. While Palestinians unanimously rejected his election, "more than half" of the Orthodox communities in Transjordan, with pro-British rulers, supported his appointment.[63]

Among the Catholics, some priests had become prominent in the national movement, notably Melkite Archbishop Gregorios Hajjar. The Orthodox community had the figure of Fr. Nicola Khoury, who served the community in Jerusalem. He joined the national ranks, becoming close to Hajj Amin Al Husseini on the national level as well as to those calling for reform in the Orthodox Patriarchate. Affiliation to either the Husseini or the Nashashibi camps was relevant during the last half of the British Mandate. Ragheb Nashashibi founded the National Defense Party (*Hizb al Difa*) and Jamal Al Husseini founded the Arab Party of Palestine. The differences between the two were immediately apparent. While Nashashibi was surrounded by mayors and other notables, Husseini was directed more to the masses of Palestine. While Nashashibi was committed to "make efforts to gain national independence for Palestine with full Arab sovereignty without recognizing any foreign obligation that would imply foreign domination or influence," Husseini set more straightforward goals: to fight in parallel against Zionism and the (British) Mandate.[64]

The Arab revolution of 1936 initiated a new chapter for British-Arab-Zionist relations in Palestine. The AHC consolidated its role as the representative of Arab Palestinians, while at the same time, the revolution made room for other groups that espoused an Islamist discourse. This line had been successfully promoted by Izz ad-Din al-Qassam, a Syrian preacher who led several attacks against British and Zionist targets in Palestine and was killed by British forces in 1935. Although the "Islamization" of the discourse by some national leaders raised concerns among Palestinian Christians, this did not prevent Christians from remaining in leading roles, including notably Yacoub Farraj.[65]

The revolution of 1936 was brutally repressed by the British authorities. Andrea Mansour, the mayor of Beit Jala, was killed by British forces as they surrounded his home where a meeting was taking place with national leaders of the resistance. Mayor Mansour had allegedly asked everyone to remain calm while he talked with the British officers. As soon as he went out of his home, soldiers opened fire and killed him. He was the first mayor considered as a martyr for the Palestinian cause.[66]

The British repression led to crimes, even in rural areas considered to be calmer than the main cities. The ancient village of Aboud on the outskirts of Ramallah contains the shrine of Saint Barbara and is surrounded by olive groves, archeological sites, and water wells on the historic path of the Holy Family from Jerusalem to Nazareth. This village had the first martyr of the Palestinian struggle for national liberation with the execution of Yacoub Anfous by the British. Similar scenes were repeated in dozens of Palestinian villages in demonstrations where the words "this country is our country!" (*w'liblad bladna*) were chanted against British rule.

An important aspect of the Palestinian struggle during that period was the demonstrations organized by Palestinian feminists. These women included a number of Christians who were active in institutions such as the Arab Women's Association, Arab Women's Union, and the Arab Women's Executive. A speech against the Zionist project delivered in 1933 by Matiel Moghannam, a Christian woman, in Al Aqsa Mosque Compound demonstrated the level of mobilization by Arab Palestinians around the concept of national liberation. A similar speech was made by a Muslim woman, Tarab Abdel Hadi, at the Church of the Holy Sepulcher. Other prominent Palestinian feminists engaged in the struggle against the Zionist project were Katrin Dib, Melia Sakakini, and Mary Shihada. Adele Azar, a Palestinian Christian, was known for organizing activities in Jaffa. Several women were arrested for violating the curfew in the city, leading to large demonstrations by thousands of people.[67] In 1933 Arthur Wauchope, the British High Commissioner in Palestine, wrote about a *"new and disquieting feature (...) the prominent part taken by women of good family as well as others (...) did all they could to urge the male members of the demonstrations to defy police orders".*[68]

Khalil Totah, the headmaster of the Friends School in Ramallah at that time, described those years in the town. As the head of an institution founded by the Quakers in 1857 and with close ties to the United States, the diaries of Totah reflect the same frustration shared by the vast majority of the palestinian population regarding the situation of Palestine: *"Raja al-Issa, whose father is Issa al-Issa, owner of Falastin newspaper, was taken by his mother today to escape to Syria where (his) father is. She said a few days ago, seven armed men (Jewish?) came to the house and burned her furniture. They took what little money she had and asked where the children were, which terrified her. Consequently, she is taking all the children and joining her family in Lebanon."*[69]

Although non-confessional and Marxist, and facing its own internal crisis due to its Jewish-Arab composition, the Palestine Communist Party also had important Christian representation. Lawyer Hanna Asfour from Haifa was one of its main leaders, alongside journalist Jabra Nicola, Boulos Farah, and notably, Emile Touma and Fouad Nassar during this turbulent period.[70]

By 1936 the Arab Higher Committee was composed of 10 members, including Ragheb Nashashibi, Hajj Amin Al Husseini, Ahmad Hilmi Pasha, Abdul Laith al Salah, Alfred Rock, Jamal Al Husseini, Hussein

Khalidi, Yacoub Al Ghussein, Fouad Saba, and Yacoub Farraj. Three of these were Christians (Rock, Saba and Farraj). The prominence of Christians in the national movement did not prevent accusations of being pro-British and even calls for a boycott of Christian businesses.[71] Nevertheless, anarchy and attacks were not confined to Christians and included many Muslims who worked with the British Mandate, as well as politicians such as the mayor of Hebron.[72]

Christian-Muslim tensions were in some cases fomented by the British authorities, and on several occasions were even financially supported by the early elements of Zionist intelligence. At the beginning of the Zionist enterprise, attempts were made to find Christian allies in Palestine but this policy failed. Some Zionist sources would attribute this to religious hatred (against Jews) or to a Christian intention to "manipulate Muslims" in order to control the country.[73]

In 1937 Ragheb Nashashibi left the Arab Higher Committee and tensions increased in the internal political situation. Palestinian efforts abroad for national liberation continued almost unhindered, even in the absence of national unity. Christians such as Henry Cattan, Emile Ghoury, Fr. Nicola Khoury or George Antonious became some of the most prominent Arab voices abroad, first as part of delegations, and later in the first Arab Palestinian diplomatic representations, including in London, New York and Geneva through an initiative funded by Iraq and initiated by Musa Alami.[74] He was born in Jerusalem in 1897 into one of the most prominent Muslim families of Jerusalem. He worked in a senior post with the British Mandate, but left the government after the revolts that took place in the 1930s.[75] Alami was educated in Christian schools (Freres in Jaffa and the American Colony in Jerusalem) and went on to study law at Cambridge University.

Musa Alami became one of the key Palestinian representatives, led by Jamal Al Husseini, at the renowned London Conference on Palestine that took place in Saint James' Palace in February 1939. This was a response by the British authorities to the great Arab Palestinian rebellion for national independence that lasted, in several stages, between 1936 and 1939. Other names in the Palestinian delegation included prominent Christians such as George Antonious, Fouad Saba, and Alfred Rock. One of the outcomes of this meeting was the White Paper, perhaps one of the most relevant demonstrations of an incipient Palestinian diplomacy, where despite the fact that Palestinian negotiators did not achieve all their goals, London would eventually declare that with the number of Jews in the country (around 450,000), the goal of the Balfour Declaration of providing Jews with a national homeland had been achieved. The White Paper of 1939 called for one independent Palestine to be ruled by Jews and Arabs within 10 years, with limited Jewish immigration and acquisition of land in Palestine. Any increase in Jewish immigration to Palestine would be conditional on Arab acceptance.[76] In fact, these terms were barely respected and there was further illegal immigration to Palestine and British tolerance of Zionist violations of the White Paper.

In Khalil Totah's diary of those days, he describes the chaos in Palestine. On June 7 and 8 of 1939 he wrote:

> *"Jews bomb railway near Tel Aviv, kill Arabs in Jerusalem & another in Tel Aviv, Jewish cinemas closed. Also cafes & curfew. It is the Jews' turn (...) Electric power station in Jerusalem bombed by Jews & 1/3 of city in darkness, Jews boycott King's birthday. That is what British get for having brought a half a million of them to Palestine."*[77]

The UN Partition Plan

With the end of the Second World War, the US became increasingly focused on Palestine. After the Anglo-American Commission of Inquiry in 1946, the United Nations had come out with recommendations on the situation of Palestine by 1947. US policy was to support Zionism and the Arab Palestinian population were not even consulted about the plans for their own homeland.[78] Palestine's demography had changed dramatically and Jews made up to one-third of the population of the country. British rule, initiated by a group of enthusiastic Christian and Jewish Zionists, was keen on the transformation of Palestine. By 1947, the Palestinian population had effectively been disarmed by the British, weakened, and left unprotected against attacks by Zionist groups.[79] It was in this context that the United Kingdom decided to turn the issue of Palestine over to the United Nations in early 1947.

In this scenario, the Holy See increased its lobbying to protect the holy sites, with the most viable alternative being a call for the internationalization of Jerusalem. This was an option that had been considered already by the Royal Peel Commission of 1937 when, for the first time, the British authorities had spoken of the partition of Palestine, considering not only Jerusalem but Bethlehem, Nazareth, and the Sea of Galilee as a "corpus separatum".[80] Under international law this concept, which is the Latin term for "separated body", refers to special treatment given to a particular region in relation to its environment. This does not mean sovereignty or independence; rather, it emphasizes the different legal and political status of the region.

When the discussions began in the United Nations, the Arab states and Muslim countries made strong arguments calling upon the organization to honor the right to self-determination of the people of Palestine, but these calls went unheard by the great powers that supported partition. The exception was the United Kingdom, which having endorsed the denial of Palestinian rights in the Balfour Declaration, decided to abstain from the discussions. The Arab Higher Committee, as the representative of the Palestinian people, notified the United Nations that they would not cooperate with the Special Committee set up by the United Nations for several reasons. In particular, because the UN was violating its own mandate by not recognizing the natural right of the Arab Palestinian population to be free in accordance with the principles of the UN Charter.[81] This message was delivered by the Palestinian representatives to the UN in New York. The representatives included three Palestinian Christians: Emile Ghoury, the right hand man of national leader Abdel Kader Al Husseini and holder of a MA in Political Science from Cincinnati University; Issa Nakheh, a lawyer from the University of London; and Henry Cattan, a renowned lawyer who had studied in the University of Paris and the University of London.

On November 26, 1947, a heated debate took place in the General Assembly (UNGA). The issue was a proposal to divide Palestine into two states. The initiative was rejected by the indigenous Arab population of Palestine as a consequence of the Balfour Declaration[82] and a violation of their right to self-determination. In other words, UNGA was debating the future of Palestine while the majority of the population of the country were opposed to any partition plans.

The General Assembly was composed of 57 states. Six Arab countries (Egypt, Iraq, Lebanon, Saudi Arabia, Syria, and Yemen) and some other nations, including the intervention of Pakistan, defended the interests of the Palestinian people. The challenge was immense as almost all the West, in addition to the Soviet bloc, favored the partition. There were documented cases of extortion to obtain the necessary votes to divide Palestine[83].

The Arab strategy was mainly focused on the illegality of the proposal Egyptian diplomacy, the oldest Arab foreign ministry, led a campaign to discredit the whole process. Egypt argued that UNGA had no mandate to divide Palestine and requested the Assembly to call for an opinion of the International Court of Justice (ICJ) on the matter. Osvaldo Aranha, the Brazilian President of the Assembly and one of the strongest supporters of the Zionist project in Palestine, largely ignored the request. When pressed to a vote, taking the case of Palestine to the ICJ was rejected on November 24.[84] The Egyptian position was based solidly on the principles of the UN Charter and those who opposed sending the case to the ICJ knew exactly what the ICJ would have said when confronted with the solid evidence gathered by Egyptian diplomats.

Ambassador Mahmoud Fawzy, Egypt's representative, stated: *"I think it must be clear by now that the General Assembly is not competent to impose any solution in this matter (...) if the General Assembly's resolution is passed, I must reiterate that we shall take it for what it is: a mere recommendation addressed to the Egyptian government. I must, in terms of no equivocation, reiterate our position (...) we are of the opinion that the General Assembly is not competent to make the proposed recommendation to Egypt or any other state (...) we requested, more than forty days ago, that UNGA should ask the ICJ or an advisory opinion. We still would like to enlighten by such an opinion from the Court; failing an advisory opinion of the ICJ, Egypt will be guided by its own views as to the powers conferred on the General Assembly by the Charter."*[85] The Pakistani representative Sir Mohammad Khan did not express himself any less strongly: *"What authority has the United Nations to do this? What legal authority, what juridical authority has it to do this...?"*[86]

After only 72 hours, the UN voted on the partition of Palestine. It was a strange moment in the Cold War where both the US and the

Soviet Union wanted the same outcome. With 33 in favor versus 13 against and 10 abstentions,[87] UNGA Resolution 181 recommended the partition of Palestine into two states, an Arab state on 43% of the land (Arab Palestinians were around 70% of the population) and a Jewish state on 56% of the land (Zionist Jews owned 5.8% of the land).[88] Jerusalem, including Bethlehem, was to be considered a corpus separatum after lobbying conducted by, among others, the Holy See.[89]

The indigenous population of Palestine were given less than half of the country, Jaffa was an isolated island in the middle of the Jewish state, the border with Syria would be lost and territorial contiguity could not be guaranteed. All Palestinian groups, with the exception of the Communist Party,[90] rejected the partition plan. Palestinian representative Walid Khalidi presented the Palestinian position in response to the UN's approval of the partition resolution:

> *"The native people of Palestine, like the native people of every other country in the Arab world, Asia, Africa, America and Europe, refuse to divide the land with a settler community."[91]*

According to the UN Partition Plan, the Jewish state would be established with 500,000 Jews and 400,000 Palestinians, in addition to 100,000 Jews living in the corpus separatum of Jerusalem[92] and 10,000 in the Arab state.

The position of the Holy See was partially adopted in UN Partition Resolution 181, which recognized Jerusalem and Bethlehem as part of a corpus separatum. When the British announced that they would leave Palestine on May 14, Pope Pius XII on May 1, 1948, issued an encyclical on the issue of Jerusalem, stating:

> *"We mean to refer to the Holy Places in Palestine, which have long been disturbed. Indeed if there exists any place that ought to be most dear to every cultured person, surely it is Palestine where, from the dawn of antiquity, such great light of truth shone for all men."*[93]

The position of the Anglican Church in Jerusalem continued to differ from that of British Protestants close to Zionism or that of the British Government. In 1947, Jerusalem's Bishop was Weston H. Stewart. Like most of the heads of churches, he did not show much sympathy for the nationalist inclinations of the Arab faithful, but also did not want to see the country turned into a Jewish state. For him, the best policy would have been to perpetuate the Mandate with a strong British presence.[94] Was this position adopted out of concern for the fate of the Palestinian congregation or due to the privileges that a British presence would provide to the Anglican Church? It can be assumed that just as Patriarch Barlassina advocated for Italian or French control over Palestine, and Patriarch Thimotheos saw himself as part of the Greek nation, Bishop Stewart also defended the colonialist interests of his country over the national rights of his congregation.

The end of the British Mandate of Palestine created a crisis for all Palestinians. The churches began to gather their communities around monasteries, convents and churches for their protection. These locations had been flourishing over previous years. For example, the Latin Patriarchate, under the leadership of a strong Louis Barlassina, had inaugurated a number of communities, including Beisan (1922) and Jenin (1935).[95] At the same time, during the British Mandate several pilgrim houses and hotels were established,[96] with pilgrims also staying in the houses of Palestinians, especially in Jerusalem.

The Latin Patriarchate had almost 30 communities in Palestine[97] and alongside the Franciscans and other Catholic congregations, had a strong network of institutions.

As Arab Palestinian society mobilized to achieve national independence, it was forced to mourn several figures even before the end of the British Mandate. In November 1940, Archbishop Gregorios Hajjar died in a car accident on his way from Jerusalem to Haifa after having delivered a passionate statement in Al Aqsa Mosque compound. His congregation did not believe it was a simple accident, nor did the rest of the Palestinians. The context of his death was not well established and the idea that the British were involved in his death became a fact for many. In effect, Archbishop Gregorios Hajjar was recognized as a martyr and his funeral was attended by thousands of people who took over the streets of Haifa to bid farewell to the charismatic religious leader.[98]

Concluding the British Mandate, Consolidating the Zionist Enterprise

After 30 years of British Mandate, it can be said that London kept its promise of supporting the Balfour Declaration: Palestine and its demographic composition had changed dramatically. If the Palestinian population in 1947 was about 1,200,000 million Arab Palestinians (Christians and Muslims) and 700,000 Jews, in British-defined Jerusalem the population was about 99,000 Jews and 64,000 Arab Palestinians. British-defined because the boundaries of the city had been changed to include a larger number of Jews. For example, inside the Old City the population was 4,000 Jews and 17,000 Arab Palestinians (7,000 Christians and 10,000 Muslims); outside the walls the population was about 95,000 Jews and 47,000 Arab Palestinians (24,000 Christians and 23,000 Muslims).[99] Urban planning during the Mandate was designed *to "privilege the colonial power's Zionist partner over the indigenous Arab community"*.[100]

John Tleel, a notable Christian Jerusalemite, wrote in his memoirs: *"Our foolish confidence finally proved wrong; on 14 May 1948 the last British High Commisioner, Sir Alan Cunningham, left Jerusalem and the three decades of British Mandate over Palestine ended. In 1917 the British entered Jerusalem to the sounds of trumpets, but left unceremoniously and without fanfare, plunging Jerusalem and the entire region into an endless state of chaos."*[101]

Palestine Begins to Fall

On Christmas Day 1947, the first Palestinian village fell to Zionist gangs: Al Mas'oudiya. The news took only a few hours to reach Jaffa, just five kilometers to the south. The fact that British troops were still in the country did not prevent Zionist organizations from attacking Palestinian civilians, and Jaffa had become one of the main targets.

Popularly known as the "bride of the sea", almost 16,000 of the 70,000 Palestinian Arab inhabitants of Jaffa were Christians. The most important communities were Orthodox and Roman Catholics, although there were also sizable Melkite, Maronite, Coptic Orthodox, and Armenian communities. Cafes such as the Venezia and Saraya were targeted by Zionist terrorists and resulted in a number of civilian casualties. The collapse of the city was only a matter of months.

Jaffa was Palestine's most important coastal city, a driving force for the national economy and a cultural magnet for regional and local singers, artists and intellectuals. It hosted some of the first cinemas in Palestine (including al-Hamra) as well as future Palestinian leaders such as Salah Khalaf (Abu Iyad) and George Habash who studied in its schools (Terra Sancta and St. Archangel Michael Orthodox School respectively). Its Orthodox Sports Club played a prominent role in the defense of the rights of the Palestinian people, to the extent that it would be closed several times by the British Authorities and members were arrested during the main demonstrations, including notably in 1936. Its strong football team was one of the most important ones in Palestine until 1948.

The fate of Jaffa was one of the most strategic decisions taken by the Zionist leadership. Taking over the city was one of the central parts of the so called Dalet Plan,[102] which contrary to Israeli claims of respect for the partition resolution, focused key operations in areas that did not fall within the Jewish state according to Resolution 181. The operations began in April with Operation Nachson (April 5-15) aimed at opening a corridor on the Jerusalem-Jaffa road on land belonging to the Arab state in the partition plan. The aim was to "occupy and destroy Palestinian villages".[103]

The Dalet Plan detailed that *"these operations can be carried out in the following manner: either by destroying villages (setting fire to them, blowing them up, or planting mines in their ruins), especially those population centers which are difficult to control continuously; or by mounting combing and control operations according to the following guidelines: encirclement of the villages and conducting a search inside them. In case of resistance, the armed forces must be wiped out and the population expelled outside the borders of the State."*[104]

The last captain in charge of the defence of Jaffa was Michel Issa, a Palestinian Christian. By May 3 he had been left alone, with some Arab irregulars leaving their positions and with many inhabitants displaced. The plans of the Arab Liberation Army (ALA) deployed in the area had collapsed in a manner as chaotic as the forcible displacement of the civilian population. Captain Issa's last attempt to save the city from the Zionist bombardments was to declare it an "open city", but this did not materialize. He ended up leaving Jaffa on May 5 with 50 soldiers left from his battalion. In his final report, he described the causes of the fall of Jaffa as being the Zionist bombardment, the mass "panicked" departure, the inability of the British to protect the population, and the spread of pessimistic rumors among the population.[105] One of the consequences of the Nakba in Jaffa was the closure of the Episcopal Church and a number of Church-related institutions that could never recover from the exile of their congregations[106].

Operation Nachson succeeded in ethnically cleansing several villages on the periphery of Jerusalem and Jaffa. Among them was Al Qastal, falling on April 9 despite the fierce resistance of Palestinian volunteers led by Abdel Qader Husseini. He was killed in the battle, which demoralized the troops of the Palestinian resistance as the struggle ended by consolidating Zionist control over what became known as West Jerusalem. Emile Ghoury, the loyalist who had accompanied Abdel Qader in organizing the resistance, was one of the leaders who had to deal with the demoralization of the various groups that composed their improvised army. With limited support from Arab countries, the Arab Palestinian militias did not have a master plan and the scarcity of resources revealed the reality: this was not an army ready to fight but ordinary people fighting to save their homes. It was the antithesis of the detailed plan, clear goals and means to achieve them that the Zionist forces had built up.[107]

On the same day as the fall of Al Qastal, Zionist forces conducted the infamous massacre of Deir Yassin, also located in the corridor that they expected to open between Jerusalem and Jaffa. In the *Ethnic Cleansing of Palestine,* historian Ilan Pappe recalls descriptions of the massacre thus: *"Jewish soldiers sprayed the houses with machine-*

gun fire, killing many of the inhabitants. The remaining villagers were then gathered in one place and murdered in cold blood, their bodies abused while a number of the women were raped and then killed."[108]

The massacre was conducted by the Irgun, a more radical faction than the official group, Haganah. Nevertheless there had been coordination between both of them in order to conduct the attack, just as would be proven to have happened in the rest of West Jerusalem. The Irgun regional commander in Jerusalem had received a note from the Haganah regional commander emphasizing that, *"I learnt that you plan an attack on Deir Yassin. I wish to point out that the capture of Deir Yassin and holding it is one stage in our general plan. I have no objection to your carrying out the operation provided you are able to hold the village. If you are unable to do so, I warn you against blowing up the village which will result in its inhabitants abandoning it and its ruins and deserted houses being occupied by foreign forces. This situation will increase our difficulties in the general struggle. A second conquest of the place will involve us in heavy sacrifices. Furthermore, if foreign forces enter the place, this will upset the plan…*"[109]

Was the message delivered by the Haganah a green light for the atrocity committed? What is clear from various sources is that more than 200 people were killed, including women and children. The Irgun would comment, *"wonderful operation of conquest (…) as in Deir Yassin, so everywhere… Oh Lord, Oh Lord, you have chosen us for conquest"*[110]. Deir Yassin resulted in the exile of thousands of Palestinians who fled in panic from the Zionist attacks, with almost no reaction from the British forces still deployed in Palestine. Later, Menahem Begin would acknowledge the importance of Zionist terror in the forcible displacement of Palestinian civilians, beginning with Deir Yassin, and stated that one of the goals of the Dalet Plan *"made it possible to keep open the road to Jerusalem. In the rest of the country, too, the Arabs began to flee in terror, even before they clashed with Jewish forces (...) the legend of Deir Yassin helped us in particular in the saving of Tiberias and the conquest of Haifa (...) all the Jewish forces proceeded to advance through Haifa like a knife through butter. The Arabs began fleeing in panic, shouting: 'Deir Yassin'."* Begin would later become the Prime Minister of Israel.[111]

The account of Menahem Begin was particularly evident in Jerusalem. During the month of April 1948, several attacks targeting Palestinian civilians took place in the neighborhoods of Talbiya, Katamon and Upper Baqaa in the west of Jerusalem. One of the most horrific of these attacks was the killing of a group of Palestinian women working in the Greek Orthodox monastery of Saint Simon.[112] The panic provoked by the Zionist massacre of Deir Yassin led thousands of civilians from these neighborhoods to flee seeking safety. Various churches played a crucial role by receiving large numbers of refugees in their buildings, especially in what was thought to be the safety of the Old City of Jerusalem. One of the churches that was most active in receiving refugees was the Coptic Monastery close to Jaffa Gate.

During the attacks to take over the west of Jerusalem, a Palestinian Christian family became a symbol of the acts of terror being conducted against civilians. In the early hours of January 6 1948, or Eastern Christmas Eve, Haganah operatives blew up the Semiramis Hotel in the residential neighborhood of Qatamon. This act of terror killed twenty-four Palestinian civilians, including the Aboussuan family, as well as Hubert Lorenzo, the son of the hotel's owner, all of them Palestinian Christians. The attack also killed Manuel Allende Salazar, Spain's deputy consul in Jerusalem.[113]

One of the Palestinians in charge of security of the residential neighborhoods of Baqaa, Katamon and Talbiya was Issa Khalil Janho, a Palestinian from a Syrian (Syriac) family. He spoke English well and had good relations with British officers. At that time some British officers had shown their opposition to the Zionist groups, particularly after the Irgun's terror attack on the King David Hotel in the summer of 1946 that killed 91 people, including British, Arab Palestinians and Jews. Janho had known some of those officers.

On February 5, Janho found himself commanding the first major Palestinian operation of sabotage against a Zionist organization. The bombing of the Semiramis Hotel had been just one of several terror attacks against Arab Palestinians in Jerusalem and Abdel Kader Husseini, the Palestinian leader, agreed that it was a moment to respond with a similar tactic. On that day, Issa Janho departed from Birzeit with a British truck full of explosives alongside three British deserters from the police and the military. The truck made its way to the strategic location of the *Palestine Post*, the main Zionist English daily, opposite a garrison used by the Palmach,[114] the Haganah's elite fighting force. The truck exploded, making the building collapse.

Zionist attacks against Arab Palestinian neighborhoods in the west of the city continued and soon, the Palestinians conducted another act of sabotage. This time it was not with deserters but with a Palestinian employee of a foreign diplomatic delegation: Anton Jamil Jeries Daoud was a driver at the US Consulate. A Palestinian Christian from Bethlehem, he had secretly joined the national movement. On Thursday March 11, 1948, he reported to work, something that some people considered strange as it was supposed to be his day off. The last time he was seen by his colleagues, he was leaving with an official car.

A few hours later, a large explosion took place. Making use of an official car and the US flag, Daoud had entered the underground of the building hosting the Jewish Agency. After he left, the car exploded, partially demolishing the building and leaving around 100 casualties.[115]

The attacker escaped an internal investigation by the consulate and made his way out of the country, settling in Kuwait.[116]

Resisting or even anticipating and preparing for a siege was not restricted to those involved with Abdel Kader Husseini. In the first months of 1948, communities organized services for the displaced and prepared for the defence of their homes with local militias. In this context, the Armenian community played an important role in the defence of Jerusalem's Old City. They organized themselves into three main groups: a militia that included engineers and bomb experts; a medical team; and a mixed team ready to help either of the other two. There was also a team in charge of securing water supplies via the dozens of water wells protected by the walls of the Armenian Convent.[117] The heads of the defenses was in the hands of Dragoman Father Hayrig and Hrayr Yergetian.[118] Almost 40 Armenians were killed in the fighting in a battle that prevented the Israeli occupation of the Armenian Quarter, where Armenians from all over Palestine had taken refuge.[119] The resistance of the Armenian Quarter was one of the key elements that prevented the fall of the Old City, especially through its proximity to Jaffa Gate.

In Haifa, the northern Galilean port with a population in 1948 of about 60,000 Arab Palestinians, including around 26,000 Christians belonging to the Roman Catholic, Greek Orthodox, Greek Catholic, Maronite, Armenian Orthodox, and Episcopal communities, the effect of the fighting in Jerusalem was felt in the panic of the civilian population over the news of the Deir Yassin massacre. Irgun leader Menahem Beguin, who always refused the claims of a massacre in the Jerusalemite village, said that *"the legend of Deir Yassin helped us in particular in the saving of Tiberias and the conquest of Haifa".*[120]

While it is difficult to affirm that the massacre of Deir Yassin was the main factor responsible for the fall of Haifa, and omitting how the British troops still in Palestine failed to protect the civilian population, the resistance was poorly prepared and there was a failure of Arab leadership. The name Deir Yassin, alongside other documented massacres,[121] was definitely a symbol of the Nakba and prompted many to flee. Before the end of the British Mandate, the city was already under Zionist control and about 50,000 of the 60,000 inhabitants had been pushed into exile. The local Episcopal community symbolized the effects of the Nakba in the city when its congregation of around 1200 faithful was reduced to around 150 people in a matter of weeks.[122]

Iconic as it was, the fall of Haifa was a defining moment in Palestinian historiography and post-Nakba cultural creation. From the classic story *Returning to Haifa* by the late Ghassan Kanafani to the poem *Ahmad Al Arabi*, the masterpiece of Mahmoud Darwish and the Lebanese composer Marcel Khalife, Haifa remained one of the most painful moments of the Nakba. The chaotic scenes of April 23 were of families leaving on boats under the tardy protection of British soldiers, and regardless of the desperate calls of the Arab Higher Committee for people to stay or of the fact that Arab countries with consulates in the city stopped issuing visas for inhabitants. Around 300 Arab Palestinians were killed during the fall of the city, with the British authorities rejecting requests to provide medical treatment, including ambulances, for at least 18 hours.[123]

Negotiations led by Palestinian notables marked the last attempt at saving the city from total collapse. They took place after the original leadership in charge of the resistance had already collapsed, giving place to members of the local elite to try to save the situation. A delegation of five members included mainly Palestinian Christians: Farid Saad, Elias Koussa, George Mu'ammar, Anis Nasr, and Victor Khayyat (also honorary consul of Spain). But there was little dialogue left. General Stockwell, the British Military Commander in Haifa, began the meeting by making clear that he was not going to move his troops against "any of the parties". According to Farid Saad, the meeting with the British General resulted in a *"printed copy of Jewish conditions"* of surrender.[124]

Archbishop Georges Hakim, the successor to Gregorios Hajjar, could do little to prevent the fall of the city and the expulsion of large parts of his community, mainly to Lebanon and Jordan.[125] Attempts to allow people to return in the following months were met with refusal by Israel. Other communities in the city, including the Carmelite community in charge of the Roman Catholic community, opened their doors to safeguard refugees and their furniture. Some of the furniture has been kept until today with the names of the families who still live in exile. When a former parish priest of the community was asked how long these belongings would be kept, his answer was "the furniture will stay until their return".[126]

The effect of the fall of Haifa on the Christian population was almost immediate. As the largest church in the Galilee, the Greek Catholic Archeparchy had its base in Haifa and a congregation that included almost 30 parishes. One of their parishes was in Safad, where all Palestinians were forced out of their homes, ending the existence of the community by the second week of May. A few kilometers to the south, following the shores of the Sea of Galilee, is Tiberias where the Arab residents were evacuated by British troops on April 18, including the local churches whose congregations were internally displaced towards Nazareth. A similar situation was witnessed in Beisan, located between Nazareth and the Jordan River, where Zionist forces forced the expulsion of all Arab Palestinians, either to Jordan or to Nazareth.

For the Latin Patriarchate of Jerusalem, the fall of Beisan represented the first time that a parish had to be closed since its second establishment in 1847. Zionist attacks against the city had begun in February 1948, with several Palestinian homes being demolished and the Haganah putting the city under an "intermittent siege".[127] The city had three churches belonging to the Greek Orthodox, Latin Patriarchate, and the Episcopal Church. One of the leaders of the Palestinians in Beisan was the Latin priest Fr. Hanna Nimri, a charismatic personality, known for his contacts with the Arab Liberation Army (ALA) who were in charge of the defence of the town. It is believed that Fr. Nimri himself took part in the resistance until the expulsion of the population became irreversible. When the village was occupied, he was one of the three notables who negotiated with the Haganah operatives[128] until the occupying forces decided to expel everyone and Fr. Nimri ended up crossing the Jordan River, later moving back to Palestine as the priest for Gaza. The three churches closed in 1948. The building that used to host the Latin Church became the headquarters of the right-wing Israeli Likud party in the city that is now called Beit Shean.

The same day that the State of Israel was created, May 14, 1948, *L'Osservatore Romano* stated: *"Modern Zionism is not the true heir of Biblical Israel, but a secular state... therefore the Holy Land and its sacred sites belong to Christianity, the True Israel."[129]* The substance of this strong statement was mainly absent from the discussions of the heads of churches in Jerusalem during the British Mandate and no theological discussion was promoted to challenge the exploitation of the Bible made by supporters of the Zionist movement. On the contrary, divisions and disregard for the national rights of the Palestinian population marked the tone of the heads of churches in Palestine. Some of those issues remain until today.

By May 14, the end of the British Mandate, large parts of Palestine were already occupied by Zionist forces. An Israeli intelligence report entitled *Migration of Eretz Yisrael Arabs between December 1, 1947 and June 1, 1948* estimated that up to 391,000 of the Arab population had "emigrated", equivalent to almost 50% of the total Palestinian refugee population by the end of the war. The same document makes it clear that the main cause of the Arab Palestinian departure was the actions of the Haganah and other groups. The document, buried for decades by the Israeli government and released by the activities of the Israeli NGO Akevot, disclosed reasons for the departure of the population from each village, including "our reprisal", "our harassment", "fear of attacks", "fear of invasion", "wanted to negotiate. We did not turn up", "our occupation", and "attack on orphanage", among others.[130]

The formal beginning of the Arab-Israeli War of 1948 was on May 14, 1948, with the announcement of the establishment of the State of Israel when hundreds of Palestinian villages were already occupied by Zionist troops. At this stage, fewer than 20,000 Arab soldiers were mobilized, notably to the areas assigned to the Arab state by UNGA Resolution 181. Over 60,000 Israeli troops[131] were deployed in the operation of the Dalet Plan.[132]

At that time, Michael Sabbah was a young student at the Latin Patriarchate Seminary located in Beit Jala, on the outskirts of Jerusalem. The fighting in the area had intensified after the Zionist occupation of the neighboring villages of Al Malha and Al Wallajeh, and large parts of the population had begun to flee the town. The seminarians were kept inside the building, which overlooks both Jerusalem and Bethlehem, and stayed there until the end of the hostilities. When Nazareth was occupied by Israeli troops on July 6, Michael Sabbah, who in 1988 became the first Palestinian Latin Patriarch of Jerusalem, was separated from his family and was not reunited until the imposition of a permit regime that operated mainly for the seminarians over religious holidays. It was not the case for everyone: near to the Latin Patriarchate Seminary, on Virgin Mary's Road in Beit Jala, families of refugees were descending towards

Bethlehem, finding refuge under olive trees or in impoverished shelters offered by the villagers.

Among those refugees coming mainly from the west of Jerusalem, were members of one of the oldest Christian communities to be forcibly displaced during 1948, from Ein Karem, the birthplace of Saint John the Baptist. By 1945 Ein Karem had a population of 3,180 people, including 670 Christians,[133] and was a prominent village on the periphery of Jerusalem with several institutions, churches, and monasteries. While the religious orders, mainly the Franciscans and the Greek Orthodox Patriarchate, were allowed to stay, their communities were not allowed to return to their homes, putting an end to centuries of an active Christian life in the village. Most of the people from Ein Karem ended up in Jordan, although until today there are several families in East Jerusalem, Ramallah, and Bethlehem.

Beit Jala was defended by a small group of Egyptian soldiers who trained a larger local militia headed by Khalil Abughattas. It included members of the key families of the city, including Farah Al Araj, Carlos Al Mohres, Emile Al Mohres, Yacoub Musallam (killed on 3 May 1949 by a landmine near to the Cremisan Valley), Anton Abuamsha, George Abuawad, Salim Yarad, Khalil Zeidan, and Fouad Kahbar.[134] The defense of the town ultimately protected Bethlehem and prevented a further wave of refugees because Beit Jala stood as the last Arab Palestinian town to the west of Jerusalem after the fall of Al Malha, Al Wallajeh, and others. Many families were preparing to abandon the town and it was the fierce resistance of the Egyptian-trained militia that prevented the Israeli occupation.

Not all attempts to resist were successful. The largest Christian community next to the border with Lebanon was in Al Bassa. With a population of around 4,000 people, the village was occupied on

May 14, 1948, and the vast majority of its people were expelled to Lebanon. The village had two churches, one for the Greek Orthodox Church and one for the Greek Catholic as well as two mosques. The village witnessed a massacre taken as revenge for resistance against the occupation.[135] Today, the people of Al Bassa are spread worldwide, although several live in the refugee camp of Al Dbayeh, which has the particularity of being the only Palestinian refugee camp left in Lebanon which is entirely inhabited by Christians. Another non-recognized camp in southern Lebanon, Al Bassa, also has families displaced from the village.

One after the other, hundreds of Palestinian villages continued to be emptied of their population, including dozens of Christian communities. By the beginning of June when the first Arab-Israeli truce took place, Israeli forces were already in control of vast areas that were supposed to be part of the Arab state in accordance with the partition resolution. After the resumption of hostilities, other cities and villages would fall, including key Christian communities.

In the same area of Al Bassa was Al Birwa, the birthplace of Palestine's national poet Mahmoud Darwish, with a population of close to 1,500 inhabitants, including 130 Christians and their church.[136] The village was entirely cleansed, including its Greek Orthodox Church. The last priest of the village, Fr. Joubran Khoury, represents the simplicity of life in the villages of Palestine. He was a respected peasant at the time when the Orthodox priest passed away. The heads of the village, all of them Muslims, went to the Orthodox Bishop of Acre asking for Khoury to be appointed as the new priest. When asked why they cared because they were Muslims, the men responded: *"We are talking about the priest of Al Birwa, not just the priest of the Christians".*[137] Nearby lies Al Mansoura, a mainly Maronite Palestinian village in which the ruins of the church remain standing.

UN Mediation Efforts

The United Nations tried to intervene by appointing its first mediator in history, Swedish Count Folke Bernadotte, who received a mandate through Resolution 186 to "promote a peaceful adjustment to the future situation of Palestine".[138] Count Bernadotte, an experienced diplomat who had saved thousands of Jews during the Holocaust,[139] made a proposal on June 28, 1948, that included the following terms:

- Arab areas of Palestine to be united with Jordan and then form a union with Israel.
- The proposal included the Naqab dessert to be part of Jordan, the Western Galilee part of Israel, Jerusalem as Arab, Haifa a free port and al-Lydd a free airport.[140]

The proposal was rejected by both Israel and the Arab countries. The UN mediator continued his work to bring about a truce that was violated several times. On September 16, he delivered his last report to UNGA before being assassinated in Jerusalem by Israeli extremists for being considered "an agent of the British government".[141] Mediation attempts continued, including the approval of UNGA Resolution 194, which was largely based on the reports of the Swedish diplomat. This resolution included the creation of the Palestine Conciliation Commission (PCC) and also reaffirmed the right of return of Palestinian refugees.[142] The international community, including the US, pressured Israel on the issue of the repatriation of the Arab Palestinian refugees,[143] a matter that was already of major concern for the churches of Jerusalem and the Holy See. The pressure put on Israel to accept the repatriation of Palestinian refugees was documented in the documents of admission of Israel as a full member of the United Nations. In May 1949, UNGA Resolution 273 granted Israel UN membership after its representative committed to respect the UN Charter and UNGA Resolutions 181 and 194: UNGA *"decides that Israel is a peace-loving State which accepts the obligations contained in the Charter and is able and willing to carry out those obligations".[144]*

Resumption of Hostilities

On July 11 Israel took over al-Lydd and the neighbouring Ramleh, with its Greek Orthodox and Catholic congregations. The forcible displacement of the people of al-Lydd became one of the most dramatic scenes of mass expulsion during the Nakba. The central mosque and Orthodox Church, located nearby, were used by the Israeli troops to concentrate the local population, while others were openly being expelled. The mass expulsion of the Palestinian population ordered by David Ben Gurion and executed by Yitzhak Rabin[145] is described by Dr. Munayyer, a Palestinian Christian doctor who served in al-Lydd during those days in the city's hospital: *"Of the 50,000 people in our city a few days before, including both regular inhabitants and refugees, only about 500 remained. They were staying near the grand mosque and the church."[146]* Dr. Munayyer also recalled the expulsion of Dr. Sami Bishara and Dr. George Habash, two Palestinian Christians who were among the four doctors who remained in al-Lydd's hospital.[147] Two decades later, Dr. Habash became the founder and leader of the Popular Front for the Liberation of Palestine (PFLP), becoming one of the main referents of the Palestinian national movement. During the Israeli attacks on al-Lydd, his sister was killed. Those moments were described by Habash in an interview fifty years after the Nakba:

> *"We buried my sister near our house because we could not get to the cemetery. Three hours later, Jewish fighters stormed the house, screaming: "Out! Out! Get out!" My mother and my sister's children - including a small child we had to carry*

- ran out, as did other relatives and neighbors. We had no idea where to go, but the Jewish soldiers ordered us to get moving. So we walked. It was a hot day in Ramadan. Some people around us were saying it was the Day of Judgment, others said we were already in Hell. When we reached the outskirts of town, we found a Jewish checkpoint where those leaving were being searched. We had no weapons. But our neighbor's son, Amin Hanhan, apparently had some money concealed on him and wouldn't let them search him. A Zionist soldier shot him dead right in front of our eyes. His mother and sister rushed to him, wailing. His brother, Bishara, had been in elementary school with me and we were friends. We used to study and play together . . . [again he is overcome with emotion]. You wonder why I have chosen this road, why I became an Arab nationalist. This is what Zionism is about. After all this, they talk about peace. This was the Zionism that I knew, that I saw with my own eyes."[148]

The expulsions from Jaffa, al-Lydd, and Ramleh had a dramatic effect in the Ramallah area, approximately 20 kilometres from the coast and al-Lydd, and where most of the refugees traveled on foot. The family of Dr. George Habash went to Ramallah, and from there to Amman. Today, it is estimated that most Palestinian Christians in Ramallah city are refugees from the coastal and central areas. Rosemary Sayigh quotes an article that appeared in *The Economist* on October 2, 1948: *"Probably the most affecting sight in the hills is at Birzeit, north of Jerusalem, where about 14,000 destitutes are ranged on terrace upon terrace under the olive trees, a tree to a family, and are forced to consume the bark and burn the living wood that has meant a livelihood for generations. Here and at Nablus, where the organization is slightly more systematic, there is at present so little milk for babies that abortion seems the kindest way out."[149]*

Among those refugees was Anton Barrouk, Abu Maher, an active member of the Latin (Roman Catholic) Church in Ramallah. Born in Jaffa in 1941, he remembers the moment that we left Jaffa when I was almost seven years old. *"In our neighborhood we could hear the bombs falling into Jaffa. People were scared. There were many killings around that time, including the news about the massacres in the villages. We were eight people in my family: father, mother, and six siblings (three sisters and three brothers). My father was a carpenter and rented a truck. We said that we would go for two weeks or so, returning when things had calmed down. We went towards Jifna because my father had been born there. We were received by the Latin Convent and they gave us a tent in the Latin School. After two or three years, when it was becoming clear that we were not going to return, we moved to Ramallah."[150]* Jifna is located near to Birzeit and both are known as traditional Palestinian Christian villages. Jifna contains a water well where tradition says that Virgin Mary stopped on her way to Nazareth.

In the Galilee, Israeli troops were assuring decisive victories, including the occupation of Nazareth on July 16. The fall of the city of the annunciation not only represented a further violation of the UN partition resolution in which Nazareth was part of the Arab state, but it put Israel in control of one of the main Christian centers of Palestine. According to Israeli historiography, Nazareth was given "special treatment" due to the importance of the town for the Christian world. This allegedly included instructions against the desecration of holy sites.[151]

Around the same period of time, other Palestinian villages around Nazareth fell to Israeli troops, including a number of Christian communities such as Ma'loul, Jaffa of Nazareth, and Kufr Kanna. Ma'loul was destroyed and its inhabitants mainly internally displaced, although the Orthodox church remains standing in the middle of a forest planted over the ruins of the village by the Israeli authorities. The village also had a mosque and a Greek Catholic church. Jaffa of Nazareth and Kufr Kanna, the place of the Biblical miracle of Jesus turning water into wine, remain standing. The occupation of Al Mujaydil on around July 15 represented another significant loss to the Latin Patriarchate, now forced to close a second community in the area after the earlier fall of Beisan. The village had a population of almost 2000 inhabitants, including 260 Christians.[152]

By October the Israeli command had already defined a scenario to consolidate the changes in Palestine. The plan included preventing Palestinian refugees from returning, the destruction of Arab villages, *"settling Jews in Arab villages and towns and distributing Arab lands among Jewish settlements"*.[153]

By the end of October, most of the Christian communities in the Galilee were under Israeli control. Some had responded to Israeli attacks with fierce resistance, such as Eilaboun close to Nazareth and Mi'liya in the upper Galilee. Acts of revenge took place by Israeli forces after the occupation, including a reported massacre in Eilaboun.[154] Other villages with Christian communities that were taken over at the end of October were Rameh, Iqrith, Kufr Bir'im, Suhmata and Jish. Of these, only Jish remains standing today. One of the Christian religious leaders in the area was Fr. Yacoub Hanna, an Arab Palestinian nationalist who was *"taken by the Israelis in a bus to the border with Lebanon"*.[155]

The Rhodes Armistice Agreement signed in 1949 put a formal end to what was known as the first Arab-Israeli War. The UN partition resolution was not respected, Jerusalem did not become a corpus separatum and Israel took over 78% of Palestine. Israel celebrates this period as its "independence". Palestinian journalist and historian Aref al Aref gave it a different name: Nakba or catastrophe. This is the name that has prevailed to describe the forcible displacement of around two-thirds of the Palestinian people and the occupation of their land.

The Holy See, who had lobbied to keep Jerusalem, Bethlehem and even Nazareth as international areas in the context of the UN partition resolution, was facing a different situation that perhaps had been feared since the time of Vatican opposition to the Balfour Declaration: Nazareth was on one side of the border while the Old City of Jerusalem and Bethlehem were on the other. Communities with historic ties had been divided and large numbers of the faithful had been displaced. The Latin Patriarchate of Jerusalem had already lost its strong Patriarch, Louis Barlassina. By the end of 1949, the Roman Catholic Church had completely lost five communities: Beisan, Moujaydil, Tiberias, al-Lydd, and Ein Karem, while others that had been prominent were reduced to fractions of their original size, such as Acre, Haifa, Jaffa, and Ramleh.[156]

The reality of the Palestinian refugee crisis led the Holy See to begin the work of the Pontifical Mission in Jerusalem, serving as a central body to support the work already being carried out by various church organizations to assist with the humanitarian situation. With convents and schools filled with refugees from all over the region, from the Old City of Jerusalem to the suburbs of Amman and Beirut, the Holy See estimated that at least 50,000 Catholics from Palestine had become refugees by the end of the war.[157]

In an effort to save what remained, the Holy See made use of its diplomatic weight to remind the international community of the importance of keeping Jerusalem outside the hostilities. Pope Pio

XII made a call on April 15 for an *"established regime guaranteed by international law, a regime which, in the present circumstances, provides of a more appropriate manner for the protection of the sanctuaries"*.[158] The Holy See was among the forces behind a vote in the UN General Assembly that took place on December 9, 1949, calling for the internationalization of Jerusalem, an initiative supported by the Catholic states and the Soviet bloc, but rejected by Israel, Jordan, Britain, and the US.[159] Approved in Resolution 303, the geographical unit defined as an international area was: *"The City of Jerusalem shall include the present municipality of Jerusalem plus the surrounding villages and towns, the most eastern of which shall be Abu Dis; the most southern, Bethlehem; the most western, Ein Karim (including also the built-up area of Motsa); and the most northern, Shu'fat."*[160]

At this stage the city was already divided. The western part was taken by Israel and almost entirely emptied of its Arab Palestinian population. A number of churches lost their communities in the west, including Catholic, Orthodox, Armenian Orthodox, and Episcopal congregations. The emphasis of the Holy See to retain the concept of corpus separatum became the position of the churches in Jerusalem.

Large Christian properties were lost on the other side of the armistice lines, including through the so-called Absentee Property Law that, since 1951, has legitimized Israeli control over Palestinian refugee property. This is how Palestinian dispossession was "legalized" by the Israeli government in a move that has been never recognized by the international community as it does not conform to Israel's international obligations. The mansions of the Palestinian elite were taken over by the Israeli authorities, including those of Christian families such as the Haroun Al Rashid Villa of the Bisharat family, whose home was, remarkably, occupied years later by Israeli PM

Golda Meir. She was the same Israeli leader who on more than one occasion negated the existence of the Palestinian people.[161]

In effect, it was both Palestine and the Palestinian people's existence that were negated by the Nakba. And it was in this context that Israeli propaganda lines would try to separate the Christian component of Palestine from the rest of the Palestinian people. But the facts are too evident as to be hidden: The consequences of the creation of Israel in 1948, the period known as the Nakba, became the closest to a mortal blow to centuries of vibrant Christian presence in Palestine.

2.

From the Catastrophe to the Disappearance of Arab Palestine (1949-1967)

The charismatic Latin Patriarch of Jerusalem, Louis Barlassina, passed away on September 27, 1947, after thirty years of leading the Catholic Church in the Holy Land. There was no time to nominate a new patriarch and Christmas 1947, the last before the Nakba, was celebrated in Bethlehem by the Apostolic Administrator Vincent Mansour Jallad. An Arab Palestinian born in Jaffa in 1885, Monsignor Jallad had served in several parishes in the central regions of Palestine, including Ramallah, Jifna, Aboud, and Nablus. A few years later, Monsignor Jallad became the first Palestinian bishop in the history of the Latin Patriarchate, although it was already significant that a Palestinian had led the Christmas service at the Nativity Church.

The route from the Latin Patriarchate in Jerusalem's Old City to the Church of Saint Catherine, the Roman Catholic section of the Nativity Church, was also part of the Status Quo observed by all the authorities. The route involved exiting the Old City via Jaffa Gate and traveling south along Hebron Road. Here, Monsignor Jallad was greeted by Palestinian families as he passed through the traditionally Arab neighborhoods of Talbiya, Qatamon, Baqaa, and Talpiyot before reaching the monastery of Mar Elias. In Beit Jala, just outside the entrance to Bethlehem and near to Beit Safafa, Monsignor Jallad was welcomed by Beit Jala's mayor, Wadie De'mes, and the Latin parish priest of the city, Fr. Yacoub Beltriti. The group then continued south through a road planted with olive trees until they reached Rachel's

Tomb, also known for centuries as the Bilal Bin Rabah Mosque. Immediately after this site, which is believed to be the burial place of the matriarch Rachel, wife of Prophet Jacob, the road to Hebron divides into a junction with the boundary of Beit Jala and Bethlehem, leading to Nativity Street. This point is also marked by the Sansour Villa, an impressive house built around 1880. The authorities from Beit Sahour and Bethlehem received the procession at this point and then proceeded for a few kilometers of olive groves through Nativity Road to Star Street, the old entrance to Bethlehem's Old City and the path believed to have been taken by Joseph and Mary upon their entrance to the city. The group arrived at the Nativity Church where, according to the Status Quo, they were received by the Mayor of Bethlehem, Issa Bandak, and by a representative of the British authorities and British forces in Bethlehem.

By Christmas 1949, much of this tradition had changed. Fr. Alberto Gori, a former priest in the Italian army during World War I and former head of the Custodia of the Holy Land, had become Patriarch in February 1949 and was leading the Christmas celebrations. Jaffa Gate was part of the new border between West Jerusalem, occupied by Israel in 1948, and East Jerusalem, controlled by Jordan, which included the Old City. With special coordination between Israel, Jordan and the United Nations, the Patriarch traveled south along Hebron Road. The families that had greeted previous processions in the Arab neighborhoods along the road were no longer there as they had been forcibly displaced by Israeli forces. The houses of these prestigious neighborhoods had been looted by Zionist forces and Israeli citizens, and most of them stood empty.

After passing Ramat Rachel kibbutz, the site of a battle between Egyptian and Zionist forces in 1948 that ended with the displacement of the Arab residents who lived in the area, the procession returned to Arab-controlled territory in Beit Safafa and arrived at Mar Elias monastery. Even here things had changed. The olive groves on the way to the Nativity Church now sheltered several families of refugees expelled mainly from areas around Jerusalem. They were living under flimsy tents or just in the trees and caves. To the east, just after Rachel's Tomb, refugees were concentrated around the Convent of Franciscan Missionary Nuns in what later became Aida refugee camp. From the Sansour Villa along Nativity Road, there were more refugee families in the olive groves, later to become Beit Jibrin (Azza) refugee camp. Arriving at Nativity Square, Mayor Issa Bandak was accompanied by representatives from the Jordanian Government. Only limited numbers of Christians living under Israeli control were allowed to cross the borders to join the celebrations.

The economic situation in Bethlehem was devastating. Just like elsewhere in Palestine, convents and schools had opened to receive refugees. Fr. Beltriti in Beit Jala received "six Palestinian Christian families" expelled from Ein Karem in his own home.[162] Dozens of families from Ein Karem, Jaffa, and al-Lydd were hosted at the parochial school. The Holy See rapidly planned the work of the Pontifical Mission in Jerusalem to support humanitarian assistance to Palestinian refugees, including chapters in Jordan, Syria, Lebanon, Cyprus, and Egypt.[163]

The Armistice Agreement and New Realities on the Ground

The changes to the historic 10-kilometer path between Jerusalem and Bethlehem, now passing through territory belonging to two different entities, had been approved in Rhodes on April 3, 1949, in a bilateral Armistice Agreement between Jordan and Israel that established the new boundaries.[164] This agreement redrew the boundaries outlined in UN Resolution 181 and introduced changes that the Holy See had hoped would be avoided under a corpus separatum that included at least Jerusalem and Bethlehem.

The majority of Jerusalem was occupied by Israeli forces. Around 30,000 Palestinians had been forcibly displaced from their villages, including the Christian community of Ein Karem and the traditionally Christian-majority neighborhoods of Talbiya, Qatamon, and Baqaa. The Episcopal Church lost its parish that hosted the Jerusalem Arab-speaking community, and several other Christian institutions, churches and church-owned land were now on the other side of the mythical Mandlebaum Gate, the only crossing between the two sides of the city. These included the Syrian Orphanage, the French Hospital of Saint Joseph, the Italian Hospital, the Convent of Saint Vincent, the Orthodox Monastery of the Cross, the Convent of the Rosary Sisters in Mamilla, the Terra Sancta College, the Bible Institute, the YMCA, the Saint Andrew's Scottish Mission, the Convent of the Franciscan Sisters in Talbiya, the Talitha Kumi school, the Capucin Convent, the Armenian Church of Gregory the Illuminator, and the Qatamon Monastery of Saint Simon. The Church of the Cenacle was left in the newly stablished "no man's land".

The Old City remained on the Arab side in what has been referred to since as East Jerusalem. The municipal council established in East Jerusalem and led by Anton Safieh had territorial contiguity defined as the Old City and the six kilometers around it. The area included Shuafat and Sheikh Jarrah to the north, the Mount of Olives and Ras Al Amoud to the east, and Silwan and Abu Tor to the south. In other words, the heads of churches remained on the Arab side.

The summary of the Arab defeat during the Nakba, or the Israeli victory, was the expansion of Israel from the 56% granted by the United Nations partition resolution to 78% of historic Palestine. This area included key cities with large Christian communities such as Nazareth, al-Lydd, and Ramleh that had been earmarked as part of the Arab state. As at least 418 Palestinian cities, towns and villages had undergone ethnic cleansing, most churches experienced a significant decrease in congregation, plus the looting and loss of property and religious sites. Church leaders took part in the meetings conducted by the UN Conciliation Commission. Armenian Patriarch Guregh Israelian, who had taken the lead in protecting his community from the Haganah bombardment, told the UN Conciliation Commission that Armenians had suffered considerable losses in Jaffa and Haifa, and asked for those refugees to be allowed to return. He was keen to request that the 3,000 Armenians left in Jerusalem should not leave the city.[165]

Several churches approached the Israeli authorities for restitution. The Latin Patriarchate conducted relations with the Israelis through the Bishop of Nazareth. Others such as the Lutheran Church had lost all their assets on the other side of the Armistice lines. For the Greek Catholic Church, the change was dramatic because most of their congregation were located in areas occupied by Israel between 1948 and 1949. The Archbishop of Haifa George Hakim, the successor to Gregorios Hajjar, led the calls for the Israeli authorities to allow their community to return from outside the country, but his requests went unanswered.[166] He visited his community of refugees in Lebanon and was reportedly willing to accept even just the return of the refugees from Haifa. The answer was still negative.

The Holy See was clearly alarmed by the new reality of Palestine and continued to elevate diplomatic efforts to save whatever could be saved. On Good Friday 1949, Pope Pius XII delivered the Redemptoris Nostri Cruciatus (the literal translation in English is "Our Tortured Redeemer") as an Encyclical on the Holy Places in Palestine. It was a response to the dramatic reports that were being delivered to the Vatican from their churches in Palestine. The Encyclical said: *"Although the actual fighting is over, tranquillity or order in Palestine is still very far from having been restored. For We are still receiving complaints from those who have every right to deplore the profanation of sacred buildings, images, charitable institutions, as well as the destruction of peaceful homes of religious communities. Piteous appeals still reach Us from numerous refugees, of every age and condition, who have been forced by the disastrous war to emigrate and even live in exile in concentration camps, the prey to destitution, contagious disease and perils of every sort (...) We are not unmindful of the considerable aid contributed by public and private agencies for relief of these suffering thousands; and We Ourselves, continuing the work of charity, organized from the beginning of Our Pontificate, have left nothing undone, within Our means, to meet the more urgent needs of this same unhappy multitude (...) But the condition of these exiles is so critical and unstable that it cannot longer be permitted to continue. While, therefore, We encourage all generous and noble souls to put forth their best effort to aid these homeless people in their sorrow and destitution, We make an earnest appeal to those responsible that justice may be rendered to all who have been driven far from their homes by the turmoil of war and whose most ardent desire now is to lead peaceful lives once more."*[167] Pope Pius XII reaffirmed the Holy See position of placing the Holy Places of Jerusalem, as well as elsewhere in Palestine, under an international regime.

The Palestinians continued their diplomatic efforts in the United Nations to little avail. One of the last delegations was in 1949 with the Arab Higher Committee that included Emile Ghoury, Raja Husseini, and Nicolas (Abu) Yarur, a wealthy businessman born in Bethlehem who at that time was the head of the prestigious Palestinian Club in Santiago de Chile. This was probably an attempt to gather greater Latin American support, which had been mainly pro-Zionist, partially due to Christian Zionist work in the region. There were large Palestinian communities of mainly Christian origin in Chile and Colombia, but Christian Zionism remained strong in other areas, especially in Central America.

Henry Cattan, the Jerusalem lawyer who officiated during this period as the Palestinian representative to the United Nations, engaged in heated arguments with Moshe Shertok particularly on the issue of the return of Palestinian refugees. "This is unthinkable" was the response of the Israeli representative, despite the moving presentation by Cattan: *"Some 750,000 Arabs living in Palestine for centuries had been driven out, stripped of their possessions and reduced to the status of refugees, whilst their houses had been destroyed and pillaged (...) Who would believe that hundreds of thousands of people had left the country of their own free will, abandoning all their goods, because they had been asked to do so by the representatives of the Arab Higher Committee or of certain Arab States?"*[168] For Palestinians, expulsion from their homes was not an invention or a propaganda tool for Arab countries, which were already suffering the consequences of what was initially thought of as a temporary resettlement. Israeli representatives remain committed to this day to the negation of the Nakba and reject any responsibility for the well-documented and disclosed forcible displacement schemes carried out in 1948. Israel still refuses to disclose most of its archives from 1948, where it is estimated that much more information about Israeli policies and crimes committed during the Nakba could be found.[169]

The integration of Israel into the United Nations was paved with commitments to achieve peace and respect for the UN Charter and Resolutions, including 181 and 194 which were specifically included in Resolution 273. Yet, it had become clear that the the reality of Palestine was rapidly being changed by the refusal to allow Palestinians to return to their homes regardless of their religion. The

UN Conciliation Commission estimated in 1951 that some 16,324,000 dunums of land belonging to Palestinian refugees had been taken by the newly created State of Israel.[170]

One year earlier, the Israeli Parliament had approved the Absentee Property Law, which made it impossible for Palestinians ever to regain control over their property. The law attempted to legitimize the Israeli seizure of Palestinian property, which according to the law, *"includes immovable arid movable property, moneys, a vested or contingent right in property, goodwill and any right in a body of persons or in its management"*. The "absentees" targeted by this law were all citizens of Arab countries, as well as Palestinian citizens living in Arab countries, including in the areas of Palestine controlled by Arab countries.[171] In other words, Israel prepared the institutional framework to take over millions of dunums of privately owned land from over 700,000 Palestinians who had been forcibly displaced during the Nakba.

Palestinian Political Organization and the New Reality

In the new reality after the Rhodes Armistice Agreement, Israel had control over 78% of historic Palestine, including vast areas earmarked for the Arab state under the UN partition resolution such as Nazareth, Acre, al-Lydd, Ramleh, and Jaffa. Around 22% of Palestine was left in Arab hands, namely the Gaza Strip and the West Bank, including East Jerusalem.

The Palestinian leadership was fragmented. What was left of the leadership of the Arab Higher Committee declared a Government of all Palestine in Gaza, with the support of Egypt and other members of the Arab League. The cabinet included Hajj Amin Al Husseini as its leader, with Jamal Al Husseini becoming formally the first Palestinian foreign minister. The cabinet included one Christian member, Michael Abcarious, as the finance minister.

Efforts conducted by King Abdullah of Jordan to obtain control over specific areas of Palestine resulted in the Jericho Conference in December of 1948 in which a number of Palestinian notables supported Jordanian control of the West Bank. The Hashemite role in the holy sites of Jerusalem and the rest of the West Bank was partially legitimized by this conference of Palestinian notables, with many giving their support as an expression of political pragmatism. The Arab League did not recognize Jordanian claims over the West Bank and several countries, including mainly Egypt and Syria, were vocal against it.

Jordan granted citizenship to all Palestinians living under their control, which facilitated integration into the political system and military forces. The parliamentary elections of 1950 included the governorates located in the West Bank. The parliament approved a motion to consolidate the union of the "two banks of the Jordan",[172] although this decision did not enjoy Palestinian consensus. The acquiescence of Palestinian figures to Hashemite rule in Palestine was the result of the conditions at that time of general demoralization and division, the shock of the Nakba, and the need to protect whatever was left of Palestine from another Israeli invasion.[173]

Some of the symbols of the old Palestinian leadership such as Abdel Qader Al Husseini's right-hand man Emile Ghoury became prominent members of the Jordanian administration. Other signs of Palestinian nationalism, such as the *Filastin* newspaper and the Issa family, were displaced from their natal Jaffa to East Jerusalem. *Filastin* became known not only for denouncing Zionist plans but also for becoming the voice of the Arab Orthodox struggle against the Greek hierarchy of the Patriarchate. *Filastin* changed its address from "Jaffa – Palestine" to "Jerusalem – Jordan".

However, another narrative was appearing among Palestinians. Several cells working underground saw the void in coordination or central command as an opportunity to disrupt the status quo. The origins of these cells were diverse and included members of the Palestinian Communist Party who were at odds with the Jordanian government. A significant number of Palestinian Christians were among the founders of the party, turning predominantly Christian populations in Bethlehem, Beit Jala, and the villages around Ramallah into centers of political activity.

Many paid the price of the political turbulence that followed the Nakba. On Friday July 20, 1951, King Abdullah of Jordan was at Al Aqsa Mosque for Friday prayers. Despite warnings of an attack, the King decided to appear in the Old City of Jerusalem, where a gunman took his life with one shot to the head.

Some blamed King Abdullah for the defeat of 1948 as had hoped, in the words of Avi Shlaim, to "effect a peaceful partition of Palestine between himself and the Jewish Agency."[174] Conspiracy theories and his early connections with Zionist officials, including meetings with Golda Meir herself, were seen as attempts to exchange parts of Palestine for control over the Arab areas. His army, the Arab Legion, put up a fierce fight for the Old City of Jerusalem against Israeli attacks, but they were blamed for losing other areas of Palestine, particularly al-Lydd and Ramleh. Many of the accusations were directed against the British head of the Jordanian army, Glubb Pacha.

One of the Palestinians wanted for the assassination was a priest. Fr. Ibrahim Ayyad was one of those blamed by Jordanian security forces for the assassination. According to one version, Fr. Ayyad was serving as parish priest at the Holy Family Latin Church of Ramallah, then went to Betunia next to his satellite parish of Ein Areeq, and smuggled the pistol that ended the life of King Abdullah to one of those directly involved in the operation. Fr. Ayyad was condemned to death. The charges claimed that Fr. Ayyad took part in a meeting in the ancient village of Aboud to plan the killing of the Hashemite monarch. In church circles the rest of the story was told with almost the same details. The Holy See got involved to ensure that no execution would take place. Two other people had particular interest in securing the release of Fr. Ayyad: Monsignor Ni'meh Samaan and Glubb Pacha himself.[175]

Fr. Ayyad was saved. The agreement[176] between the Holy See and Jordan stated that Fr. Ayyad could not stay in the country and the church sent him to Beirut. There, he became the head of the Ecclesiastical court of the Catholic Church, the same position he had held during the British Mandate in Jerusalem, and a position that allowed him to build a strong network of relationships in favour of the Palestinian national movement. In the years to come, Fr. Ayyad was to return to the frontlines of Palestinian diplomatic efforts. He consistently denied any involvement in the killing of King Abdullah. He admitted to a close group of confidents that he knew about the plans to kill the King, but denied that he had anything to do with the pistol that ended the monarch's life.[177]

Fr. Ayyad was not the only person to be arrested. One after the other, cells operating underground in the West Bank were disbanded by the Jordanian security services. Several Palestinian Christians were among those arrested, with some of them escaping to join relatives abroad. This campaign caused tensions and disputes within the new Jordanian political elite that resulted from the Nakba. Prime Minister Samir Rifai, a refugee from Safad, resigned from his position after the executions took place.[178]

King Abdullah's son, Talal, who was popular among Palestinians, became the new Jordanian monarch but only for one year. Allegedly a "schizophreniac", King Talal was deposed by the Jordanian Parliament and his throne given to his young son Hussein, who effectively took over his father's functions in 1953. Jordanian control over the West Bank did not weaken. In fact, regional political developments consolidated this role further. The revolution that took place in Egypt on July 23, 1952, known as the Revolution of the Free Generals, deposed King Farouk and imposed a new regime that espoused Pan-Arabism as a policy for the rest of the region. The main challenger to Jordanian control over Palestinian affairs, the Government of All Palestine, had never been able to fully exercise its functions and was dissolved by Egypt when President Gamal Abdel Nasser declared the United Arab Republic with Syria in 1958.

The New Reality for Local Churches

The dramatic demographic changes in Palestine were particularly severe among the Christian population. From making up around 10% of the population in 1948, the percentage was reduced by almost half in the territory of historic Palestine. Palestinian Christian refugees from the Galilee left mainly to Lebanon while many others, especially from Jaffa, al-Lydd and Ramleh, did the same to Jordan. The change was felt by the local churches in Amman. If by 1947 the population of the Latin Church in Amman was about 800 people, by 1952 the numbers were around 7,000. The northern city of Irbid also received a significant number of Palestinian refugees, including many Christians from the Galilee. One of them was Afifeh Musah, a pregnant woman who had escaped the siege of Haifa. Soon after arriving, in July 1948, she gave birth to her son Maroun Lahham, who decades later became one of the most senior Vatican envoys in the Arab world and the Latin Bishop of Jordan. In that city the Latin

Patriarchate appointed Fr. Hanna Nimri, the last priest of Beisan, to help the Palestinian refugees gathered in the city. The Latin parish of Irbid was only founded in April 1949 mainly to serve the spiritual needs of the Palestinian Christians who found themselves there.

Some of the institutions that for decades had served Palestinian communities, particularly Christians, felt the dramatic changes of the post 1948-reality. The Saint Joseph School of Jaffa never recovered and ended up closing and being sold decades later. The monks in charge of the Terra Sancta School saw that many of their students from schools in Jaffa, Haifa, Acre, Ramleh, and Jerusalem were about to lose their academic year as they were displaced. This prompted them to open an emergency branch of the school in the Jabal Amman neighborhood of the Jordanian capital, one of the areas that received the largest numbers of Palestinian refugees. The school was soon moved to Jabal el-Weibdeh where a branch was formally established. A similar move was made by the Latin Patriarchate of Jerusalem to authorize the inauguration of De La Salle College in Amman in 1950, first in Jabal Amman, then relocated in Jabal Hussein, another neighborhood with a large number of Palestinian refugees. The headquarters of both schools in Jerusalem, Terra Sancta and De La Salle, had experienced the changes first hand. While the Terra Sancta School in Talbiya had been occupied by Israeli troops, De La Salle at New Gate in the Old City had become part of the armistice lines of 1949.

The Holy See established the Pontifical Mission in Palestine as a response to the humanitarian situation of refugees and distributed branches in Lebanon, Syria, Egypt, Jordan, Palestine, and Cyprus. The committees included assistance to internally displaced people inside Israel and were composed of representatives from all denominations of the Holy See. The Israel branch had as its head the Melkite Archbishop George Hakim, whose church had seen many in the congregation go into exile and had closed several chapels.

While some of the displaced people managed to return after a few weeks, including in the communities of Eilaboun and Rameh, for the majority the displacement was permanent.

Resettlement of Palestinian Christian refugees was mainly coordinated by the churches, whether through local parishes or through the Pontifical Mission, which helps to explain why Palestinian Christian refugees did not live in refugee camps in Palestine. The coordination in their work with refugees was unprecedented and involved almost all the resources available to the churches. The social impact was shocking as many people moved from the luxurious neighborhoods of Al Musrara, Talbiya and Qatamon in the west of Jerusalem to overcrowded monasteries in the Old City. The new design of Jerusalem included the renowned Mandlebaum Gate as the only passage between East and West Jerusalem, as well as a large area of no man's land between Damascus Gate and New Gate. The Notre Dame building opposite New Gate was virtually destroyed and had to be rebuilt later as a consequence of fighting during Israeli attempts to occupy the Old City.

The Mandlebaum Gate was the entry point to a reality that few could have imagined. The qualitative perspective of the considerable number of Palestinian towns and villages that witnessed the forcible displacement of their inhabitans between 1948 and 1949, with numbers ranging from around 400 to 536 villages, was to realize that Arab Palestinian society had been effectively disbanded. Communities that had lived together for centuries had been wiped off the map, their properties and land looted and taken by the recently created State of Israel. About 80% of the Arab Palestinians who used to live in what became the State of Israel (of the Rhodes Armistice of 1949) had been expelled. The 20% left, about 110,000 people, were placed under military rule, with almost a third of this number internally displaced.

This was the reality for dozens of Christian communities. Nazareth became the only Palestinian city occupied by Israel where the majority of the population managed to remain. It became a center for the resettlement of internally displaced people, including significant numbers from the forcibly displaced Christian communities of Beisan, Tiberias, Mjeibeh, and even the legendary Sereen and the ancient village of Al Shajara. The latter was the birthplace of the famous Palestinian caricaturist Naji al Ali and two Christian families made up the community of the Greek Orthodox Church in the village. Nazareth and the nearby Jaffa of Nazareth also received significant numbers of people from the Christian communities of Ma'aloul. The community of Jeish, near to Lebanon, had been almost entirely displaced, but then received many of those displaced from the mainly Maronite village of Kufr Bi'rim, in addition to some who managed to return. Other northern Palestinian Christian communities that managed to remain standing included Fassouta, Mi'iliya, Abu Snan, Tarshiha, Buqeia, and Shafa Amr', as well as the cities of Haifa and Acre.

However, many people were exiled. The Greek Orthodox community of Al Rameh saw their priest, Fr. Nicola Hanna, exiled by the Israeli authorities due to his involvement with the Arab Higher Committee. Many members of his family also left the village and ended up as refugees in Syria[179], the same destination as some of the prominent Christian families from Beisan and Tiberias. Among them was the Sayegh family, including the family of the renowned intellectual Fayez Sayegh, the son of a Presbyterian pastor who years later became the general director of the Palestine Research Center in Beirut.

Demographic changes also affected the areas of Palestine that were under Jordanian control. Areas that traditionally had mainly Christian populations such as Bethlehem, Beit Jala, Beit Sahour, Ramallah, Birzeit, Jifna and Ain Areeq, experienced an unpredicted increase in their populations from Palestinian refugees. This was particularly evident in Bethlehem where refugee camps were established at the northern and southern entrances of the town (Aida, Beit Jibrin and Dheisheh) in the expectation that displacement would not last for long. Perhaps the only indirect benefit of the Nakba for Christians in the Bethlehem area was the funding of a new Latin parish in Beit Sahour: Fr. Domenico Veglio had become the parish priest of al-Lydd in 1945 but did not have a proper church to serve, making use of a house for services.

The ancient Christian community of al-Lydd were mainly Greek Orthodox and even the idea of a Latin community was not welcomed by some in the birthplace of Saint George. Yet Fr. Veglio, then a young priest in his early thirties, served his community with devotion and committed himself to the construction of a church. He went to Italy to seek funds, but on July 11, 1948, al-Lydd fell to Israeli forces and all of his community were expelled. Some found refuge in the Latin parish of Ramallah while others kept moving to Jordan. Fr. Veglio found himself without a community and was sent as an administrator to the Latin parish of Beit Sahour, where he ended up using part of the money that had been collected for a church in al-Lydd. The other part was given to the humanitarian work of the church with Palestinian refugees.

Ramallah, the village that in 1873 was described by Soeur Emilie de Vialar, founder of the Congregation of Sisters of Saint Joseph, as *"a small place about three hours on foot from Jerusalem"*,[180] saw its population of around 5,000 people almost double after 1948. According to the Bible, it was in this area that the young Jesus got lost from his family as it was part of the summer trail followed by the Holy Family between Jerusalem and Nazareth (the winter trail was through the Jordan Valley). By 1948 the city had four Christian denominations. The oldest and largest was the Greek Orthodox, with the Orthodox Church of the Transfiguration built in 1807 with stones from an older church. There was also a Greek Catholic community with a church built about 500 meters from the Greek Orthodox Church in 1895. The Saint Andrew Episcopal community was established in 1860[181], while the Latin community began its presence in 1873 with the mission of the Saint Joseph School. All these institutions received refugees and witnessed dramatic changes in the composition of families in the parishes.

The economic conditions resulting from the war pushed dozens of families from Ramallah to join relatives who had emigrated during the Ottoman period, mainly to the United States, while thousands of refugees from al-Lydd, Jaffa and Ramleh became the new parishioners. The hall of the Orthodox Church in the Old City became the "school of the refugees", a transitory place for children who were about to lose their educational year. Those students were later integrated either into the public schools of the city, the Al Ahliyya College (Latin school), the Saint Joseph School for girls or the schools established by the United Nations during the fifties (UNRWA). Some went to the school established by the Quakers in 1889 known as the Friends School which had also served as a transitory camp for refugees. An additional educational institution was added in the fifties with the opening of a Lutheran mission in Ramallah, the Church of Hope.

The Christian presence in Gaza has existed since the early years of Christianity. The Orthodox Church of Saint Porphyries, originally built around the year 425, its most vivid testimony. By 1948 there were two churches in Gaza City, the Greek Orthodox and a Latin church, in addition to a few Armenian families. The Latin priest at the time also served communities in Khan Younis, the port of Asdud (turned into Israel's Ashdod after 1948) and Beir Al Saba' (or Israel's Beersheva after 1948). Both communities totally dissapeared during the Nakba. In 1948 the Latin Patriarchate had plans to build a church in Asdud but only succeeded in conducting a few projects before the Nakba.[182]

The Pontifical Mission efforts to support Palestinian refugees had an important chapter in Gaza, which included the construction of a refugee camp over five dunums of land in the Deir Zeitoun area over an old Christian cemetery. Fr. Shukri Srour played an important role in serving refugees in Gaza, who included people from Jaffa and al-Lydd. Later, the Egyptian authorities donated a piece of land for the Christians on the shores of Gaza, with UNRWA support, popularly known as the "Christian's camp", between Al Shati refugee camp and the Shifa Hospital.

Between the Wars of 1956 and 1967

At the end of 1956, the United Kingdom, France and Israel conducted a trilateral attack against Egypt to gain control over the Suez Canal, recently nationalized by the government of Gamal Abdel Nasser. Despite the magnitude of the aggression, Egypt did not surrender and counterattacked the foreign troops on its soil. President Abdel Nasser asked for Arab support and the preparation of a new front in order to weaken the Israeli attack, anticipated to come from the east of the Jordan River.

This is how the idea of a counterattack materialized through plans for an operation called "Beisan", designed to liberate the city of the same name located between Nazareth and the Jordan Valley with a combined force of Jordanian and Syrian troops with the aim of splitting Israel into two halves.[183] Such plans were not necessary as the US intervened and the tripartite British – French – Israeli aggression ended with Egypt regaining full control over all the territory occupied by the foreign forces, including the withdrawal of Israel from Gaza.

It was in Gaza that an enthusiastic priest, Fr. Hanna Nimri, head of the Latin community in the coastal city, had found consolation after the fall of Beisan in 1948, the city he had defended to the end. An Arab nationalist known for his charismatic personality, he soon became one of the most prominent personalities in Gaza, with close connections to the Egyptian government. What would have happened if the war had not ended and Operation Beisan had actually taken place? Some of his former colleagues believe that he would have immediately reopened the church he had been forced to leave eight years earlier. However, Operation Beisan did not take place and Fr. Nimri organized a celebration in the parish hall of Gaza to welcome the return of the Egyptian forces.

Palestinians in Israel under Military Rule

The Palestinians who remained in the State of Israel were placed under military rule. There were approximately 170,000 of these Palestinians, including around 35,000 Christians.[184] Military rules, many of them based on laws from the British Mandate period, were implemented to enclose Palestinian villages, towns, and neighborhoods. This policy allowed the new rulers to deprive Palestinians of their land for the building or expansion of Jewish towns. Nazareth lost its agricultural land in 1957 to make way for the the city of Nazaret Illit (Upper Nazareth, today known as Nof HaGalil or "View of Galilee") which was built on land belonging to the city of the biblical annunciation.

The military rule lasted between 1948 and 1965 and although justified by Israel as a security measure, it was used to permanently change the demography of the country. It included the Military Emergency Regulations of 1948, the Civil Emergency Laws and Regulations which allowed land to be declared "absentee property" even in cases where the owners remained in the country, and the Land Acquisition Law.[185] This was the experience of the Palestinian Christian communities of Iqrit and Kufr Bir'im. Close to 500 people inhabited the Melkite community of Iqrit and another 700 in the Maronite community of Kufr Bir'im. All of them were asked to leave their homes temporarily following the Nakba of 1948.

What was supposed to be an absence of a few days became a permanent situation. Some of the villagers moved to Lebanon while the majority stayed in caves around the villages or in other Palestinian communities that had not been destroyed such as Jish and Rameh. The villagers began to mobilize as the commitment of the Israeli authorities had been broken.

By 1951 the villagers tried to find a solution through the Israeli legal system and the court ruled that the villagers should be allowed to return. However, a political decision was taken not to allow them to return. One day in December 1951, a group of elders from Iqrit returned to the village with an order from the Israeli court. The officer in charge argued that they needed time to leave the village and the villagers could return on December 25, meaning Christmas Day for the community. On Christmas Day no return was possible as the families witnessed the bombardment of their village, which was destroyed before their eyes.[186] All the buildings were destroyed apart from the church and the cemetery. A similar event took place in the village of Kufr Bir'im, and only the church and the cemetery remained. Other villages such as Qaddita, Deir Hanna, and Ghabissiya were also demolished.[187] The policy was clear: Israel would prevent Palestinians from returning to their homes despite the fact that these people had become part of the newly created state.

Up to five thousand civilians were killed trying to return to their homes.[188] Families were divided and church officials could do little to remonstrate with Israeli officials. Despite the fact that some refers to "special considerations" given to some Christians, whether out of fear of the consequences for Israel's foreign relations or for domestic reasons,[189] the situation ended in catastrophic consequences.

Attacks against Palestinian property in Israel continued, including the desecration of 73 tombs in the Christian cemetery of Haifa on Good Friday 1954.[190] Regular complaints were made by local churches, including about the holy sites located in destroyed villages. Requests to access the tombs in the Christian cemetery of the destroyed village of Ma'aloul, whose inhabitants were mainly internally displaced in the Nazareth area, were continually denied.[191]

Jaffa, formerly known for its thriving economy and institutions, shrank into small neighborhoods for the few inhabitants and internally displaced people who remained. One prominent institution, the Saint Joseph School for Girls, ended up closing a few decades after the Nakba of 1948 having served the people of Jaffa for almost a century. Soeur Emilie de Vialar, the founder of the Order of Saint Joseph, described their educational work in Jaffa since 1849. *"Of all the schools in Palestine, this is the one which gives us most consolation. The good Sisters of Jaffa have asked me repeatedly for a hospice to be built for the sick and poor. Before I left, I received the vows of a Sister of Sr. Joseph, born in Jaffa. Her example will have a favorable influence on her young companions and will give rise to vocations to the religious life."[192]*

Despite the fact that military regulations dominated the lives of Palestinians in Israel between 1948 and 1966, those with valid IDs were still allowed to vote in parliamentary elections. Tawfik Toubi from Haifa was elected as part of the bid of the MAKI, Israel's Communist Party. In 1951 the renowned writer Emile Habibi entered the Knesset as part of the same list. In 1949 an Arab list supported by

MAPAI (David Ben Gurion's party) and called the Democratic List of Nazareth also participated in the elections and won two seats.

The Heads of Churches

The head of the Greek Orthodox Patriarchate during the Nakba was Patriarch Timotheos. He had experienced resistance from his Palestinian congregation about disregard for Arab rights, but retained Jordanian support due to his role as Bishop of Transjordan during the first years of the British Mandate of Palestine. Patriarch Thimotheos was rather silent about the new realities imposed by the Nakba and his Patriarchate did not play a major role in the humanitarian work of sheltering refugees, although his local congregations, often headed by Arab priests, did give refuge to thousands of people. The Greek Patriarch, supported by the British authorities prior to 1948, counted on the diplomatic cover of the Greek diplomats in Tel Aviv and in Jerusalem, who made the explicit point that they represented "the only Greek Orthodox state in the world".[193] This is the period when Greek diplomacy attempted to play a role similar to that of the Catholic countries in the Status Quo agreement (France, Italy, Spain and Belgium) as the Greek Orthodox Patriarchate and its considerable properties represented an asset for the Hellenic Republic. Greece, a country that had opposed the partition of Palestine in the United Nations, now, had to balance its diplomacy between the Greek's people strong support for the Arab cause and the protection of the Greek hierarchy of the Greek Orthodox Patriarchate.

The Holy See appointed Alberto Gori as Latin Patriarch of Jerusalem in 1949. The choice of an experienced priest with thorough knowledge of the region and the holy sites -- he was the head of the Franciscan Order in the Holy Land -- was not a coincidence. The Vatican understood the importance of having a representative with sufficient experience to deal with the new political situation in the region. Unlike the Greek Orthodox Patriarchate, the Latin Patriarchate of Jerusalem was created to focus on the communities they served rather than on religious shrines. Patriarch Valerga's historic words upon his arrival to Palestine, almost a century earlier, of *"a patriarchate without a local clergy is a mockery of itself"* seemed to be a direct reference to the way that other religious heirarchies in Jerusalem dealt with the local communities.

Patriarch Gori shared the concern of the Holy See about the status of the holy sites after the Nakba, yet one of his most important tasks, after engaging in mediation efforts, was to lobby for freedom of worship for the Christians left under Israeli control. He was respected by the Israelis and was received with full honors when he made his first pastoral visit to Jaffa on March 23, 1950, an occasion also used to meet with foreign diplomats, and which reaffirmed the important role played by the Catholic Church in diplomacy in the region. Despite the problematic situation, Patriarch Gori continued the process of expansion of the Latin Patriarchate, particularly the translation of liturgical texts into Arabic for the benefit of the faithful in Palestine and elsewhere in the Arab world.[194]

The Armenian Patriarchate of Jerusalem also had to elect a new patriarch during the period of Jordanian control of East Jerusalem. A regular election to one of the most important churches party to the Status Quo of the Holy Sites turned into a political competition between Yeghishe Derderian and Tiran Nersoyan. The struggle involved bribes, arrests, various Armenian political parties, and deportations as Jordan made use of its powers to prevent the rise of candidates seen as "pro-communist" due to their ties with Moscow. The United States was also partially involved through its Consulate General in Jerusalem, with some sources in the Armenian Patriarchate going as far as accusing the CIA of being involved.[195] The election ended with the appointment of Yeghishe Derderian in 1960 after close to five years of rivalry that almost caused the demission of Jordanian Foreign Minister Musa Nasir, a Jordanian Christian who opposed with how the Jordanian authorities had dealt with the issue.[196] Patriarch Derderian took over a Patriarchate that had suffered from a dramatic shrinking of numbers due to the Nakba. Dynamic communities were almost wiped out in cities such as Jaffa and Ramleh, while keeping a small presence in Haifa, Nazareth and areas under Jordanian control, mainly Jerusalem, Bethlehem and Jericho. The losses of the Armenian community were particularly striking in Jerusalem.

The Greek Catholic Church had a small congregation in the Jerusalem and Jaffa areas. Most of its congregation relied on the Archeparchy of Acre, based in Haifa and serving the Galilee. The Greek Catholic Patriarchate of Jerusalem still played an important role in Jerusalem and in the neighboring Ramallah and Bethlehem areas, particularly in Beit Sahour where it had established a seminary. This was also the home town of Archbishop Gabriel Abu Saada who served as Patriarchal vicar for the Greek Catholic Patriarchate between 1948 and 1965, being the first Palestinian to lead the Patriarchate in Jerusalem. He was very committed to both his community and the national cause. One of his first steps was to build housing projects in Bethlehem and Beit Sahour that benefited not only his community but also members of other Christian denominations and Muslims. He expanded his congregation by building the Greek Catholic school in Beit Sahour and a church in Taybeh, the biblical Ephraim located between Ramallah and Jericho. In 1962 he was invited to an international peace conference in Germany but refused to speak because the Israeli flag was on the podium. Once the flag was removed, he said: *"We came to talk about peace. As long as there is Israel, there will be no peace."*[197] The only parish under Abu Saada's jurisdiction left in Israel was Jaffa's "Annunciation" Church, which was reduced to 120 parishioners after the Nakba.

The Episcopal or Anglican Diocese of Jerusalem led by Bishop Weston Stewart was active in supporting Palestinian refugees. His own community had lost more than one chapel, including in the northern city of Acre and in West Jerusalem where the Saint Paul Church, built in 1873 for the benefit of the Arab congregation of Jerusalem, had been occupied by Israeli forces during the forcible displacement of the residents of the neighborhood.[198] In 1957 Bishop Campbell MacInnes became the head of the Church in Jerusalem, though in 1958 the local community finally celebrated the appointment of an Arab Bishop, Rev. Najib Cubain, who served as an assistant Archbishop in Jerusalem. After the war, the Episcopal Church maintained a presence in the territories controlled by Israel, mainly in Jaffa, Nazareth, Haifa and Shafa Amr, in addition to their communities in East Jerusalem, Ramallah, Nablus and Zababdeh, all under Arab control. This was not the case with the Lutheran Church which lost all its properties in West Jerusalem (what was left of the Schneller Orphanage, the Deaconess Hospital, and the Talitha Kumi School) as well as almost 3,000 dunums of land in Asdod, close to Gaza, and 28,000 orange trees between Ramleh and Jaffa.[199]

The Lutheran Church had been weakened by the expulsion of German citizens during the Second World War, although the involvement of the Lutheran Church in the US empowered its presence in Jerusalem, especially through Rev. Edwin Moll who arrived in Jerusalem in 1947 in his capacity of secretary of the board of foreign missions. Rev. Moll stayed in Palestine longer than initially expected as the Lutherans joined other churches in helping the humanitarian efforts after the Nakba, including turning the Augusta Victoria Hospital on the Mount of Olives into a hospital for refugees. Rev. Moll coordinated humanitarian work on behalf of the World Lutheran Federation with the Jordanian authorities, the Red Cross, and the United Nations.

This was particularly important because most Palestinian hospitals, including those run by churches, were located in West Jerusalem and Augusta Victoria became the only hospital serving the Arab Palestinian population of Jerusalem in 1948. This gave the Lutheran Church important status that led to the Jordanian authorities officially recognizing the Church as the Evangelical Lutheran Church in Jordan and the Holy Land in 1959. While most of the work of the Lutheran Church in Palestine was providing services rather than seeking to convert members of other denominations, their work with orphans and students created several communities. By the time of their official recognition as an independent church in Jerusalem,[200] there were communities in the parishes of Jerusalem (Old City), Beit Jala, Bethlehem and Beit Sahour, adding Ramallah after a few years.

Pilgrimage to the Holy Land and Arab Tourism under Jordanian Control

During the late fifties and early sixties, a tourism industry grew around religious pilgrimage centered in Jerusalem. Of the three most important churches in Christianity, the Annunciation Church in Nazareth, Nativity Church in Bethlehem and Church of the Holy Sepulcher in Jerusalem, the last two had remained in Arab hands. This was a positive asset for Jordan, now in control of the West Bank, and tourism developed to benefit many Palestinian Christian families. One of the first steps taken was to establish a tourism office in Jerusalem for the production of brochures, and to promote cities and the holy sites. This helped various churches that had invested considerable resources in the resettlement of Palestinian refugees, and it strengthened ties between Jerusalem and other Arab countries.

Religious pilgrims arrived daily from Lebanon, Syria, Iraq, and Egypt. Jerusalem airport, located north of the Old City at Qalandia, welcomed three daily flights from Beirut, two from Kuwait, Cairo and Damascus, in addition to flights from other capitals. The presence of the airport was vital for the development of the Arab tourist industry in Jerusalem and beyond. After 1948 Arab tourists stopped using the northern borders at Ras Naqoura with Lebanon or the Sea of Galilee with Syria, or the ports of Haifa and Jaffa, but many arrived in their own cars or using buses departing from Aleppo in Syria and Baghdad in Iraq. While the emphasis was on Christian pilgrimage from these countries, Muslim pilgrimage also took place, including to Jerusalem and to Bilal Bin Rabah Mosque (Rachel's Tomb) in Bethlehem, and the Ibrahimi Mosque in Hebron. These pilgrims would arrive by bus from as far away as Pakistan.

The high season for Arab pilgrimage was Easter. Arabic accents were *"easily distinguished, Egyptians, Lebanese and particularly Syrians coming from Aleppo"* according to Henry Khoury, a devoted Roman Catholic who worked at that time for Kuwait Airlines in Jerusalem.[201]

Tourism and pilgrimage were not confined only to the Arab world and thousands of Western tourists also made their way to the Holy Land. In many cases, they arrived at Beirut airport and continued by car to Jerusalem. Others made connections from Beirut to Jerusalem airport. It was common to see cars from Arab countries in Jerusalem. During that period, Western tourism took the form of small groups, mainly families, visiting religious sites. Dozens of hotels were built in Jerusalem, Bethlehem and Jericho, as well as in other cities such as Ramallah.

For tourists from the Arabian Gulf or even from the Hashemite royal family, Ramallah was a prime destination thanks to its altitude of 800 meters above sea level, its proximity to Jerusalem, and its natural beauty, including large olive groves and ancient trees decorating its quiet streets. By the fifties, Ramallah had experienced a large influx of refugees. Some of the original families had immigrated to the United States at the beginning of the century and with the resources obtained abroad, many families built large villas that became characteristic of the city, especially during the 1920s. These distinguished buildings include the Al Hamra Hotel, built by the Batteh family, one of the Palestinian Christian families that were to disappear from Palestine years later following the Israeli occupation. The hotel was built close to the Mouqatah, the location chosen by the British Government to establish its Ramallah governorate. Unquestionably, the Ramallah Grand Hotel was typical of that era: built on the highest point in the city just a few meters from the Manara, the landmark square decorated with five stone-carved lions in 1951 to represent the original Christian families of the city. The traditional Rukab Ice Cream, established in 1952, was only fifty meters away.

The Grand Hotel opened in 1907 as a guest house serving Lebanese teachers working at the Friends School, the Quaker school in Palestine. Given its strategic importance, the building was occupied by British troops in 1938. At the end of the British Mandate, Jordanian troops made the building their headquarters until the hotel was returned to the family in 1952. Ms. Aida Odeh, a graduate in political science from the American University of Beirut and a devoted parishioner at the Ramallah Holy Family Latin Church, used to work in the US Consulate in Jerusalem and took over responsibility for the building, successfully saving her family from the economic calamities that Palestine was suffering after the Nakba. She managed to bring regular visitors to the hotel through an Armenian-Lebanese agent called Mr. Babadouzian. The hotel hosted King Hussein himself. Other visitors included the renowned Egyptian couple of acclaimed actors Omar Sharif and Faten Hamama. The engineer behind the renovation of the hotel was Joubran Joubran, a Palestinian Christian from a traditional Ramallah family. His career reflected the transformations that Palestinian society was undergoing. From designing bathrooms for tourists in a successful Ramallah hotel, two decades later he took part in building underground facilities in Beirut for the Palestine Liberation Organization.[202]

Under the British Mandate, Bethlehem had not been able to exploit its full touristic potential. Local leaders complained to the Mandate authorities about tourists not spending a single night in Bethlehem and prioritizing overnight stays in Jerusalem. Nevertheless, Bethlehem did receive local Palestinian and Arab tourists. Foreign pilgrims used the services of the Casanova Pilgrims' House, established by the Franciscans in 1906.

By the end of the British Mandate, the Orthodox Society of Bethlehem had managed to build the Orient Palace Hotel, right outside the Nativity Church. This was possible despite the opposition of the Greek Orthodox Patriarch Thimotheos, and only through the determination of Mayor Issa Basil Bandak, a veteran of the Arab struggle against the Greek domination of the Patriarchate and one of the strongest Christian figures in the national movement. He made use of his popularity and his good relations with the Jordanian authorities[203] to finish the hotel "overnight". The Orient Palace was considered to be the best hotel in Bethlehem during that period. It was managed by the Sawalha family, a well-known Arab Orthodox family from Jordan.

Other well-known hotels during the sixties were the Handal Hotel (today renamed the Shepherds) located close to the Carmel monastery, and the Samer Hotel of the Khoury family near to Rachel's Tomb. The Everest Hotel in Beit Jala was located on the top of a hill overlooking Jerusalem and Bethlehem. In Beit Jala there was also a smaller hotel called the Panorama, known for its afternoon parties. After the 1967 occupation, it was turned into an Israeli military base. Another hotel was the "Normandi", property of the Kunkar family, located on the main road connecting Beit Jala to Bethlehem.

Bethlehem's real distinction in tourism was its souvenirs. The oldest documented souvenir from Palestine is a reliquary book from the sixth century containing rocks from various holy sites, including the Milk Grotto and the Nativity Church. Today the book sits in the collection of the Vatican Museum. The Catholic Church began training artisans, turning Bethlehem into one of the main producers of mother of pearl art from the beginning of the 15th century. Star Street was the location of the first souvenir shop in Palestine (opened by Italian priest Antonio Belloni to finance his orphanage). It was imitated by several families: Michel, Dabdoub, Abu Fheleh and Canawati were some of the families that opened major stores by the 19th century. The Kattan family went as far as opening stores with souvenirs made in Bethlehem, mainly of mother of pearl, in Ukraine and the Philippines.[204]

These activities were partially interrupted by the taxes imposed by the British Mandate on imports of mother of pearl stones to Palestine (of close to 400% of their value) and several producers were forced to close down. Under Jordanian rule these taxes were removed, which allowed more families to produce souvenirs.

Jerusalem, or its eastern part, was the center of tourism for the region. During the sixties, there were around 4,000 hotel rooms (compared with around 1,000 in Israeli-controlled West Jerusalem) and around 40 hotels and guest houses, in addition to pilgrim houses managed by churches such as at the Schmidt School, Saint George's Cathedral and with the Lutheran Church. The Jordan Express Tourism Transportation Company (JETT), created in 1964, alleviated some of the intense demand for tourist buses in the city. The growth in demand led a group of Palestinian hoteliers, including Khalil Nazzal and Ibrahim Salameh, to create the Arab Hotels Association in 1962. Some of the most famous hotels that have survived to the present day include the Jerusalem Hotel, the Petra, the Zahra, the National, the Casanova, the

American Colony, and the Ambassador. Others have changed names such as the Intercontinental (today the Seven Arches) and the YMCA (Legacy). Others simply disappeared under Israeli occupation such as the Mount Scopus, Ritz, the Orient House and the Shepherds' Hotel, today turned into part of a complex for Israeli settlers in the Sheikh Jarrah neighborhood.

The Visit of Pope Paul VI

In January 1964 Jerusalem received its first papal visit. Pope Paul VI became the first of his title to conduct a pilgrimage to Palestine. The political context was of extreme concern during the preparations for the visit. On the one hand, the Holy See had opposed the Balfour Declaration, had called to protect Christian populations, and had lobbied for the corpus separatum of Jerusalem, all requests that had not been fulfilled. The Catholic Church had witnessed several of its communities being ethnically cleansed and institutions closed at the very time that Pontifical Mission programs were continuing to provide protection for Palestinian refugees. The majority of Palestinian Christians had emigrated either to Lebanon or Jordan, where dozens of churches and church-related institutions had been built for their service. At that time, the Holy See had full diplomatic relations with Jordan, including the Apostolic Delegation in Jerusalem.

Pope Paul VI arrived at Amman airport on January 4, only three days before Eastern Christmas. In Palestine he visited Jerusalem and Bethlehem, then went through the crossing controlled by Israel to visit Nazareth, the Sea of Galilee and Megiddo. He spent a total of 11 hours in Israeli-controlled territory.[205] While in Jerusalem, he met Patriarch Athenagoras I of Constantinople, known as the main representative of the Orthodox Church worldwide, in one of the historic steps taken to unify the churches.

The visit served as an opportunity for Pope Paul VI to see the situation on the ground. Significant resources had been invested in supporting Palestinian refugees and developing institutions after 1948, yet the main focus of talks was about church unity. Still, this visit encouraged the Pope to take further steps to support the Palestinian people, particularly in light of Christian emigration, and planted the seeds for the creation of Bethlehem University almost a decade later.[206]

Foundation of the Palestine Liberation Organization

It was in one of the hotels referred to above, the Ambassador, where on May 28, 1964, the Palestine Liberation Organization (PLO) was founded. With dozens of Palestinian groups spread all over the region, the need had become evident for organizations to form one entity that could represent the people of Palestine politically. However, there were several difficulties, including the rivalry between Jordan and Egypt with regard to Palestine. The Egyptian government, led by Gamal Abdel Nasser, was the main driver behind the creation of the PLO, but Jordan argued that it could continue to represent Palestinian interests until a solution would be found. Jordan had annexed the West Bank and had control over the Haram Al Sharif in Jerusalem, with the West Bank providing significant economic advantages for the Hashemite Kingdom.

With much political manoeuvring, the PLO held its first session in Jerusalem. The person leading the process was Ahmad Shukeiri, a lawyer originally from Acre who had graduated from the Arab American University of Beirut and was a veteran of the Arab Higher Committee. He had served in the Palestinian mission in Washington before the Nakba and later had served as a diplomat for Saudi Arabia and the Arab League at the United Nations. He was seen by Jordan as someone close to Egypt, yet he found a formula to win Jordanian support, including reaffirming the importance of relations with Jordan and inviting King Hussein to deliver a speech at the inauguration of the council. Other considerations were also addressed in efforts to create an umbrella as representative as possible of all Palestinians.

One of the founders of the PLO was Dr. Fayez Sayegh, a refugee from Tiberias whose father was an Evangelical pastor. Dr. Sayegh had a prominent career, first as the director of the Palestine Research Center in Beirut, and then as a professor in the US. He also worked for Arab embassies in Washington and at the United Nations.[207] Archbishop Gabriel Abu Saada was also one of the participants in that meeting. Other prominent Palestinian Christians involved in the creation of the PLO were Said Khoury and Hassib Sabbag, refugees from Safad who had established the successful Consolidated Contractors Company (CCC) based in Beirut. Among the 24 women who attended the first PNC (out of 422 delegates) was Lidia Al Araj, a 34-year-old teacher born in the United States but originally from Beit Jala. She also became the first treasurer of the General Union of Palestinian Women (GUPW).

The first PLO Executive Committee included Palestinian figures such as Abdel Mohsen Qattan, in charge of the Palestine National Fund, Haidar Abdel Shafi, Abdel Majid Shouman (the founder of the Arab Bank), and Khaled Al Fahoum. Nicola Al-Durr, an experienced journalist born in Shafa Amr in 1908 to a Palestinian Christian refugee family that now lived in Lebanon, became a member of that first Palestinian cabinet. In Beirut he edited the Arab affairs section of the prestigious *Daily Star* newspaper. A graduate of the Terra Sancta School in Jerusalem, he played a key role in the formation of the Voice of Palestine radio that broadcast from Cairo. He also became the first Deputy Speaker of the PNC.

Another prominent figure in the formation of the PLO was Raji Sahioun, a journalist born in Haifa in 1920 who worked in the Palestine Broadcasting Corporation (PBC) under the British Mandate. After the Nakba he became an assistant director at the Jordanian Broadcasting Corporation, later moving to Beirut to obtain a master's degree in Political Science from the American University of Beirut. In 1964 he was a delegate to the first PNC and became one of the names that alternated in the Executive Committee during this initial period.

Ahmad Shukairi understood the importance of working with Arab communities in the West. Before 1948 Issa Bandak, perhaps the most notable politician from Bethlehem during the Mandate period, headed the only Palestinian publication, *Sawt Ash Sha'b* (The People's Voice), that reached out to the communities that had been formed since the Ottoman period in Latin America. This experience probably played a rolefor the Hashemite Kingdom of Jordan to designate him as ambassador to Chile in 1954. Shukeiri himself addressed the Palestinian community of Chile in 1960 as a representative of the Arab League.[208] It was not surprising then that as PLO Chairman, he decided to send a number of diplomatic envoys outside the Arab world, including two Palestinian Christians who went to Latin America: Ms. Victoria Araj from Beit Jala who was asked to fundraise with the Palestinian community in Honduras, and Zuhdi Tarazi, originally from Gaza but raised in Jerusalem, who was dispatched to Brazil as part of the Arab League mission. A decade later, Tarazi became the first permanent PLO representative to the United Nations.

Revolutionary Forces

The first PNC of 1964 included a group of young members of an organization funded in Kuwait in 1957 called the Palestinian National Liberation Movement, whose inverted initial words in Arabic *Harakat Tahrir Al Watani al Falastini* form the word "Fatah". While their presence at the PNC was not based on their political affiliation but on their geographical presence or mass front, they made clear to Ahmad Shukeiri that they were part of the same movement. Among those young representatives were Mohammad Ragheb Gheim (Abu Maher), Rafik Natsheh, Khaled al Hassan, and a 33-year-old engineer representing Palestinians in Kuwait called Mohammad Abdel Ra'ouf Arafat Al Kidwa Al Husseini, known by his comrades as Yasser Arafat.

When Fatah was created, Palestinians were mainly divided into three ideological camps: the pan-Arabists, the independent seculars, and a minority inclined towards the Muslim Brotherhood. There were also communists who were largely accused of "following orders from Moscow". In this context, Fatah aimed to provide an independent Palestinian voice that was not subjugated to any other capital and could bring all these ideologies together, a place where people like Yasser Arafat, Khalil Al Wazir (Abu Jihad) and Salah Khalaf (Abu Iyad), originally linked to the Muslim Brotherhood, could fight for return and freedom in Palestine alongside Palestinian Christians, communists or pan-Arabists such as Farouk Kaddoumi (Abu Lutof). This concept was close to what most of the founders of Fatah, including Arafat, had implemented with the foundation of the General Union of Palestinian Students (GUPS) in Cairo, 1952, to promote the organization of Palestinians in the Arab world.

Young members of other tendencies also participated in the PNC, including followers of the Arab Nationalist Movement (ANM) founded by Dr. George Habash, the refugee from al-Lydd who had turned into a charismatic political leader, creating several branches in the Arab world. While Fatah included non-Palestinians in the movement, the ANM was more Arab-centered. During the second half of the sixties, a number of divisions turned the movement more

Palestine-focused while moving towards Marxism. Some of the main figures who took part in this process alongside Habash were two Christians originally from Melkite backgrounds: Nayef Hawatmeh, a Jordanian, and Dr. Wadie Haddad, originally from Safad. He had met George Habash while studying medicine at the American University of Beirut and together they had funded a medical clinic in Amman, Jordan.

The oldest organized Palestinian political movement remained the Communist Party, yet after 1948 it suffered from several splits. Palestinians left inside the newly created State of Israel became part of the Israeli Communist Party alongside Jewish citizens; while the Party recognized Israel, it did not declare itself a Zionist party. The majority of the communists in exile and those in the West Bank merged with the Jordanian Communist Party.[209] The Secretary General was Fouad Nassar, a charismatic leader originally from a Christian family from Nazareth who, after being persecuted by the Jordanian government, ended up exiling himself for a second time. Unlike Fatah, the ANM or the structures created by the PLO, the Communist Party did not endorse the armed struggle as part of their political charter. This, in addition to the persecution suffered by communists in various parts of the Arab world, ended up isolating the party, including from the development of representative institutions for the Palestinian people.[210]

It was at this time that pan-Arabist political marketing by President Gamal Abdel Nasser used famous Arab artists to propagate the message of Arab unity and anti-Imperialist struggle. This including legendary songs such as *Al Watan al Akbar* (The Greatest Homeland) and *Sawt al Jamahir* (Voice of the Masses), whose section on Palestine included the words "*the hour of revolutionary work has arrived to Palestine in the name of the masses*", a song arranged by Mohammad Abdel Wahhab whose words were interpreted by the Egyptian talent Fayda Kamel. These were symbols of the post-Nakba Palestinian revolution, including military training in Algeria, China, Egypt, Iraq, Syria, Vietnam, and even Cuba. But many contradictions remained between the "independent Palestinian decision making" advocated by Fatah, and the importance of Arab unity declared by the pan-Arabist groups. By 1966 Syria also got involved in the Palestinian political arena by creating Al Sai'qa, a Palestinian branch of the Baath Party, with a well-trained and funded military branch alongside the Syrian army.

Events were being followed from Beirut by Fr. Ibrahim Ayyad, the stoic Palestinian nationalist exiled due to his alleged involvement in the assassination of King Abdallah of Jordan a decade earlier. Fr. Ayyad was in charge of the Ecclesiastical Court of the Roman Catholic Church in Lebanon. One day towards the end of 1964, he received an unexpected visit: Yasser Arafat and Khalil Al Wazir appeared at his convent asking for his blessing to launch the armed struggle. In the years to come, Fr. Ayyad became an important figure in the Palestinian national movement, returning to the central role he had played with the Arab Higher Committee prior to the Nakba of 1948. Fr. Ayyad allegedly responded to them, *"You are late, but you have my blessing".*[211]

On January 1, 1965, Fatah launched its first military operation against Israel in an attempt to destroy Israeli water pipelines near to Eilaboun in the Galilee. These pipelines were being used to divert water from the Sea of Galilee, thereby shrinking the Jordan River and taking water resources from Jordanian-controlled territory in a project inaugurated in 1964. With poor weaponry and hand-made explosives, the operation was more to "make noise" as revealed by one of the combatants who took part in its planning.[212] The first statement issued by *Al Assifa* (the storm), Fatah's military branch, stated: *"The wings of the striking forces moved on Friday night 12/31/1964, carrying out established operations in the occupied land, and returning safely to their camps. We warn the enemy against taking any measures against Arab civilians wherever they are, because our forces will respond to the attack with similar attacks (...) Long live the unity of our people and long live the struggle of our people to restore our dignity and our homeland."[213]*

The Palestinian movements became more prominent, established relations beyond the Arab world, and enjoyed the sympathy of wealthy Arab states and of Palestinian communities in the region, mainly in Kuwait, Saudi Arabia and Jordan. While the PLO was still seen as merely a "bureaucratic" structure with little connection to the people on the ground, the new structures that were created, including the PNC, Palestine National Fund (PNF), and the Palestine Liberation Army (PLA), became institutions that revived the name of Palestine.

Two months after the launch of the first symbolic attack by the Palestinian *fedayeen*, Melkite Archbishop Gabriel Abu Saada suffered a stroke and passed away in Jerusalem at the age of 57. Having been a strong supporter of his national cause, Arch. Abu Saada left a legacy of several institutions built under his mandate. On July 30, Hilarion Capucci was elected Archbishop and Patriarchal Vicar for the Melkite Church in Jerusalem. Born in Aleppo, Syria, in 1922, he studied at the Saint Anne Seminary of Jerusalem, a French-protected monastery by Lion's Gate opposite Al Aqsa Mosque, where he witnessed the last years of the British Mandate. This was the site attended by Melkite seminarians from all over the Arab world. His classmates remember how touched he was by the struggle of the Palestinian people for their country. His own adopted name of "Hilarion" (his original name was George) was a saint from Gaza. His childhood in Syria was under the French Mandate, which he also opposed. Archbishop Capucci made use of his position to serve the Palestinian cause from the very beginning.

The War of June 1967

Michael Sabbah, the young priest in charge of the Latin Patriarchate schools in Jordan and what was left of Arab Palestine, had arrived from Amman to Jerusalem to perform some administrative matters, including buying office materials. That warm and sunny morning of June 5, 1967, Michael Sabbah went walking from the Patriarchate (close to Jaffa Gate) to Salah ad-Deen Street to buy materials to take back to Jordan, but found that it was not possible: *"When I arrived I found the shops closed. I realized that something strange was taking place. When I made it back to the Patriarchate, I could see from my bedroom a group of Jordanian soldiers shooting over the walls of the Old City. I realized that this was war."*[214]

It was past 10:00 am. At 8:50 am the Royal Palace in Amman had received information that the Israeli Air Force had attacked Egypt, but the cable lacked the details of the devastating Israeli aggression that had destroyed almost all the Egyptian Air Force while it was on the ground. The operation had begun after 7:40 am. The information received by the Jordanians was that almost 75 percent of the Israeli planes that had participated in the attack had been destroyed and that Egyptian troops were stopping an Israeli land invasion.[215] The Voice of the Arabs, the powerful Cairo-based radio broadcasting to all the Arab world, was narrating a successful counter-attack and divisions of tanks moving towards Tel Aviv in response to the Israeli aggression. Yet none of these reports proved correct: Israel had carried out a powerful and well-prepared attack that destroyed most of the strongest Arab air force within a few hours.

On June 6, 24 hours after the first Israeli attack, Jordan gave the order to withdraw its forces. Henry Khoury, the organist of the Ramallah Holy Family Latin Church, saw the soldiers withdrawing from Latroun on their way to the east. *"We have been abandoned,"* they said as they asked for food and clothes. From the same road in Ramallah, also known as Jaffa Road, a day later they saw tanks with Iraqi flags. *"It was weird, how were the Iraqis coming from west to east?"*[216] Weird indeed. Those were not Iraqis but Israeli tanks camouflaged to take control of Ramallah on June 7. On that day, Iskandar Hinn, a Palestinian Christian refugee from Jaffa whose family had been displaced to Ramallah in 1948, was standing with a neighbour on Rukab Street opposite his apartment when Israeli soldiers spotted them. *"Do you know where the Odeh Hotel is?"* the soldiers asked about the Ramallah Grand Hotel. It was only a few meters away. "They knew where they were going." This was how the hotel of Aidah Odeh was once again occupied and used as center of operations for an army.

In Bethlehem there were dramatic scenes as Israel bombarded the city despite the lack of resistance. The area most affected was that of the Old City market where dozens of civilians were killed. Dr. Victor Batarseh, elected as Bethlehem's mayor in 2005, was at that time the director of the Jordanian emergency military hospital, located in the French Hospital on the Jerusalem-Hebron road and at the corner known as *Bab Zqaq*, the traditional border between Bethlehem and Beit Jala. Batarseh's Jordanian colleague, a new graduate from London, did not listen to advice to stay in the hospital instead of withdrawing with the army. His jeep was targeted by Israeli forces, killing him. A similar incident took place with Dr. Tarazi, another Palestinian Christian, who was killed with napalm in Jerusalem. *"The Israelis targeted the hospital three times, once near the statue of the Virgin Mary and another time over the roof of the room that we were using to operate. There I saw images that I'll never forget. We received a victim of a bombardment whose face could not be recognized, yet he was still alive. He ended up being my own friend Sameer Qattan, an engineer. I will never forget a girl from the Hosh family who arrived at the hospital with her chest opened by a bomb. When the Israelis entered the operations room, I was with Dr. Michel*

Dabdoub, another Bethlehemite, amputating the leg of a victim of their first attack against the hospital."[217]

On June 7, Israeli forces entered Bethlehem after days of aerial bombardments that had left a dozen martyrs, mainly in the Old City market area close to the Nativity Church where many families had found refuge. Around 30 civilians were either killed or injured before Mayor Elias Bandak surrendered the city to the occupying power. The first martyr from Bethlehem in 1967 was Shukri Saqqa (known as Abu Charlie), killed when Israeli forces raided his house close to Mar Elias monastery to the north of the city. One after the other, the casualties arrived at the French Hospital, also known as Saint Joseph, located between Bethlehem and Beit Jala, and which was turned into a military hospital by the Jordanian authorities for this emergency.

At the moment that Israeli forces entered the hospital, Dr. Victor Batarseh was conducting surgery to save a victim of the Israeli shelling of the hospital that had taken place a few hours earlier. Bombs had hit at least three parts of the building, including the iconic statue of the Virgin Mary nearby.[218] *"They brought someone who I couldn't recognize because he had been hit in the face. Later, I realized it was a close friend of mine, engineer Sameer Kattan (...) I will never forget a lady from the Hosh family whose chest had been opened by a bomb"*, recalled Dr. Batarseh. With no organized resistance, the Israeli bombardment of Bethlehem proceeded against a defenseless city.

The Jordanian forces protecting Jerusalem, less than five thousand in number, fought fiercely for the city. There were few units remaining in the mountains around the city from where the shelling of West Jerusalem could have opened another front, and inferiority in numbers and weaponry were factors that led to the defeat known as the "Naksa", the translation of which is something along the lines of "setback".

Hundreds were killed and in the streets of Jerusalem, Archbishop Capucci buried the martyrs alongside a Muslim religious authority. In the Latin Patriarchate there was a scene of particular symbolism when they discovered that two Jordanian soldiers had been killed on their roof; one of them was Christian and the other Muslim. Both were buried in a discreet ceremony organized in the Patriarchate. The Armenian Catholic Convent at the Third Station of the Via Dolorosa had served as a military command for the defence of the city. Just as in 1948, the churches opened their convents and institutions to receive refugees and injured people. Augusta Victoria Hospital, the property of the World Lutheran Federation, had a strategic location overlooking both the Old City and the Jordan Valley, as well as being close to the Israeli enclave of Mount Scopus. This key site became a battlefield just a short distance from the Mount of Olives. Yet, from some churches there was silence. The Greek Orthodox Patriarch of Jerusalem Benedict I did not issue any public statement in defence of his congregation.

The Jerusalem municipality, located in a building owned by the Greek Orthodox Patriarchate, had collapsed. It had held four elections under Jordanian rule (1951, 1955, 1959, and 1963). In 1967 the mayor was Rawhi Khatib and his deputy was Dr. Amin Majaj, a Palestinian Christian from Ramallah, although he had lived most of his life in Jerusalem. Another prominent member of this circle remained Anton Safieh, the saviour of whatever could be saved from the Jerusalem municipality of 1948 and who had remained in the municipality. There was also Hanna Atallah, the first Chairman of the Board of the East Jerusalem YMCA, created in 1951 after the original building had been occupied by Israel in 1948. Anton Atallah was a former deputy mayor who continued to provide support to the city and its council. Atallah was a lawyer from the American University of Beirut who in the sixties became Jordan's representative to the United Nations and foreign minister.

He supported the struggle for Arab rights in the Greek Orthodox Patriarchate of Jerusalem. Ibrahim Tleel, another prominent member of the Greek Orthodox community, was also a member of the municipal council in 1967.

What was left of Arab Palestine in 1948 had vanished within hours. The Israeli victory of June 1967 was a shock to the Arab world. While hundreds of thousands of Palestinian and Syrians became refugees, the Israeli flag was raised in the Old City of Jerusalem and the prospects of an Arab counter-attack were almost minimal. The defeat prompted the resignation of Egyptian leader Gamal Abdel Nasser, although he remained in power as masses of Egyptians took to the streets and called on him to stay. What changed was the Palestinian perspective: June 1967 marked the end of hopes of an Arab military victory. The result for the churches was also disastrous from a humanitarian perspective. For example, the Latin Church in Birzeit, north of Ramallah, had received substantial funding to finish its construction but the funding had to be redirected to help refugees. The Catholic Church opened a branch of its charitable organization CARITAS in Jerusalem to assist with the new situation (in 1948 it had been the Pontifical Mission). As more families crossed the destroyed Karamah crossing (Allenby) over the Jordan River, a new political reality was being formed.

3.

After the Fall of Jerusalem

Archbishop Hilarion Capucci was sitting in his office in the Greek Catholic Patriarchate of Jerusalem, behind the Imperial Hotel and a few meters from Jaffa Gate. One week had passed since Israel occupied the city, a week the Archbishop had spent burying martyrs and trying to raise the morale of the people. His nationalistic tendencies were known to the Israelis who had dealt with him prior to 1967 during his visits to Jaffa to the community there who remained under the responsibility of the Jerusalem Patriarchate. The quiet moment in the office was interrupted by an invitation to meet the person responsible for Christian affairs from the Israeli government. The Archbishop responded immediately: he could not accept an invitation from an authority he did not recognize.

Not all Christian religious authorities in Jerusalem adopted the same attitude. Greek Orthodox Patriarch Benedictos had no problem in establishing cordial relations with the occupying power from the outset. On June 27, 1967, one day before Israel announced measures to annex occupied East Jerusalem, the Patriarch participated in an event hosted by Israeli PM Levi Eshkol and praised Israel: *"We have heard with pleasure of the free access to the holy sites and we deeply appreciate your kind wish (...) I believe that I speak on behalf of all my brothers and fellow leaders here tonight, if I say that we are pleased with the behaviour of the Israeli army. All of its men have shown us kindness and a willingness to serve us. Everybody has displayed respect for the Holy Places and churches. (...).[219]"* Patriarch Benedictos became close to the Israeli authorities, disregarded the rights demanded by the Arab congregation, and continued to enter into land deals with Zionist and Israeli organizations. This further angered the Orthodox community and the larger Palestinian population.

The changes in the Holy City began almost immediately. While Israel committed to respect the Status Quo of the Holy Sites, including Al Aqsa Mosque compound, it immediately began the destruction of the Moroccan Quarter in order to expand the Buraq Square, known by Jews as the site of the Western Wall. Rebuilding the small Jewish Quarter, vacated since 1948 after its inhabitants were evacuated during the war, was also a priority but it was not the same quarter the inhabitants had left in 1948. The Jewish Quarter was expanded towards the Armenian Quarter, also taking over parts of the Syrian neighborhood established around the historic Syrian Orthodox church and monastery of Saint Mark.

The New Israeli Rulers

The request to meet heads of churches in Jerusalem was a strategic step taken by Israel to avoid any threat to its rule over the Holy City from Western countries supposedly concerned about the status of Christianity in Palestine, including the Holy See. As in 1948, assurances of respect for holy shrines and freedom of worship were overshadowed by the forcible displacement of the majority of the Palestinian people, including Christians, and the destruction of several Christian and Muslim religious communities.

The belligerent Israeli aggression that led to the victory in June 1967 did not have the same dimensions as that of 1948 with regard to the expulsion of the Palestinian population. In 1967 the world was different from 1948: the IV Geneva Convention had been introduced and the Soviet Union was no longer on Israel's side. This did not prevent Israel from attempting to empty vast areas of the newly occupied territories of as many people as possible, particularly in the Syrian Golan, where Christians constituted over 12% of the total Syrian population yet most of them were forcibly displaced, including from Ein Qiniye and Majdal Shams.

Some argue that Palestinians had learnt the lessons of 1948 and remained at home. Dr. Victor Batarseh remembers that, *"Only five families from Bethlehem left in 1967 when the Israelis started calling upon people to leave"*.[220] Those were the moments when Israeli loudspeakers were offering a bus "service" to shuttle people from cities to the border with Jordan.[221] It is estimated that the 1967 war created approximately 200,000 new Palestinian refugees, including a percentage of Christians. This figure does not include Palestinians who were stranded outside the country when the war took place.

This reality of forcible displacement did not appear in Israel's narrative to the world. South African-born Abba Eban, Israel's foreign minister and known as one of Israel's strongest diplomats, presented a number of arguments to the United Nations without offering any sort of evidence. He denounced the "aggression", ignoring the fact that Israel had begun the war, and compared the Arab states to a continuation of Nazi Germany: *"June 1967 was to be the month of decision. The 'final solution' was at hand"*.[222] This strategy helped to neutralize Western reaction to the Israeli aggression of 1967, but it did not change international opposition to the acquisition of land by force, as clearly stated in UNSC Resolution 242, approved in November 1967.[223]

Israel made its own interpretation of the new reality but this was not because the Israeli government was unaware of its obligations under international law. It understood these very well; when the Israeli government asked its foreign ministry about the possibility of building settlements in the occupied territory, the legal opinion they received was unambiguous: *"From the point of view of international law, the key provision is the one that appears in the last paragraph of Article 49 of the Fourth Geneva Convention. Israel, of course, is a party to this Convention. The paragraph stipulates as follows: 'The occupying power shall not deport or transfer parts of its own civilian population into the territories it occupies (...)'. The prohibition therefore is categorical and not conditional upon the motives for the transfer or its objectives. Its purpose is to prevent settlement in occupied territory of citizens of the occupied state."*[224]

Israel exploited the ambiguities and referred to the occupied territory as "administered" or sometimes "disputed" to avoid the legal obligations of an occupying power, while launching a fully fledged colonial settlement enterprise. This is how the Israeli government, led by the Labor Party, began the occupation. Recalling the quote by Israel's founder, David Ben Gurion, of *UN shmom* ("UN Nothing" in Hebrew), Israel's "progressive party" and the favorite of European social democracy initiated an enterprise that was summarized by Justice Minister Yacoob Shapira: *"We set about Jerusalem with our eyes open and contravened the Geneva Conventions in the most blatant way."*[225]

The first maps of the colonial settlement enterprise in the newly occupied territory appeared one month after the beginning of the occupation. In July 1967 a plan was presented by Yigal Allon, known as the Allon Plan, which formalized the intention to immediately annex the Syrian Golan Heights and East Jerusalem. The plan also identified several areas of the occupied West Bank such as the Jordan Valley, Latroun, and western Bethlehem as zones to be retained by Israel.[226] Under the plan, the population centers would be returned to Jordan in the context of peace negotiations. The pre-1948 theme of "a land without a people for a people without a land" was simplified by 1967 to "the land without the people", in other words, taking as much as land and natural resources as possible while minimizing the number of Palestinians.

The Allon Plan was part of attempts to redefine relations between the occupied population and the occupier. The Israeli authorities met with religious leaders, local leaders and key notables to seek their collaboration. A few initiatives were introduced such as the written paper delivered by Aziz Shehadeh, the renowned lawyer born to an Episcopal family and expelled from Jaffa in 1948. Shehadeh proposed that the State of Palestine be a full member of the United Nations with borders based on the 1947 partition plan, with border modifications agreed between the parties. The capital of the State of Palestine would be East Jerusalem, with the Old City administered by a joint Israeli-Palestinian body, and economic treaties would be signed between both states. There would also be a Palestinian port in the Mediterranean and guarantees of independence made by the United Nations.[227]

Some Palestinian personalities were willing to cooperate with the new Israeli rulers. These figures were mainly mayors in the southern West Bank, including most notably the mayors of Hebron[228] and Beit Jala.[229] Leaders in Ramallah, Nablus, and the rest of the West Bank also met with the Israelis but refused to collaborate in establishing a body to administer the occupied territory that did not include an end to the Israeli occupation. One of the few personalities from Ramallah who accepted the Israeli invitations, after being arrested and allegedly tortured, was Khalil Janho, who had actively participated in the resistance of 1948 in Talbiya and Qatamon, and in blowing up the *Palestine Post* building. In Jerusalem, the opposition to cooperation was overwhelming.

Expansion of Jerusalem

The Palestinian mayor of Jerusalem, Rawhi al-Khatib, continued the distribution of humanitarian aid and the collection of weapons for delivery to the Israeli occupation. His logic was that the municipal council had been trusted by the people of East Jerusalem and he would continue to exercise his role just like any other municipality in the occupied Palestinian territory. However, from the beginning Israel did not treat Jerusalem like the rest of the occupied cities and towns. On June 27, 1967, the Israeli Parliament passed a law declaring the unilateral expansion of the "Israeli" Jerusalem municipal boundaries, effectively annexing occupied East Jerusalem. In addition to the territory of the old Jerusalem municipality, Israel expanded the city in every direction, including areas such as Beit Hanina and Qalandiya on the way to Ramallah to the north, and large parts of the hinterland of Bethlehem to the south, annexing approximately 20,000 dunums of land mainly from the towns of Bethlehem, Beit Jala, and Beit Sahour. These were the first steps towards the construction of a ring of colonial settlements intended to separate Jerusalem from the rest of the occupied West Bank.

Almost a week after the Israeli decree was announced by the Israeli Parliament, the United Nations approved Resolution 2253 *("The General Assembly (...) Deeply concerned at the situation prevailing in Jerusalem as a result of the measures taken by Israel to change the status of the City (...) Considers that these measures are invalid (...) Calls upon Israel to rescind all measures taken and to desist forthwith from taking any action which would alter the status of Jerusalem").*[230] The Resolution was approved by 99 votes in favour and 20 abstentions with no vote against. Among the abstentions were Australia, Italy, South Africa, and the United States. This was the beginning of several UN resolutions reaffirming international opposition to annexation and Israeli attempts to change the status quo of the Holy City.

Israel's response to international criticism without concrete sanctions was to continue with its plans. As David Ben Gurion stated: *"What matters is not what the Gentiles will say, but what the Jews will do".*[231] Members of the Palestinian Jerusalem municipality were invited to merge with the Israeli municipality of West Jerusalem, consolidating the annexation of the city. The response of the East Jerusalem municipal council came in a letter: *"The mere discussion of the question of joining the Jerusalem Municipal Council under the Israel rule proclaimed by the Israeli authorities constitutes an official recognition by us of the principle of the annexation of Arab Jerusalem to the Israeli occupied part (...) Since the annexation is an illegal act, we demand the restoration of the situation to that existing prior to 5 June 1967. Consequently we regret to inform you that we are unable to accept the invitation to meet you and hold talks with you on this subject."*[232]

This rejection and support to the people of Jerusalem came at a price, including the deportation of mayor Rawhi al-Khatib in March 1968. These were moments of a dramatic reconfiguration of Jerusalem. Jerusalem residents who were abroad at the time when Israeli forces occupied their hometown struggled to return, either by crossing "illegally" into their own country or through coordination with the Red Cross. A large number were unable to return and their residency rights were revoked following the census conducted by the Israeli authorities in June 1967. The census included questions that focused on the displacement of the Palestinian population such as, *"Had the individual lived prior to the 1948 War in the area that became the State of Israel?"* or *"Was the individual living in or outside of a refugee camp at the time of the 1967 enumeration?"*[233]

Among the newly displaced was Afif Safieh, nephew of Anton Safieh. After graduating from the traditional Catholic College des Freres, Afif went to study Political Science and International Relations in the

Catholic University of Louvain. Afif, son of one of the most traditional Catholic families of the city, remembered his father Emile, a member of the Jordanian Parliament representing Jerusalem and one of the founders of the Palestine National Council, saying, *"In 1948 we lost our country and in 1967 we lost our children"*,[234] a direct reference to the fact that two of his three children could not return home to Jerusalem.

The Israeli occupation of 1967 also marked a new cleavage between foreign heads of churches and the local Christian communities. Almost a year after the occupation, with thousands of deportations, displacements and home demolitions, the head of the Catholic Custody of the Holy Land, delivered a statement saying: *"Thanks be to God, pilgrimages to the Christian Shrines are increasing in number from day to day, and pilgrims make their visits as they did a year ago. Only occasionally they are advised, though not prevented by force, to omit the visit to the River Jordan, on account of some danger of shooting in that zone"*.[235] The emphasis was on foreign pilgrimage while the rights and concerns of the local Christian community were not addressed. This is reflected in a comment heard from Palestinian Christian clergy: *"Many foreigners come to this land because they care about stones, but what about the living stones that have kept those holy sites functioning for centuries?"*.

The Palestinian Revolution

Ironically, the Arab defeat of 1967 symbolized a revival for the Palestinian national movement. In addition to Fatah, which symbolically launched its first military operation in the early hours of January 1, 1965, the Arab Nationalist Movement became the Popular Front for the Liberation of Palestine (PFLP), inspired by the Algerian National Liberation Front aimed at bringing several revolutionary organizations under one single umbrella. Dr. George Habash, the refugee from Saint George's al-Lydd, became its leader. Palestinians had begun to grow more independent from the Arab governments.

Most Palestinian Christians identified politically with the left, although at that time the Communist Party had lost much of its relevance, whether due to persecution or for its refusal to endorse armed struggle, and it remained outside the Palestine National Council and the discussions that were taking place between the "revolutionary" factions. Many did find their place in the PFLP for a variety of reasons, from the secular ideals to the intellectual discussions that were taking place, as Christians were known for their high educational rates. These same reasons served as barriers for their membership in Fatah as despite its embrace of a secular Palestine, Fatah had failed to provide any ideological umbrella, and some of its founding leaders came from the Muslim Brotherhood.

This explains why Fatah did not have a single Christian member on its first Central Committee at the same time that key PFLP leaders were Christians: George Habash, Nayef Hawatmeh, and Wadie Haddad. Nevertheless, several Christians gradually began to join Fatah. This process was accelerated after March 21, 1968, with the Al Karameh battle where a group of Fatah commandoes confronted thousands of Israeli soldiers as they invaded a training camp in Jordan. The support of an anti-aerial brigade of the Jordanian army prevented Israeli bombardments and prompted an Israeli withdrawal: Israel had been defeated for the first time in a battle since the 1967 war. The victory prompted euphoria and almost 20,000 new volunteers joined the ranks of Fatah within the first 48 hours after the battle. A few months later, the PFLP captured an El Al plane flying from Rome to Tel Aviv and diverted it to Algeria. After 40 days of negotiations, a prisoner exchange was made and 16 Palestinian prisoners left Israeli jails. Wadie Haddad was behind this operation.

The battle of Al Karameh marked a turning point for the Palestinian resistance, and particularly for Fatah. Inflicting strategic losses to the Israeli forces was seen as an achievable goal and thousands of enthusiastic Palestinians, mainly those who were children at the time of the Nakba or born after it, answered the call by joining cells. One of them was Hanna Mikhail, born in Ramallah in 1935, who studied at the prestigious Quaker's Friends School and later obtained a PhD in Political Science from Harvard University. He began a prominent career teaching at Princeton University and the University of Washington, Seattle, but the resurgence of the Palestinian revolution convinced him to leave academia and join Fatah. Nabil Shaath, who was close to Mikhail, said that his decision to join Fatah was mainly because *"they speak the language of the people, simple language. It is a secular movement yet it still uses some religious rhetoric. This could aspire to mobilize the nation more than a Marxist movement"*.[236] Coming from a Christian family, Mikhail adopted the name Abu Omar, which could be seen as typically Muslim, and became a top official in charge of international relations. The majority of the Christians who joined Fatah at that time were clearly identified with the left-wing of the organization. Naji Alloush, originally from a Christian family from Birzeit, was identified as a Marxist and became a prominent Fatah leader.

In 1969 Yasser Arafat officially became the chairman of the Executive Committee of the Palestine Liberation Organization. It consolidated a process in which a new generation took over the national movement, a generation that had begun political activism in the General Union of Palestine Students (GUPS) or in military training camps. Unlike the first PLO leadership, this was based on people training to take the lead in providing the Palestinian people with the means for national liberation without depending on any foreign support. While the Palestine Liberation Army (PLA) remained under the sponsorship of the Arab nations that were hosting them (Iraq, Syria, Jordan and Iraq), a new guerrilla movement was bringing together thousands of Arabs to fight for Palestine under a Palestinian leadership. Among those Arabs who joined the Palestinian resistance was Nayef Hawatmeh, a Jordanian born in Salt, originally from a Greek Catholic family. He led a split from the PFLP in 1969 to form the Democratic and Popular Front for the Liberation of Palestine, later known just as the Democratic Front (DFLP). Some prominent Christians from the Arab world who joined Fatah were Lebanese writer Elias Khoury and Egyptian analyst and intellectual Raouf Mikhail, known as Dr. Mahjoub Omar, perhaps the most prominent Coptic member of the Palestinian revolution.

Military Operations and the PLO Arrival in Lebanon

Archbishop Capucci had a known commitment to the Arab cause. His boycott of the Israeli occupation authorities was not the only sign he gave of his support for Palestinian freedom. While there is no agreement on when he officially became involved with the national movement, his relations with Fatah dated back to before 1968. In that year Mustafa Issa, known as Abu Firas, the head of the western sector of Fatah in the occupied territory, contacted the archbishop to request his cooperation. The western sector was the operative branch of Fatah for the occupied territory in charge of committing acts of resistance, including sabotage and guerrilla operations against Israeli targets. It was headed by Khalil Al Wazir, Abu Jihad, who operated as the military mastermind of Fatah. Salah Khalaf, Abu Iyad, was in charge of security, which included the Palestinian intelligence services and operations outside Palestine.

Abu Firas was born in the village of Lifta, west of Jerusalem, and his family was forcibly displaced alongside Deir Yassin and other villages in the west of the city during the Nakba of 1948. He joined Fatah from the beginning and was part of the coordination for the legendary clandestine visit of Yasser Arafat to the occupied West Bank after the June 1967 war. His main task was to create military cells to fight the Israeli occupation and for that purpose, he contacted Archbishop Capucci, someone who had already met Abu Jihad. The diplomatic status of the Melkite leader in Jerusalem, including the diplomatic plates of his car, were a precious asset for a local resistance needing to smuggle weaponry. This is how Archbishop Capucci began to carry weapons inside his Mercedes Benz and participated in the creation of the first armed cells of Fatah in Jerusalem and the rest of the occupied Palestinian territory. His role became more prominent after Israeli forces arrested and deported Abu Firas to Jordan.

Archbishop Capucci was leading a church that, unlike others hierarchies, identified deeply with the idea of being a local church. Therefore, he naturally identified with the struggle of his people just as church representatives had identified with struggles against Latin American dictatorships, South African apartheid or anti-Soviet resistance in Poland. However, some believed that the role adopted by Archbishop Capucci of direct involvement in the armed struggle of the Palestinian people was not compatible with the position of the church regarding the use of violence. The Catholic Church does espouse the idea of "just wars" and this is how some members of the clergy became involved with the Palestinian resistance in various ways.

Archbishop Capucci was a symbol but he was not the only one. Stories of combatants and weapons being hidden in churches were not confirmed by religious sources, but were also not denied. It was confirmed that some priests were known to carry weapons, including Fr. Hanna Nimri who served as the last Latin priest of Beisan in 1948 and became the parish priest of Gaza, becoming one of the most prominent figures in the city.

The organization of the resistance movements was mainly taking place outside Palestine, external but the Israeli occupation took strong action to prevent the articulation of any kind of resistance inside the country. Mass arrests, beatings, and random attacks were the response of Israeli forces to any kind of resistance or political organization. In a letter dated September 21, 1969, the Jordanian ambassador to the UN, Mohammad Al Farra, denounced the mass arrests of *"large groups of Arab women and teenage girl students from Nablus, Gaza and Jerusalem. Mrs. Isam Abdul Hadi, President of the Palestine Women's Union, was also arrested and imprisoned. More than 250 people, including elderly women, were imprisoned and tortured"*.[237] It was in the first half of September that Israeli forces arrived at the Anglican (Episcopal) Church in Ramallah, at the traditional "Rukab" street across the Latin Convent, to arrest Rev. Elia Khoury. In fact he was not only arrested but was deported to Jordan, accused of participating in an attack against a supermarket in West Jerusalem that killed two people.[238] The priest, born in Zababdeh in the north of the West Bank, always denied his involvement in any act of violence but his alleged role in passing messages from the national movement in Jordan to people in Palestine, including foreign diplomats, was what eventually led the Israeli authorities to deport him. This deportation provoked demonstrations in Jerusalem, Ramallah, Bethlehem, and Beit Sahour that included hunger strikes.

Around the same period of time, Israeli forces severely beat dozens of schoolgirls in Bethlehem and the secretary of Bethlehem municipal council during a peaceful sit-in demonstration against Israeli policies. Mayor Elias Bandak protested to the military governor, as registered in UN records, yet such acts did not end. The Israeli authorities crushed any movement aimed at ending the occupation.

Many believed that a non-violent approach against the occupation would not deter Israel from entrenching its control. Palestinians of all social backgrounds began to leave the occupied territory to join the resistance abroad; some returned to organize acts of resistance while others stayed abroad. Thousands of Palestinian professionals from engineers to medical doctors gathered around Palestinian revolutionary groups to provide their services. An example was Shafika Al Saqqa, a nurse from Beit Jala who worked in the clinic of Wadie' Haddad in Amman, providing free services to Palestinian refugees.

Those coming from the West Bank to join Fatah mainly joined the western sector commanded by Khalil Al Wazir (Abu Jihad). One of his lieutenants was Raji Musleh, a native of Beit Sahour. Born into a traditional Greek Orthodox family, he became particularly prominent in the activities of the western sector. There was also Nabil Aburdeneh, born to a Christian family from Bethlehem, who studied law at Cairo University, then joined Fatah and served under Abu Jihad's orders. His name became known internationally decades later when he became the presidential spokesperson for Yasser Arafat, and later for Mahmoud Abbas. Some of the Palestinian Christians who participated in the formation of the first Fatah guerrilla units could not be identified due to security precautions adopted by the organization. For example, one of the most qualified trainers in the combatant camps of Jordan was simply known as "Abu Fadi". It is known that he was originally from Birzeit and trained some of the most renowned Palestinian officers. Another Fatah recruit of those years was Hanna Muqbell, born in Jerusalem and known as one of the most important journalists in the early revolutionary press of Fatah and the PLO. A similar role was played in Jordan by May Sayegh, a Palestinian Christian from Gaza.

Unlike Fatah, the PFLP did not become as prominent in the guerrilla fighting against Israel. Some people did not forget that instead of joining the Fatah forces in the Al Karamah battle, the PFLP leaders ordered their forces to withdraw to the hills of Amman. Wadie Haddad was developing relations with revolutionary movements worldwide to create a more extensive map for operations. The successful hijacking of El Al flight 426 on its way to Tel Aviv from Rome in the summer of 1968 and the liberation of Palestinian political prisoners was a sign of what became official PFLP policy by the late sixties.

It is in this context that a few months later, Jael Al Arja arrived at Arturo Merino Benitez International Airport in Santiago de Chile. The Chilean capital had become a major center for Palestinians in a process that had begun in the last years of Ottoman control over Palestine, but increased significantly after the Nakba of 1948. Palestinians had become part of the Chilean social fabric; the Palestino Football Team competed in Chile's premier league and the textile factories of Yarur, Sumar and Hirmas, among others, provided jobs to thousands of Chilean workers. At passport control, Jael told Chilean police that he was going to stay with one of his relatives. Indeed, the house of Musa in Avenida Peru, the heart of a neighborhood full of Palestinian immigrants, was the house of a relative, but Musa was not his brother, his father or first cousin. He was a distant relative from the Al Ehsenat clan that traces its roots to an area close to the Mar Elias monastery to the north of Bethlehem, and that for several centuries had been one of the most traditional Greek Orthodox families of Beit Jala. Chile's Palestine community was largely composed of Palestinian Christians from the Bethlehem area.

Unlike his distant cousin Musa and the other relatives he visited, Jael's intentions were not to settle in Chile and start a new business. He contacted a handful of young members of the Palestinian community to introduce them to the PFLP. He had been sent to Chile under direct instructions from Wadie Haddad for two purposes: to create PFLP cells and collect funds for the resistance, and Jael succeeded. The fact that the PFLP was led by George Habash, also a Palestinian

Christian, served as an incentive for other Christians to join the organization. Thus, while Fatah was strengthening its position among Palestinian communities in Arab countries, the PFLP managed to extend its influence to Latin America and built ties with revolutionary movements such as the Tupamaros and the MIR. Soon, the name of Ilich Ramirez, known as Carlos the Jackal, a Venezuelan national, became one of the most prominent additions to the external operations of the PFLP, although this had little to do with the activities of Jael Al Arja in the Palestinian communities; Ramirez was recruited in the Soviet Union. Patrick Arguello, a 27-year-old US-Nicaraguan citizen of Irish descent and member of the Sandinistas, became one of the first martyrs of the PFLP as he was shot attempting to take over an El Al flight flying over London in early September 1970. Leyla Khaled was arrested in the same operation. She had posed as Patrick's wife when boarding the flight with Honduran passports, another country with a prominent Palestinian Christian community.

The Palestinian revolution continued to escalate, led by a PLO that had already succeeded in unifying dozens of groups dispersed in various countries with the main goal of returning to Palestine and establishing an independent state. It succeeded in monopolizing political representation to become the "sole and legitimate representative" of the Palestinian people. The infrastructure and networks that were built in the Arab world and beyond included a significant level of involvement by Christian clergy, from a Patriarchate in Jerusalem to a small church in Zarka, Jordan. In 1970, the Melkite Archbishop of Galilee, Joseph Raya, wrote: *"Through no fault of their own, the Christians of the Holy Land became victims of injustice, discrimination and cunning persecution. Their only escape is to leave their country and go to more secure places"*.[239] For other Christians, the response was to fight to recover and return to their country.

From Amman to Beirut

On September 6, 1970, the PFLP carried out one of the most spectacular operations ever conducted by the Palestinian resistance. With the approval of George Habash and planning headed by Wadie Haddad, two hijacked planes arrived at the "airport of the revolution", the name given to an abandoned British military airport known as Dawson located in the Jordanian desert east of Mufraq city. A fourth plane was taken to Cairo. They made use of Jordanian soil to take an action involving not only Israel but also the United States (TWA flight 741 from Frankfurt) and Switzerland (Swissair flight 100 from Zurich). On September 10, BOAC Flight 775 (a British state-owned company) departing from Bahrain was also taken to Dawson airfield. The holding of hundreds of foreign citizens in the Jordanian desert was a real problem for the Jordanian government. The events around this action represented "a final straw" for King Hussein.[240]

At the same time, Dr. Abdullah Abdullah was in Chile as part of the PLO delegation to the inauguration of President Salvador Allende, the first ever democratically elected Marxist President. This distinguished delegation from the incipient PLO diplomacy was in the middle of an international event full of delegations from dozens of countries when the news broke from Jordan. Abdullah immediately called headquarters in Amman and spoke with Kamal Adwan, a Fatah Central Committee member. *"Can you please tell me what is going on?"* said the young Abdullah. Adwan concluded his explanation of the situation by saying, *"This is not good"*.[241] Within a few days, Adwan's analysis proved correct when the Jordanian army launched an offensive with 65,000 well-trained soldiers against 15,000 Palestinian guerrillas[242] in what was known as Black September.

The Jordanian narrative presents Black September as an internal dispute between the forces of law and order and those trying to create a "state within a state". Palestinians were, in fact, the majority of the population, had contributed significantly to the development of state institutions, made up the majority of the business community and occupied significant posts in the Jordanian military forces as well as in the government. In 1970 the Jordanian foreign minister was Anton Atallah, a Palestinian Christian born in Jerusalem who had used his seniority to champion the Palestinian cause in international forums. He still viewed the activities of the Palestinian revolution as irresponsible, as did other Palestinian Jordanians who remained in the government and opposed the PLO forces.

However, several government officials submitted their resignations and a few hundred army officers left their barracks to join the Palestinian groups. Nicola, a Palestinian Christian from Beit Jala, was a distinguished soldier in the Jordanian Armed Forces. When the conflict began, he simply left his weapon in his office and left on foot: *"It was not like I had an option. I had no previous involvement with Palestinian groups but I was still Palestinian and could not handle the incitement against my people I heard from some of my superiors (...) I left my weapon and credentials and left walking without knowing where to go. There was fighting all over Amman, shootings here and there (...) When I arrived to Jabal Hussein where my house was I realized that I could be killed for leaving my post (...) I decided to pass by the Fatah offices and enrol with them. Soon I was on my way to Syria."*[243] A large number of those who deserted from the Jordanian Army, including some Jordanians who remained loyal to the PLO, joined a new battalion called "The Yarmouk Forces", known for the professionalism and skill of its well-trained officers.

For many Palestinians whose families had been divided in 1967, the situation in Jordan was terrifying as there was no communication. Fayez Saqqa was a 17-year-old Fatah member in Bethlehem with a family that reflected the political and social complexities of Palestine. His father was a renowned leader of the Communist Party while his mother was a devoted Roman Catholic. The communist membership of his father helped his three older brothers to find scholarships in the Soviet Union, but their return to Palestine was made difficult after 1967. During Black September, the family lost contact with Adel, who had been working as a medical doctor in Amman while waiting for a permit via the Red Cross to return home. The young Fayez decided to go to Jordan to look for his brother. He did so smuggled in a truck from the famous Abu Aita plastic company based in Beit Sahour. Once in Amman, Fayez managed to find his brother but returning to Palestine seemed impossible as he had not exited through the regular channels. Fayez contacted other Fatah members and left for Spain to begin his university studies. It was the beginning of a career that would take him from a military leader in Lebanon to a special envoy for President Yasser Arafat.[244]

The Jordanian-PLO struggle lasted until 1971 when the last Palestinian forces were expelled from northern Jordan and the events left deep wounds that took years to heal. The events of 1970 were a determining moment for the Palestinian revolution, which moved from Jordan via Syria to Lebanon, where an agreement signed through the Arab League granted a base for the PLO. The country of the cedars already had an important Palestinian population, mainly from Jaffa and the Galilee, and hosted some of the finest Palestinian intellectuals and businesspeople, many of them graduates from its prestigious American University. A new era began with the Palestinian presence in Lebanon, one that involved a fierce struggle against attempts to eliminate the Palestinian national movement.

Palestinians in Israel: Iqrith and Kufr Bir'im

The Nakba of 1948 fragmented Palestinian society with forcible displacement and exile, imprisonment, arbitrary and discriminatory legislation, suppression of institutions, and banning of expressions of national identity. The Palestinians left in Israel, approximately 110,000 by 1949, lived under military rule until 1966. While Palestinians were allowed to vote in Israeli elections, large areas of their land were expropriated, thousands of families were divided, and many were forced to leave their homes. About a third of the Palestinians left in what became Israel identified as internally displaced.

The Palestinian leadership left in the country included several prominent Palestinian Christians, mainly leaders in the Communist Party, which was not viewed favourably by church leaders. Some became strong advocates of the Arab-Palestinian cause from their own church circles, including through the magazines printed in several communities. A few Christians accepted to work with Israeli Zionist institutions, notably Elias Nakhleh, a member of the Israeli Parliament until 1969 and an adviser on Arab affairs, as well as prominent members of Nazareth municipal council that allied with Zionist parties (mainly Ben Gurion's Mapai). At a time when proclaiming support for the PLO was a criminal offense that could result in jail, several Palestinian leaders in Israel were persecuted. These included Mahmoud Darwish, from a Muslim family of Al Birwa, Samih Al Qasem, from a Druze family in Rameh, and Sabri Jiries, a Palestinian Christian from Fassouta. Both Darwish and Jiries left Israel to join the PLO in Lebanon.

To the south, the Christian community left in Israel was located in Jaffa, with some remaining in al-Lydd and Ramleh. The greatest concentration was in the Galilee, including Nazareth, the city of the annunciation which became the only Arab city left in what became

Israel. The largest congregation was that of the Greek Catholics (Melkites), followed by the Orthodox Church, and a significant Latin community (represented by its Vicariate in Nazareth). Maronites, Episcopals, Armenians, Copts and a few Syriac families were the other communities left. The leader of the Melkites in 1970 was Archbishop Joseph Raya, who had replaced Archbishop George Hakim, and was a strong figure who opposed the Communist Party (the main party supported by Palestinian citizens in Israel) while strongly advocating for the right to return of members of his community.[245] Archbishop Raya wrote a comprehensive report on the situation of his community, signed on January 12, 1970. In the introduction he describes the effects of the exile on the church and added:

"The Church was deprived of her elite and the Christians "beheaded" from their leaders. Many churches and the best schools had to be abandoned or sold (...) This from the Greek Catholic diocese alone, 28,000 Christians left for good and more are ready to follow them (...) unjust and cunning laws promulgates between 1948 and 1962 make possible at any time expropriation in favour of Jewish immigrants. Compensation has been and still offered to the dispossessed, but it is so unjust and humiliating that people refuse it and prefer to starve than to subject themselves to its degrading conditions (...) there are too others who were later on dispossessed for no other reason than the fallacy of "security reason". For instance the two villages of Ikreth and Kafar Birem were completely dynamited and plowed for no reasons. The Supreme Court of Justice of Israel studied and discussed their case and gave back the right for the people to return. But the court injunction was completely ignored by the government which still has possession of these two villages in favour of future Jewish immigrants."[246]

There were cases of internal displacement in almost every corner yet Iqrith and Kufr Bir'im became the key symbols of this reality.

The excuse that villagers had joined armed resistance against Zionist gangs could not be used in their cases as they had left peacefully in coordination with the military commanders who had committed to let them return after a few weeks. The destruction of Iqrith, a Greek Catholic village, on Christmas Day 1952 was a clear indication by the Israeli authorities of their intention to block any return. The main pretext for ignoring the ruling of the Israeli Supreme Court of Justice to allow villagers to return was "security". The legal procedures had begun in July 1951. In practical terms, the Israeli government did not want to set a precedent for the return of Palestinian refugees regardless of their place of displacement or religion. Kufr Bir'im, a village mainly inhabited by Palestinian Maronites, suffered the same fate. In both cases, the only buildings that remained standing were the church and cemetery.

The villagers did not want the compensation offered by Israel but to exercise their right of return. They had witnessed the destruction of their ancient villages and wanted to rebuild them. There are reports that Archbishop Hakim eventually accepted compensation for the church lands lost in Kufr Bir'im but the matter is still part of negotiations between Israel and the Holy See.

In August 1972, almost two decades after the Israeli court ruling in support of their return, blocked by successive Israeli administrations, the villagers joined with Archbishop Raya and organized a march towards the Israeli Prime Minister's office. Only a few weeks earlier, the villagers had been brutally evicted by Israeli police when they tried to repair their churches. They were supported by left-wing Israeli Jews and by Palestinian leaders in Israel.

The demonstration was the tip of the iceberg in increased efforts led by Archbishop Raya, who had already engaged in equality activism during his stay in the United States, where he became famous for confronting the Ku Klux Klan.[247] His efforts involved briefings with diplomats and media, and even an attempt to persuade Israel's PM Golda Meir. In response to strong opposition from the Israeli leader, Archbishop Raya stated: *"Because you have killed justice in Israel we will declare next Sunday a day of mourning. We will not pray the Sunday prayers nor will we celebrate the Eucharist. We will only toll the church bells as a sign of mourning for the death of justice in Israel."*[248] That following Sunday, Melkite churches were not opened for prayers in what became a firm symbol of defiance to the Israeli government, which had been careful to convince the West that Christians were thriving under Israeli rule.

The "civil rights movement" model by Palestinian citizens of Israel was different from the struggle of the Palestinians living in the occupied territories of 1967 or those displaced elsewhere. Israel had granted the former citizenship but was attempting to deal with the contradictions of being a Jewish state as well as a self-proclaimed "democracy". From the very beginning, Palestinian citizens of Israel did not have equal rights with their Jewish neighbours. The case of Iqrith and Kufr Bir'im was a clear example of that. In July 1972 an Israeli columnist of *Yediot Aharonot* newspaper highlighted some of these issues in the context of the civil disobedience promoted by the leaders of the Greek Catholic Church in Israel: *"It is the duty of Israeli leaders to explain to the public with clarity and courage a number of facts that have been submerged with the passage of time. The first of these is the fact that there is no Zionism, settlement, or Jewish state without the eviction of Arabs and expropriation of their lands".*[249]

The struggle of the people of Iqrith and Kufr Bir'im remains unresolved today (we will return to the topic in the next chapter), but the case revealed Israeli discrimination against its Arab Palestinian population and the reality faced by the Christian population living under its control. It also highlighted the contradictions presented by foreign Christian leaders who support Israel, even financially, as a duty while ignoring the situation of the indigenous Christian population living under Israeli control. Archbishop Raya explained with an example: *"Since the establishment of Israel, we have known so many Catholic missionaries – priests, nuns, brothers, laymen – who became enthusiastic about their study of the Hebrew language. They follow the Oulpans, do research, and expect a great deal of energy to satisfy an intellectual desire to know and speak Hebrew. They do it with great pride. However, these same missionaries spent long years living and working in Arab communities. They neither understood nor spoke a word of Arabic, the native language of the Christians. On the contrary, they forced these people to speak their own language. Is it any wonder that the Christians feel discrimination, condescension, paternalism and colonialism from the Church and its representatives?"*[250]

Latin Bishop Giovanni Marcuzzo, who served in Nazareth for many years, explained: *"Politically we are forgotten. Some special Christian communities, especially in the United States, support the Zionist movement and forget or deny the existence of Palestinian Christians. For example, an evangelical preacher from the United States recently brought twenty million dollars, not for the Christian community here but for the so-called "Zionist" movement. It is a problem less because of the material help than because of their way of reading the gospel."*[251]

Palestinians in Lebanon

Before the Nakba of 1948, relations between northern Palestine and Lebanon were close. Many families were inter-married and commuted from one area to the other. A significant number of Lebanese Christians had found refuge in the Palestinian Galilee from the sectarian violence and clashes between Druze and Christians in 1860. At the same time, many members of the Palestinian elite sought their higher education in Beirut, notably at the American University.

The Nakba changed the nature of those relations as a border was imposed, connections were cut, and families were divided. Lebanon received thousands of refugees in dozens of refugee camps. By 1970, some of them had obtained Lebanese citizenship, mainly Palestinian Christians, but the vast majority were discriminated against in a country where the balance between almost 18 religious communities was an extremely sensitive issue. Not all Palestinian Christians had been granted citizenship. Thousands were living in refugee camps where various churches and Christian organizations, mainly the Greek Catholics as well as the Pontifical Mission, provided them with services, in addition to the work of the UNRWA. A significant number of Palestinian Christians lived in refugee camps, including notably in Al Dbayeh, Mar Elias, Jisr Il Basha, and the unrecognized camp of Al Bassa near Tyre in southern Lebanon.

Among those who received citizenship were members of a distinguished business class that had thrived in pre-1948 Palestine, including both Christians and Muslims, but Christians obtained Lebanese citizenship more easily. This policy fulfilled two interests of the Lebanese government: to increase the number of Christians and to inject investments into the Lebanese economy. It is estimated that between 1949 and 1958 about 31,000 Palestinian Christians obtained citizenship in Lebanon.[252] These people included the Gargour family from Jaffa who were traders and who obtained the Mercedes Benz franchise for the Middle East; the Khoury family from Jaffa who owned orange plantations (they made the first shipment of "Jaffa Oranges-Palestine" to Germany); the Talamas family (also traders from Jaffa); Tannous (from Jerusalem) who moved to Lebanon after losing their properties outside Jaffa Gate (the General Motors franchise); Mounir Haddad from Jerusalem; Fritz Marroum from Jerusalem; Emile Mousallam from Haifa; and Yousef Beidas, the son of Palestinian writer Khalil Beidas and known as "the Genius of Jerusalem" due to his ability to make money as one of the most successful bankers in Beirut. Beidas later suffered harassment from the Lebanese state and it is believed that one of the reasons was because of his financial support for Fatah; Batshoun (Jaffa, groceries and textiles); Hreish (Jaffa, glass); Bouri (from Jaffa, cement king regionally); Daoud Abdo (from Jerusalem, one of the most prominent photographers in Palestine); Hassib Sabbah and Said Khoury, both from Safad and founders of the largest regional construction company, the Consolidated Contractors Company (CCC); Assad Nassar, CEO of Middle East Airlines (Lebanon's carrier) until the sixties was a Palestinian Christian from Nazareth; Dr. Fouad Khoury was a medical doctor from Jerusalem who established a hospital; Dr. Charles Ayyoub from Haifa; and Antwan Abdelnour, a wealthy businessman from Jaffa.[253]

In addition to the churches established in the refugee camps of Mar Elias, Dbyaeh, Jisr Il Basha and Al Bassa, Palestinian Christian refugees congregated in a church for the Orthodox community in Al Seide, Ras Beirut, where Fr. Hanna Sakkab was the parish priest, also of Palestinian origin. In the 1950s, Fr. Ibrahim Ayyad arrived in Lebanon after being pardoned by Jordan for his alleged role in the killing of King Abdullah in 1951. The Latin Church was not a large congregation in Lebanon and the arrival of Palestinian Christian refugees from Jerusalem, Jaffa, Haifa, and Acre significantly contributed to its numbers.

Political Organizations
and Military Operations

An agreement was reached on November 3, 1968, between the PLO and Lebanon under the auspices of the Arab League to allow Palestinian forces to operate in Lebanon. This was the basis for Palestinian forces to start relocating to southern Lebanon. For the PLO it was strategic to maintain a presence on the borders of historic Palestine and therefore, the PLO-Lebanon agreement was of vital importance to Palestinian interests.

Before the arrival of the PLO leadership in Beirut, the main Palestinian political figures were independent figures such as PLO Executive Committee member Shafiq Al Hout, the PLO representative, whose Lebanese ancestry facilitated his access to Lebanese political circles, including from the right-wing. Almost all Palestinian political groups were organized in the refugee camps. In 1970, when the first leaders of factions began to arrive to Beirut, the scenario gradually changed in an already troubled Lebanon. More military training camps were established where thousands of Palestinian, Arab and foreign volunteers were trained to join the Palestinian revolution. In some cases, fighters with groups such as the Armenian Secret Army for the Liberation of Armenia (linked to the PFLP) or the Uruguayan Tupamaros (linked to Fatah) were trained as a contribution to their own struggles without necessarily having to conduct operations on behalf of Palestinian groups.

The idea of turning Southern Lebanon into a new "Hanoi" for Israeli forces was repeated by some Palestinian fighters, a reality that some Lebanese politicians saw as the destabilization of their country. It is a fact that there was no Palestinian consensus on what military involvement would take place in the country but Lebanon became the headquarters of the Palestinian national liberation movement and a location for military training (in addition to other training sites elsewhere in the Arab world).

Military training was a key part in the formation of Palestinian cadres and a significant number of Palestinian students would spend their summer breaks preparing for what was seen as the national liberation struggle. The General Union of Palestine Students (GUPS) became a central place for recruitment in Western countries, and served as the basis for Palestinian diplomatic representation in locations that still refused to open PLO missions. Many of these students formed the legendary Students Batallion (*Al Ktaiba il Tul'labiya*) discussed later in this book, and whose "godfather" was Naji Alloush from Birzeit.

Palestinian citizens of Israel also crossed the borders with Lebanon to join the PLO. This was the path taken in 1972 by Therese Halasseh, an 18-year-old woman from Acre and an activist in the Israeli Communist Party. She made the journey with a group of people who shared the same goal. They crossed from Kiryat Shmona (the northern Israeli town built on top of the Palestinian village of al-Khalisa that was ethnically cleansed during the Nakba) to Al Matala, and from there to Lebanon, arriving in Marjayyoun (one of the most important Christian towns in Southern Lebanon) and walking until they found a Fatah patrol. The journey took them *"three nights and two days"*.[254] Therese's father was descended from a major Jordanian Christian tribe and her mother was Palestinian.

Rima Tannous was a Jordanian Christian who joined Fatah when she was 20 years old: *"The motive behind my joining the Palestinian revolution was the human aspect of the Palestinian cause, not the fact that I am an Arab. The issue of humanity is universal and cannot be divided."*[255] Both Therese and Rima took part in an operation that was unusual by Fatah standards: the hijacking of a plane, an act that had mainly given prominence to the military branch of the PFLP.

The operation took place on May 8, 1972, when four Palestinians (Therese and Rima joined by Ali Taha Abu Sneineh and Abed Aziz Al Atrash) took control of Sabena flight 571 en route from Vienna International Airport to Israel's Lod International Airport (al-Lydd). They made the plane land at the Israeli airport and immediately made their demand for the release of Palestinian prisoners from Israeli jails.

The Palestinians called for the Red Cross to transmit the messages and allow food to be provided to the passengers. On May 9, a group of Israeli commandoes dressed as ICRC staff stormed the plane, killing Abu Sneineh and Al Atrash, and capturing Therese and Rima. In the brief fight, Therese Hallaseh managed to shoot and injure Israeli soldier Benjamin Netanyahu, later to become Israel's Prime Minister. Both women spent over a decade in jail until they were released in two separate prisoner exchanges. They had initially been condemned to life imprisonment. Years later, a Palestinian security official with knowledge of the planning of the operation said: *"The biggest mistake was having played in their playground. Our people were excited to enter Palestine, but it could have been dealt with differently (...) extending the dialogue with the ICRC envoys who were either collaborating with the Israelis or were Israelis disguised as ICRC officials, which allowed them to plan a successful rescue operation that prevented us from freeing hundreds of prisoners."*[256]

One of the centers for Palestinian student unions in Western Europe was in Spain, a country that had no diplomatic relations with Israel and cordial relationships with many Arab countries, although not yet as friendly with the PLO which had identified with the struggle of those fighting the Franco regime. The recruitment of spies was a priority for the Mossad. Palestinian student Samir[257] was particularly vulnerable as he came from a poor family and was dependent on a scholarship that he risked losing due to his low marks. He initially agreed to collaborate with Israel but later confessed to the Palestinian intelligence apparatus operating in Madrid. The person in charge of his detention was George Salameh, a Palestinian Christian from Beit Jala, known as a strong and committed militant.

The decision about what to do with this case was not easy as collaboration would most probably be paid with the collaborator's life. Yet the instructions they received from Abu Iyad in Beirut were different: *"Make him a double agent and let him bring as much information as possible"*. The move worked and Samir gained the trust of his Israeli counterparts: *"George and others would tell Samir to give details about a car with weapons parked at a particular address. The Israelis would go and see that the car had weapons, but they did not suspect that this was all planned."*[258] With his reputation growing in Israeli circles, Samir was contacted by Baruch Cohen, the person in charge of Mossad in southern Europe.

Within a few days, George, following Abu Iyad's instructions, had prepared a trap for the Israeli official in which Samir would shoot him and leave. This is precisely what happened in the Nebraska coffee shop on Madrid's Gran Via on January 23, 1973. A PLO operation ended with the death of the highest-ranking Israeli intelligence officer killed since 1948 while Samir escaped. "Black September" claimed responsibility for the attack as a response to the Israeli assassination of the PLO representative in Rome, Abdul Wael Zuaiter, and of Mahmoud Hamchari, the Palestinian representative in Paris.

Israel's assassination campaign of Palestinian leaders stretched from Paris to Beirut. One of its most prominent victims was Kamal Nasser. An intellectual born in Gaza in a family originally from Birzeit, he graduated from the American University of Beirut as a political scientist in 1945 before returning to Palestine. He engaged in politics supporting the Baath party and its Pan-Arabist ideology. Having been an elected member of the Jordanian parliament representing

Ramallah, he joined the PLO in 1968 after being expelled from Palestine in 1967, becoming a member of the Executive Committee in 1969.

The old Episcopal church of Birzeit, a beautiful and humble stone building, was where Kamal demonstrated his talent for playing the organ. Nasser came from a prominent Palestinian Episcopal family strongly linked to the development of the Birzeit College, and later the University. Kamal was in charge of PLO communications in Beirut when on April 10, 1973, Israeli forces executed him in his apartment in West Beirut. That night, three other Palestinians were assassinated by the same forces: Kamal Adwan, Mohammad Yousef An Najjar, and his wife Rasmiyya An Najjar.

Resistance inside Palestine

Fatah, the largest Palestinian group, operated mainly through Yasser Arafat's two closest aides: Salah Khalaf (Abu Iyad) who built up the Palestinian intelligence apparatus, and Khalil Al Wazir who was in charge of the Fatah military forces and operations inside the occupied homeland. The western sector (*Kata' Al Gharbi*) became famous for its operations inside Palestine, and one of its key members was the Greek Catholic Archbishop of Jerusalem, Hilarioun Capucci. He participated in the recruitment of fighters and coordination of the organization. He is best remembered for smuggling weapons from Lebanon into Palestine using the diplomatic immunity of his car.

Archbishop Capucci was not the first Christian religious leader to carry weapons in the context of a national liberation struggle. However, in the context of Jerusalem, with an office just 300 meters away from the Holy Sepulcher, a number of questions arise. The Latin Patriarch of Jerusalem at the time was Giacomo Beltriti, an Italian who had arrived at the age of 16 to study at the Latin Patriarchate Seminary of Beit Jala. He was fluent in Arabic and is remembered as being very dedicated to his Palestinian congregation. He had a rather cold relationship with the Israeli authorities and provided the Holy See with extensive information about the human rights situation in the occupied Palestinian territory. Nevertheless, Capucci's political engagement was seen by Patriarch Beltriti as a deviation from their role as religious leaders. Someone who had repeatedly crossed such lines was Fr. Hanna Nimri, known as an Arab nationalist. After the occupation in 1967, he withdrew from political activities, perhaps following instructions from the Latin Patriarchate after the Bishop of Nazareth Hanna Kildani visited him at the church in Gaza, accompanied by Israeli officers.

Fr. Nimri's sudden withdrawal and the relations he built with Israeli authorities, allegedly done to facilitate the life of his community were viewed with suspicion by some. In February 1973 a single assailant entered the Latin Convent in Gaza City and assassinated Fr. Nimri with a shot to his heart. The crime was never resolved, at least not publicly. Fr. Manuel Musallam, at that time the priest of Jenin and later appointed as the Gaza Catholic priest, remembers an announcement on Al Assifa[259] radio that Fr. Nimri had been executed for collaborating with Israel. *"In the same report they remembered his patriotic work but said that he had changed during recent years."*[260]

Fr. Nimri's burial took place in Ramallah and was attended by relatives and members of his congregation. The city had a population of almost 15,000, a number that included many refugees who had tripled the population in only 22 years since 1948. The mayor since 1972 had been Karim Khalaf from one of the traditional Ramallah families whose beautiful villa located in the Ein Munjed area overlooked what was then a valley of olive and apricot trees on the way to the municipality. The elections of 1972 had been the first elections after the Israeli occupation of 1967 and were intended by Israel to be a propaganda tool to show normality, as well as to provoke divisions between the PLO in exile and the "moderate Arabs" living under Israeli control.

The 1972 elections had been largely boycotted by the organized national forces and only 26,000 people participated.[261] Nevertheless, they highlighted the need to organize people inside the occupied homeland beyond the traditional activities of resistance, particularly the importance of local government. In 1973 the PLO decided to create the Palestinian National Front made up of members living inside Palestine to coordinate activities against Israeli attempts at absorption. This step encouraged the meetings already taking place between representatives of various Palestinian factions.

The Arab Jerusalem municipality had been dissolved by decree of the Israeli authorities and was excluded from the elections. Other major municipalities elected Palestinian Christians as their heads, including Elias Freij in Bethlehem, a known pro-Jordanian figure, and Farah Al Araj in Beit Jala. Al Araj had taken part in the defense of the city in 1948. Neither had known relations with the PLO, stayed away from national politics, and focused mainly on providing services, which earned them an initial sign of approval from the Israeli authorities. Elias Freij replaced Elias Issa Bandak, a member of a prominent Bethlehem family, while Farah Al Araj replaced Jabra Khamis, the mayor of Beit Jala since 1957 who had earned the hostility of nationalistic sectors. Both the leaderships of Freij and Al Araj were considered by the nationalistic camp as "traditionalists". This was not an isolated event in the 1972 elections and became the case in some of the key cities.

Despite the fact that the 1972 municipal elections were largely boycotted by the nationalistic camp and mainly participated in by traditional local leaderships, the outcome was a path contrary to that anticipated by the Israeli authorities. Separation between the "radical" PLO in exile and the "moderate" local leaderships was seen as a priority, yet 1972 marked the beginning of a serious internal dialogue between members of organized Palestinian groups in the occupied territory and the PLO leadership.

In 1973 the PNC gave formal endorsement to the political organizations inside the occupied territory and a Palestinian national front was created to coordinate actions between leaders who represented Palestinians inside the occupied territory. The movement involved coordination between the local cells of Fatah, the Communist Party, the Democratic Front for the Liberation of Palestine and Al Saiqa. Independents, newly elected mayors, trade unionists, and students also got involved, while the PFLP decided not to participate. The movement was seen by Israel as a strategic threat to its rule over the Palestinians and reacted harshly, imprisoning and exiling its leaders. One of those exiled was Hanna Nasser, the grandson of an Episcopal priest whose role in the student demonstrations that took place in Birzeit University was not underestimated by the Israeli authorities.

The development of local institutions continued in October 1973 with the founding of Bethlehem University, funded with support from the Holy See and seen as one of the main outcomes of the pilgrimage of Pope Paul VI a decade earlier. While it rightfully describes itself as *"the first registered university in the West Bank"*, it was not the first institution of higher education in Palestine: the Latin Patriarchate Seminary of Beit Jala had also offered higher religious education since 1856. In Birzeit, north of Ramallah, a college had been functioning since 1942, mainly through the initiative of the Nasser family. Extending Palestinian access to higher education had been one of the strategic goals of the national movement, with thousands of scholarships received from the Arab world, the Soviet Union, Europe, and Cuba. The establishment of proper universities in Palestine served several goals, from facilitating access to higher education for women to preventing emigration. This was one of the main goals of the Holy See in the establishment of Bethlehem University, whose first graduates numbered merely 63 students under the presidency of Brother Joseph Neary.

The 1973 War and a New Regional Context: Between the Rifle and the Olive Branch

When Egyptian President Gamal Abdel Nasser passed away at the end of September 1970, the Palestinian national movement lost one of its main supporters. Archbishop Capucci raised black flags over the Patriarchate at Jerusalem's Jaffa Gate, all churches of Jerusalem rang their bells in mourning, and all mosques called for prayers at the same time for only the second time in history.[262] Thousands of people mourned Abdel Nasser. *Al Quds* newspaper, the main Arab national newspaper printed in the occupied Palestinian territory, issued several editions with paid advertisements of condolences. The first major Palestinian demonstration in the occupied territory after 1967 marked the loss of one of Palestine's main allies. But not much was known about Anwar Sadat, Abdel Nasser's successor who had been vice-president since 1969 and had previously played an instrumental role in the 1952 revolution that brought an end to the Egyptian monarchy.

Almost immediately, the new Egyptian President launched a secret plan to change the comfortable status quo that Israel had enjoyed since 1967, and that had allowed it to construct settlements in the occupied Egyptian territory of Sinai. Sadat finally managed to articulate a strong attack, in coordination with Syria, on their respective territories occupied in 1967. Cairo had already shared peace proposals with the US but this was not enough to change the situation. "Jordan, which had already begun secret contacts with Israel, did not participate in the Arab plans, although they were briefed about the strategic goals." In December 1972, Jordan's PM Zaid Rifai secretly visited Anwar Sadat. The Egyptian President told him: *"I know I am not Tarzan. I realize my limitations. I am not good at blitzkrieg. The Israelis are good at blitzkrieg. I will fight a war of political reactivation and not of military liberation. I will wage a limited war: cross the canal, secure a bridgehead and stop. Then I will ask the Security Council to call for a ceasefire. This strategy will ensure my victory in the battle, cut my losses and reactivate the peace process."[263]*

The scenario described to the Jordanian PM in December 1972 materialized almost 10 months later with a fulminant Egyptian and Syrian offensive over their occupied territories. The excitement of Arab forces crossing the Suez Canal and overlooking the Galilee from the Golan made millions of Arabs take to the streets of their capitals while Voice of the Arabs, the pan-Arab radio owned by Egypt, reported victorious battles and played nationalistic and revolutionary songs. These included a song by Abdel Halim Hafez: *"If the whole world slept, I would wake up with my weapon"*, or the popular *"Your lands and farmlands, your sun and moon, your poems and tunes, your Nile and pyramids, by my blood I recompense and shall repel all feuds and I shall recompense my soul for you oh Egypt (...) going forth, carrying a weapon, going back, raising the banners of victory."*

The popular mobilization throughout the Arab world was not a synonym for coordinated Arab military strategy and not even Syria truly knew the scale of the Egyptian plans. Limited Arab reinforcements came only after the war had begun. Jordan stayed out of the fighting and the PLO had not been included in the preparations (although a delegation composed of Yasser Arafat, Farouk Kaddoumi and Salah Khalaf had been briefed by the Egypt and a Palestinian battalion fought in the Syrian front). There were no acts of sabotage that could have been carried out by Palestinian commandoes to change the scenario of President Sadat's limited goal of gaining back Egyptian occupied territory[264]: this war was not about Palestine.

In Egypt the powerful Coptic Orthodox Church was led by Pope Shenouda, who was marking his second year in charge. Born in 1923, he studied History at Cairo University and was part of the army that fought the war of 1948 in Palestine. He had strong nationalistic views and a very emotional connection to the Palestinian cause. He also had a strong case to make regarding Coptic rights in Jerusalem. In 1971 the Israeli authorities were complicit in the Ethiopian Church taking over the Coptic possession of Deir es Sultan on the roof of the Holy Sepulcher Church. Both Ethiopian (Orthodox) and Coptic (Orthodox) were in full communion and effectively the Ethiopian religious community had arrived in Jerusalem as guests of the Copts.

That was the status in the Coptic Convent but a combination of religious disputes and political opportunism led Ethiopian monks to change the keys of the site, taking it over as the Coptic clergy were celebrating mass in the main church of the Holy Sepulcher during the Easter celebrations of 25 April 1971. Subsequently, the Copts denounced Israeli complicity as persecution against their Egyptian identity and demanded support from the Egyptian authorities.

In October 1973 thousands of Egyptian soldiers crossed the Suez Canal and destroyed Israeli defences known as the "Bar Lev" line. Egyptian engineers built several bridges that within a few hours had been crossed by hundreds of Egyptian tanks onto the other side of their occupied territory. Israeli flags being lowered were the images broadcast from the battlefields during the first days of fighting, which took place during the Jewish holiday of Yom Kippur and the Muslim month of Ramadan. Meanwhile, the Syrian Army, including the mobilization of Palestinian forces, had managed to penetrate the occupied Golan Heights. That was the moment when Washington intervened with an unprecedented supply of weapons to Israel, which counterattacked and recovered control.

The ceasefire signed on November 11 had already changed the geopolitical situation and Israel awakened to a new reality that it was no longer the invincible power it had believed itself to be since 1967. It could not continue to ignore the offers to sign a peace treaty that involved the return of the occupied territory of Sinai to Egypt. President Sadat had achieved the first part of his plan to recover the Egyptian territory occupied by Israel. This was not going to be part of a comprehensive peace treaty that included Palestine, nor even the sensitive case of Deir es Sultan in occupied East Jerusalem. Pope Shenouda and his Palestinian friends were soon to be divorced from the Egyptian president.

1974
From Capucci's Arrest to the United Nations

Archbishop Capucci departed from his mother's home in Beirut for Jerusalem, driving his Mercedes Benz with diplomatic plates through the Israeli border crossing of Ras al-Naqura. This time though, the Israeli officer asked to search the car. The crossing on that sunny and warm August 6, 1974, was not normal. The Melkite Bishop of Jerusalem felt that something was wrong and returned to Beirut. He contacted the Apostolic Delegation to make the required contacts with the Israelis to respect his diplomatic status, and then returned to the border and crossed normally. However, the Israeli intelligence services were already after Capucci. He was subjected to surveillance, and the Bishop noted it. Two days later, the Archbishop was driving his car when he was stopped by Israeli forces in Jerusalem. No diplomatic protocols were followed but the Israelis knew what they were looking for. They went straight to one of the doors and found two pistols. In other parts of the car there were four Kalashnikov rifles, 220 pounds of dynamite and several detonators.[265]

The Archbishop's detention provoked a turmoil in the local church and immediately there were demonstrations calling for his release. *"Release our bishop"* was heard outside the district court of Jerusalem in Salah Ed-Deen Street, next to Saint George Episcopal Cathedral, as some remembered the deportation of Rev. Elia Khoury in 1969 for his alleged cooperation with the Palestinian resistance. Patriarch Maximus declared from Damascus that East Jerusalem had been illegally taken by Israel. On September 20, the Melkite Church gathered in the Syrian capital and adopted a defiant tone against the Israeli decision, including references to the efforts made to silence voices against annexation and occupation, and even an accusation against Israel of attempts to blackmail the Holy See.[266]

The case against Capucci became an iconic moment for the resistance inside the homeland. Israel had made efforts, including the 1972 municipal elections, to give an impression of normality to the international community. A court case against an archbishop accused of smuggling weapons to the resistance made many question the reality of Israel in the occupied territory of Palestine. Archbishop Capucci was aware of the importance of this moment and tried on every possible occasion to deliver a message of defiance that questioned the legitimacy of Israeli rule in Jerusalem. This included theatrical elements such as dismissing his lawyer in front of the court in order to delay events. His lawyer, Aziz Shehadeh, knew well what Capucci was trying to do as they had discussed this previously. The Archbishop was attracting more attention and managed to gain access to international media. *The New York Times* published an article titled *Arabic Cleric Defies Jerusalem Court.*[267]

On December 9, 1974, a few days after the beginning of Advent and the entry of the recently appointed Custos Maurilio Sacchi to Bethlehem, an Israeli court sentenced Archbishop Capucci to 12 years in prison. Statements of condemnation poured in from all the Arab world, particularly from Christian religious leaders. While the Holy See made no immediate comment, the PLO issued a statement saying that the Palestinian National Movement would spare no efforts to free the Archbishop. In his last statement to court, Capucci delivered a eulogy of his role as a religious person in the struggle for justice and claimed that if Jesus had been there, they would have *"wept together".*[268]

Exactly one month earlier, PLO leader Yasser Arafat had addressed the UN General Assembly for the first time. It was a historic moment that marked a turning point for Palestinian diplomacy. The Palestinian representatives to the United Nations, including Jamal Al Husseini, Henry Cattan, Musa Alami and Emile Ghory, had not addressed the organization since 1949. Some of those who had served as Palestinian diplomats (under the Arab Higher Committee) during that period had been absorbed by the Jordanian Foreign Ministry. Others had simply ended up working for other Arab countries, including Saudi Arabia and Kuwait. With the creation of the PLO, some Palestinians were dispatched to Arab League missions worldwide but at the UN the presence of Palestinians had been reduced to a minimum. Some Arab countries provided accreditation to a few Palestinians to create a lobby, namely Issa Nakhleh, a Palestinian Christian lawyer born in Beit Sahour. He was the author of the *Encyclopaedia of the Palestine Problem* and served for a while as Arab League Representative to Argentina. Some believe that he maintained the institutional memory of Palestine in the United Nations during the years of official Palestinian absence.

In November 1974, the PLO made a significant move in the UN with an advanced team led by Nabil Shaath and a group of senior officials, including Jaffa-born Shafik al-Hout (who served for years as Palestine's representative to Lebanon), Abdul Jawad Saleh (former mayor of Al Bireh who was deported by Israel in 1973 in its campaign against Palestinian organizations in the occupied territory, an economist, former follower of the Baath Party, and member of the PLO Central Council), and Farouk Kaddoumi (Abu Lutof). The Palestinian participation was possible after the approval of Resolution 3210 which invited the PLO to participate in the deliberations that included the question of Palestine.[269] This Resolution was approved by 105 countries with only four votes against (the United States, Israel, the Bolivian dictatorship of Hugo Banzer, and the Dominican Republic).

The arrival of the delegation was coordinated by the FBI which was concerned about possible terrorist attacks against the Palestinians. Demonstrations were held in front of the UN by Zionist organizations opposed to the presence of Yasser Arafat in New York. When briefed about the slogans displayed in the demonstration, diplomat Shafik al-Hout focused on one particular banner that read "Arafat Go Home". He told a group of journalists, *"This is precisely why we came here, to go home"*. The irony was evident, including US protection of a PLO delegation listed as a "terrorist organization" by Israel.

The event proceeded very successfully for the Palestinians and for over an hour, Yasser Arafat addressed the assembly and made several references to anti-colonial struggles worldwide. He described the status of Palestinian citizens of Israel and referred to the massacre of Kufr Qassem, and the struggle of the villagers of Iqrith and Kufr Bi'rim, the two ethnically cleansed Palestinian Christian villages that were symbols for almost one-third of the internally displaced Palestinians left in Israel. Arafat also referred to Archbishop Capucci as a *"brave prince of the church (...) Lifting his fingers to form the same victory sign used by our freedom fighters, he said 'what I have done, I have done that all men may live on this land of peace in peace".*[270] The address ended with the historic words: *"Today I have come bearing an olive branch and a freedom-fighter's gun. Do not let the olive branch fall from my hand. I repeat: do not let the olive branch fall from my hand".*[271]

After that address, the PLO became part of the UN debates. Its first permanent representative was Zuhdi Tarazi, a Palestinian Christian from Gaza and graduate from the Terra Sancta College in Jerusalem who had previously served in Brazil as one of the first Palestinian envoys to Arab League missions after the creation of the PLO.

The Hot Winter of 1976

On January 1, 1976, Fatah conducted a military parade to mark the 11th anniversary of the Palestinian revolution, or the first military operation launched by their organization. While the environment was festive and the offices of Yasser Arafat, Farouk Kaddoumi and Salah Khalaf[272] had received congratulatory notes from several governments and revolutionary moments worldwide, the situation was tense. There were sporadic clashes in Beirut between right-wing Lebanese forces (mainly but not exclusively composed of Maronite Christians) and left-wing forces (from the Communist Party, with several Christian leaders, to the socialists of the Druze Kamal Jumblatt). The demographic composition of Lebanon and its political representation was leading to an irreparable crisis. The PLO felt closer to the left-wing camp and some of its groups had participated in clashes. On many occasions though, as revealed by Palestinian representative Shafik Al-Hout, their role was mainly to fill the vacuum left by the Lebanese security forces, including preventing criminal gangs from operating in the city.[273]

Palestinian responses to the Lebanese crisis were also affected by their own divisions. The PLO had undergone several splits and tensions that were mainly provoked by regional interference. At the 12th Palestinian National Council celebrated in Cairo in June 1974, the PLO adopted a "10 point program" that maintained its position in support of *"all means, first and foremost armed struggle"*[274] and complete rejection of Zionism, but accepted for the first time the liberation of "any part" of the occupied homeland as a step towards the fulfilment of the PLO program (of liberation and return). This was considered by some as a step towards normalization and recognition of Israel. It led to the creation of a "rejectionist front" and some organizations left their posts on the PLO Executive Committee, the most prominent being the PFLP led by George Habash.

Fatah maintained a strong position of support for "independent Palestinian decision making" and highlighted its difference versus other movements that functioned in coordination with or under the orders of specific Arab regimes such as Syria, Iraq or Libya.

In addition to the PFLP, the Democratic Front for the Liberation of Palestine (DFLP, at that time called the Popular and Democratic Front for the Liberation of Palestine) was also Marxist and enjoyed privileged relations with several left-wing governments worldwide. They were seen by Fatah as more pragmatic than the PFLP and supported the 10-point plan.

These three movements (Fatah, PFLP and DFLP) were the most prominent Palestinian factions and had a significant presence in both Palestine and the diaspora. Other groups were influential only in particular countries. Al Saiqa and the PFLP – Command General of Ahmad Jibril[275] were fully supported and trained by Syria (Al Saiqa is in fact the Palestinian branch of the Syrian Baath Party). The Palestinian Liberation Front (PLF) had left the PFLP and was also close to the Arab nationalist Baath ideology (over the years it moved between Syria and Iraq). The Arab Liberation Front (ALF) was heavily supported and trained by Iraq, acting almost as the Iraqi Baath Party's Palestinian branch. Another member of the rejectionist front was the Palestinian Popular Struggle Front (PPSF), funded by Samir Ghosheh, a Jerusalemite who was also close to both Syria and Iraq. The rejectionist front included Sabri al-Banna (Abu Nidal), a Fatah dissident who having created a split (supported mainly by Iraq at the beginning), became an organization with mercenary characteristics at the service of various Arab governments. The Communist Party, though it enjoyed a significant national membership, was not accepted in the PLO, nor was it part of the rejectionist front mainly due to its opposition to armed struggle.

In this scenario it was difficult for the PLO to maintain one coordinated military strategy but it still tried to achieve this and the military parade of January 1 served as a means for Fatah to show its strength. A declassified CIA report made public later that decade estimated that Fatah had more commandoes than all other organizations combined.[276] The PLO's military was nominally under the command of Zuheir Mohsen, who belonged to Al Saiqa, yet the Fatah forces led by Abu Jihad were operationally more active and reliable.

Lebanon's capital Beirut was heavily divided between east and west. Most Palestinians were in west Beirut with a few thousand in the eastern part, including the refugee camps of Tel al Zaatar, Jisr Il Basha, Miye Miye and Al Dbayeh, as well as the neighborhood known as Karantina. Some of the camps were located in strategic positions and leading right-wing Lebanese leaders considered taking over these sites as a priority. A siege of Palestinian areas in east Beirut that had begun in 1975 strengthened in 1976 and it was only a matter of time before fighting began. One of the first acts took place in Al Dbayeh refugee camp where right-wing Lebanese militias led by Dany Chamoun bombarded a refugee camp entirely made up by 3,000 Palestinian Christians who were mainly from Al Bassa in the upper Galilee.

From January 4 heavy bombardments of the camp caused severe damage, including to the Saint George Melkite Church, the camp's only religious site. Unlike other concentrations of Palestinians, Al Dbayeh residents did not have many weapons and the camp's geographical location in the heart of East Beirut prevented the possibility of reinforcements arriving. When Chamoun's forces tried to take over the camp, they faced strong resistance that made them believe there were dozens of forces resisting. In fact the resistance was mainly made up of two people: Mamoun Mreish and his assistant, known by Palestinian guerrillas simply as "Tony".[277]

At the end of the assault when the resistance, referred to as "heroic" by Palestinian eyewitnesses, had ceased and the camp surrendered, almost 60 Palestinian Christian refugees had been killed, including some who had been executed. The local priest, Fr. Nicola Nasrallah, who had served in Jerusalem under Bishop Capucci,[278] was beaten by the Lebanese group and the funeral of the victims was disrupted by provocations inside the church by another Lebanese Christian fighter.[279]

News of Al Dbayeh and Mreish's resistance reached the PLO headquarters. Yasser Arafat called his personal security chief, Ali Hassan Salameh, with an urgent request to save Maroun Mreish and bring him to Arafat. Salameh, nicknamed the Red Prince by Israeli intelligence, made use of his contacts among right-wing Christian Lebanese and managed to bring Maroun and Tony to Yasser Arafat. They then continued to work under the orders of Abu Jihad. Ali Hassan Salameh was one of the best-loved Palestinian figures in right-wing Christian Lebanese circles and he built influential relationships that concluded with the first security contacts between the PLO and the US Embassy in Beirut. He married a Lebanese Christian and Miss Universe, Georgina Rizek, and, against the advice of his team, maintained regular routines in Beirut. Salameh was assassinated by the Israeli intelligence in 1979 when his car was blown up shortly after leaving home.

The Jisr al Basha camp, also in East Beirut, was set up in 1952 and hosted around 3,000 Palestinian Christians mainly from Jaffa, Haifa and Acre. The residents included people from various denominations that ranged from Catholic to Orthodox and Armenian who had been moved there by UNRWA in coordination with the Orthodox Church. The siege of the camp began at the same time as Al Dbayeh and lasted until the end of June, when the camp fell amid another massacre of Palestinian civilians. In this camp, more Palestinians took part in the resistance, which was very strong despite the fact that they were heavily outnumbered by the right-wing Lebanese militias. Those who survived were relocated and the right-wing attackers achieved their goal of eliminating the refugee camp. Fr. Boulos (Melkite), the priest of the refugee camp, was beaten by the right-wing Lebanese Christian militias.[280] The fall of Jisr al Basha opened the way to intensify the siege of Tel Al Zaatar, the largest Palestinian camp in east Beirut. At the same time, the Syrian Arab Army entered Lebanon to support the right-wing militias.

Before the fall of Jisr al Basha and the intensification of the attacks against Tel al Zaatar, the neighborhood of Karantina, largely inhabited by Palestinian refugees, was the site of a massacre. It is estimated that over a thousand people were killed as part of the right-wing offensive against Palestinian positions in East Beirut. This provoked tensions between Palestinian factions and there were calls to respond to what were massacres of civilians rather than attacks on military targets. It is in this context that one of the darkest episodes in Palestinian military history took place: the massacre of Damour.

Members of the Lebanese National Movement, also known as the progressive groups, joined Palestinian troops from different factions to attack a stronghold of support for right-wing Lebanese forces. The Palestinian forces included troops from the Palestine Liberation Army, As-Saiqa, and Fatah with a battalion led by the prominent commander Said Al Muragha (Abu Musa). What began as the takeover of a strategic location on the Mediterranean coast turned into a massacre of over 100 Lebanese civilians and the displacement of hundreds of people. The magnitude of the crimes led to bitter disputes between Palestinian leaders. A group of fighters from Fatah's western sector led by Commander Abu Rateb arrived at Damour to reinforce the Palestinian attack. When they saw what was taking place, they withdrew and presented a complaint against the commander leading the attack, Abu Musa. The complaint reached Yasser Arafat himself.

During the assault on Damour, many Lebanese civilians found shelter in the nearby Moussa Castle by the Shouf mountains. Dany Chamoun was besieged there. Maroun Mreish arrived to open a dialogue. He was the very same Palestinian Christian combatant rescued by Chamoun from Al Dbayeh camp after a request by Arafat. Chamoun sent a message requesting a helicopter and the PLO forces facilitated the entry of a helicopter to get him out.[281]

Journalist Anton Mansour, a Palestinian Christian citizen of Israel (a Maronite himself), had the opportunity to visit the areas that were under PLO control in Lebanon and concluded that while atrocities such as Al Damour had taken place, *"they were apparently revenge for similar actions carried out by 'Christians' in Karantina, Tel al-Zaatar, in the Beirut area and Khiyam (near Metulah)"*. It was, in fact, in the areas controlled by the Phalange and other right-wing Lebanese, mainly Christian, militias that all "non-Christians" were being driven out.[282] In the areas under the PLO and allied Lebanese forces, there was no policy to expel Christians. This can be explained because the majority of the groups allied to the PLO were not "communal" but *"profess a universalist Arab, Lebanese or socialist ideology"*.[283] Atallah Mansour was born in the village of Jeish, became a refugee during the Nakba at the age of 14, stayed in Lebanon with his family for a while but eventually managed to return to the Galilee. He became one of the most important Palestinian journalists in Israel.

While some believe that the PLO acted with ambiguity regarding the events in Damour due to what had happened in Dbayeh and Karantina, others affirm that Yasser Arafat was extremely upset and even threatened to execute the Palestinian officials involved in the massacre.[284] Damour certainly increased the contradictions that many Palestinian leaders felt regarding their engagement in the Lebanese Civil War. In effect, Damour became a symbol for supporters of Lebanon's right-wing parties and part of their propaganda against the Palestinian presence in the country.

When a Fatah unit composed mainly of Palestinian university students occupied the town of Bhamdoun, one of Lebanon's mountain resorts on the Beirut-Damascus road, the mayor, a Lebanese Christian, hosted the Palestinians in charge of the unit. The leader Mahmoud Al-Aloul explained the system for ensuring that all inhabitants had enough food to survive. After the meeting, the mayor came to the Fatah commander and asked, *"Are you really like this?"* "Like what?" replied Al-Aloul. The mayor explained: *"The people who came with you are all students or graduates of the American University. You are not massacring people and you are concerned about their safety. We didn't know you were like that."* Al-Aloul replied that they were just guests in Lebanon, dragged into a civil war that was not theirs, and that their goal was simply to return to Palestine.[285]

In Kmatieh, a mountainous area not far from Beirut, one of the most fiercely fought battles took place between the Lebanese Falange and the PLO. The Student's Batallion (*Al Kataiba il Tul'labiya*) composed of Palestinian students from different worldwide branches of the General Union of Palestine Students (GUPS) lost four members who had come together from Yugoslavia: Hazem Radwan, Mohammad Younis, Mohammad Hindi, and Anton Abu Aita. Anton, a Palestinian Christian from Beit Sahour, was a civil engineering student. No religious ceremonies were observed and the four of them, three Muslims and one Christian, were buried with military honors at the martyrs' cemetery of Burj Al Barajneh refugee camp. *"At that time we didn't know who was Christian or Muslim until the day of their funeral,"* said one of their comrades who survived the battle.[286] Anton had left Beit Sahour a few years earlier with the same revolutionary dreams as many other young Palestinians yet he ended up being buried in Lebanon.   It was around this time that Nabil Shaath resigned from his post at the PLO Planning Center in Beirut and left for Cairo. *"It was a difficult decision but I just couldn't take the situation. We were not in Lebanon to be part of a sectarian war but as a temporary base in our path back to Palestine. It's true we were provoked in many occasions and the massacres against our refugees in 1976 left us in a difficult position, as this became more about protecting our own people. Yet I remember how many times some of my students at the American University of Beirut, whether Muslims or Christians, had to ask me for help in order to cross checkpoints. I didn't believe in that and in the summer I ended up moving to Egypt."*[287]

The 1976 Municipal Elections
and the Rise of New Leadership
in the Occupied Palestinian Territory

In 1976 Israel allowed municipal elections to take place in the occupied territory. The exception once again was East Jerusalem as the Arab municipality had been dissolved by the Israeli authorities a few weeks after the 1967 occupation. On this occasion the rules were different from 1972 as more people could vote than in the previous elections, which had been subject to the Jordanian Electoral Laws that were in place in 1967 (dating back to 1955). These laws restricted the participation of vast swathes of society, including women and adults below the age of 21. This law was even contrary to the rules created by the PLO within the PNC, which shows how progressive the Palestinian national movement was at that time in comparison with many Arab countries.

Once again, there was an internal discussion within the PLO about the elections. Some believed that the Israeli aim was to consolidate its control by promoting a class of leaders within the occupied territory who would be willing to accept their plans for limited autonomy rather than national independence. Israel had already found a limited yet existing class of traditional leaders who were willing to move in that direction.

From the other side, there were those who believed that the elections were an opportunity to show the PLO's strength and use the municipalities as organizational tools to oppose the occupation. While Israel had banned the PLO and any of its movements from legally operating in the territory under its occupation, PLO members had managed to find alternative forms of popular organization, as proven after the 1972 elections. The formation of the Palestine National Front back in 1973, with representatives from municipalities, trade and student unions, served as the basis for a unified leadership at home. It had been formed with mainstream independent support and politically backed mainly by Fatah and the Communist Party (rejected by the PFLP). Israel responded by jailing and deporting the leaders, including Abdul Jawad Saleh, mayor of Al Bireh, and Hanna Nasser, who had initiated the process of turning Birzeit College into Birzeit University. Saleh remembered how soldiers went to his home and told him: *"Please follow us. The military governor wants to talk with you for five minutes"*. He was then blindfolded, handcuffed, and put in a vehicle of the Israeli intelligence that took him to the Jordan River. The vehicle held eight Palestinians for deportation, including two Palestinian Christians.[288]

Abdul Jawad Saleh had become the mayor of Al Bireh in 1967, a few months before the occupation. The city, with an overwhelming Palestinian Muslim population has biblical importance (an old Byzantine church lies on the site believed to be part of the path of the Holy Family) and had welcomed the Rafidi family, Christians from the Nablus area. Saleh had close relations with the mayor of Ramallah Nadim Zaru, a Palestinian Christian. This strong combination of two popular local leaders blocked the attempts of a minority who wanted to cooperate with the Israeli military governor. Ramallah became a center of nationalistic activity and planted the seeds of the national front. Many meetings took place in an Evangelical Church in Al Teereh neighborhood, and two Palestinian Christian clergymen were particularly prominent: Rev. Odeh Rantisi, a refugee from al-Lydd, and Rev. Elia Khoury (deported in 1969).

Ramallah Mayor Nadim Zaru was deported in 1969 after protesting the demolition of Palestinian homes. In some accounts, he is also said to have provided logistical support to Palestinian resistance organizations. He accused the Israeli military governor, Col. David Brinn, of torturing and harassing Palestinians following instructions from Moshe Dayan, Israel's Minister of Defense.[289] At that time Israel was particularly worried by Palestinians who had good connections with international parties. Zaru was making good use of Ramallah's special relationship with the United States (by 1969 hundreds of Ramallah residents had US passports) and kept updating the US Consul General in Jerusalem, Mr. Peter Sutherland, of Israeli human rights violations, including accusations of torture.[290]

On October 6, 1969, Zaru was expelled to Jordan alongside nine other Palestinian personalities.

The deportations did not end and by the 1976 elections, several mayors and potential candidates had been deported by Israel, including the mayors of Jerusalem, Ramallah, and Al Bireh. A delegation from the National Front met Yasser Arafat in Beirut to explain that the PLO needed to support the elections as it would result in it being empowered. At that time, Abdul Jawad Saleh had become a PLO Executive Committee member and was living in a room in Tel Al Zaatar refugee camp. He joined the efforts to lobby Arafat: *"I told him that the PLO had to make a decision. We either call for people to boycott the elections, and nobody votes, or we call to participate and we ensure that the PLO will come out strengthened. I supported the second option and eventually Yasser Arafat was convinced as well."*[291]

With the PLO approval, the nationalist candidates quickly organized into one list of consensus per city. Eventually, each local election had candidates from two main lists: one the unofficial PLO and a second of local leaders known as "traditional" or who were not mainly concerned about national liberation but about day-to-day issues. Some candidates who were openly accused of collaboration with the Israeli occupation ran in the second lists.

In cities and towns with a strong Christian background such as Bethlehem, Beit Jala, Beit Sahour and Ramallah the results took different shapes. Elias Freij, a strong pro-Jordanian figure was elected as mayor of Bethlehem, defeating the pro-PLO list led by Hanna Nasser, a businessman from the textile sector. The nationalist side suffered from a lack of discipline and key figures in the national front, such as trade unionist George Hazboun, did not run in the list coordinated with the Palestinian factions. This, in addition to lack of a serious efforts among family clans, helps to explain the Bethlehem results.

A similar scenario took place in Beit Sahour where the list headed by Hanna Atrash, a combination of family/clan leaders, won the municipality, defeating the pro-PLO list led by Jamal Bannoura. The only member of the second list who succeeded in being elected was Atallah Rishmawi, a member of the Communist Party and who at that time was in an Israeli prison. Family pressure and solidarity made the people of Beit Sahour vote for Rishmawi as they thought this would pressure Israel to release him from jail. Rishmawi remained in prison.

It was in Beit Jala where the pro-PLO candidates struck a major blow to the interests of the Israeli military governor. The town was largely identified with left-wing parties, mainly Communists and the PFLP. While the latter was not part of the national front behind the nationalist lists, it eventually decided to support its candidates. Instrumental in the work for the list were figures such as Atallah Abu Ghattas, whose father Khalil had led the local resistance against Zionist attacks in 1948, and Communist Party member Fuad Rizek. The list was headed by Bishara Daoud, an independent nationalist who won strong popular support. Part of the team who mobilized the popular support were disciplined militants from various family clans, including Saba Hadweh, Jeries Qunqar, Daoud Matar, and Jadallah Abu Jeries. The second list failed to gain any significant representation. A few years later, this changed, and not exactly through new elections.

In Ramallah, the national front endorsed incumbent candidate Karim Khalaf. A lawyer from Cairo University, Khalaf eventually moved towards the pro-PLO camp after endorsing the idea of a two-state solution (which was not official PLO position at the time). Although he was not a party member of any PLO faction,

Khalaf espoused the stance of the national front not to collaborate with the Israeli authorities. Ramallah was a strategic target for the Israeli authorities as they had already invested heavily in defeating the strong National Front presence, including detentions and deportations, but their attempts failed. In Ramallah, the National Front list won eight out of nine seats.

One of the figures articulating the pro-PLO list in Ramallah was Yousef Farhat, a Palestinian Christian from one of the original Ramallah families and a member of the Communist Party. He coordinated the work of the list directly with Bassam Shakaa, the candidate from Nablus who had appeared as a natural leader of the pro-PLO lists. Farhat's wife, Doris Khoury from Jerusalem, had recently served a five-year jail sentence for her activities as one of the PFLP leaders in the occupied territory.

The other main list in Ramallah included prominent figures but only Khalil Musa was elected to the municipal council. Khalil Janho, the former Palestinian fighter who had become one of those closest to the Israeli authorities, did not manage to win a seat. Despite the fact that he had gained significant power locally, Janho lost miserably. One of those elected to the council was Rev. Odeh Rantisi who became Ramallah's deputy mayor.

The Israeli occupation never repeated this exercise ever again. The 1976 municipal elections failed to create an "alternative leadership" to the PLO and had actually strengthened the nationalist camp. Of all the main cities, only Gaza, Tulkarem and Bethlehem retained "traditional" leadership after the elections. Others such as Nablus, Hebron and Beit Jala succeeded in replacing the traditional mayors and the nationalist "tsunami" could be seen everywhere. Three-quarters of the newly elected authorities were considered to be nationalists.[292]

The New York Times summarized the results thus: *"A new, militant leadership dominated by Palestinian nationalists and Arab radicals emerged on the occupied West Bank (...) Communists, Syrian Baathists and candidates sympathetic to the Palestine Liberation Organization swept to power in many town and villages."*[293] While Israel's Defense Minister Shimon Peres tried to hide the defeat of his ministry's strategy in the occupied territory by emphasizing that the elections were not a "day of mourning in Israel", in reality he worked to weaken the authority of the democratically elected Palestinian mayors.[294] Ramallah's Karim Khalaf said, *"The vote shows the whole world that the West Bankers are Palestinians who want to establish their own national entity and put an end to the Israelioccupation."*[295]

The newly elected authorities quickly organized around the figure of Nablus mayor Bassam Shakaa. Their new leaders increased efforts to become more independent from the occupation authorities and succeeded in increasing their outreach to diplomats. Consul Generals were visiting elected Palestinian authorities in the occupied West Bank, not as part of Israeli-arranged tours, and could witness and report home the reality of life under occupation. This approach also brought financial support from abroad, including from both Jordan and the PLO.

In 1977 a new government was elected in Israel. The right-wing Likud party was led by Menahem Begin, known to the Palestinian people for his leading role in the infamous massacre of Deir Yassin. Begin expanded the colonial-settlement project initiated by the Labor Party and introduced an aggressive policy in the occupied territory. When Begin spoke of "autonomy" for Palestinians, it was about "people but not for territory",[296] in a clear reference to Israel's control over the land. It is in this context that the newly elected Beit Jala municipality called for a first conference of Palestinian municipal engineers, held at the legendary Everest Hotel, to study and block Israeli settlement plans. The Israelis planned to limit the municipal boundaries of Beit Jala as a means to cement the annexation of land around Jerusalem. In addition, the planned construction of bypass Road 60 was intended to isolate the west of Bethlehem; this project remained frozen until it was implemented 20 years later.[297]

Beit Jala municipality opposed the settlement plans and Road 60 but the Israeli authorities insisted that the municipalities were not there to deal with "politics". Bishara Daoud, Beit Jala's democratically elected mayor, was ousted by an Israeli military order in 1978.

Land Day and the Revolution
by Palestinian Citizens of Israel

The Palestinians who survived the Nakba in what became Israel achieved citizenship after almost two decades of military rule. They were allowed to run for election and some joined Zionist parties of their proxies, mainly from the Labor Party. The majority embraced the *yabha* (Front) whose driving force was the Communist Party. Having been through several transformations, the communists were a source of concern for the traditional leadership, including Christian clergy, yet a significant number of Christian youth who became involved in politics at that time did so through the *yabha*. Joseph Raya, the Melkite Archbishop of Haifa who spoke constantly about the discrimination suffered by Palestinian citizens of Israel, wrote in an internal report: *"With the existence of Israel as an independent country, the only voice they hear now loud and clear for justice and equality, if it be in the Knesset of Israel or in the daily papers, is the Communist voice, which is really strong and articulate. They are disappointed in the Church and they turn towards those who seem to be taking their cause to heart. From all indications, we can say that the Christians of the Holy Land seem to be unwanted and undesired by the government. They are being squeezed out. Unjust laws, cunning laws (...) suspicion, subtle persecution and sometimes plainly expressed hatred on the part of the government seem to drive the Christians away from their normal, traditional and rightful hoes and lands. So far, they have no hope for a better future. They are seeking it somewhere else.''[298]*

This was the context that mobilized organized groups of Palestinian citizens to rebel. Some increasingly identified with the PLO's call for full national liberation, while others supported the communist calls to end the occupation that began in 1967 and achieve equality for all citizens within Israel. By the mid-seventies, these people were all "full Israeli citizens" but the meaning of citizenship was still disputed by dozens of discriminatory laws. One of the most important issue up to that moment was that of internally displaced people, particularly those of the Christian villages of Iqrith and Kufr Bir'im. Israel had continued to push an active campaign of land expropriation for the benefit of Jewish settlements. Nazareth was one of the first cities to suffer from that phenomena with the expropriation of vast areas of its land for the construction of the new city of Nazareth Illit. Services were not provided to many villages, which led, for example, to the decline and ultimate destruction of the Palestinian – Armenian village of Sheikh Bureik near Haifa[299].

In 1976 the Israeli government pushed for a plan to expropriate 20,000 dunums of land from villages around the triangle of Deir Hanna, Arrabeh and Sakhnin in order to expand the Jewish settlement of Karmel, built in 1956 on land that had been already expropriated from Palestinian villages. Palestinian citizens organized their communities and created the Committee for Land Defence headed by Rev. Shehadeh Shehadeh. Born in Kufr Yassif, Rev. Shehadeh was an Episcopal pastor living in Haifa. The young 36-year-old reverend participated in the first meetings that took place in Haifa to find ways to protect the lands and future of the Palestinian citizens. He became involved in the community efforts to protect their land and in the internal political issues that concerned the Palestinian minority in Israel. He went against the line of most Palestinian mayors in Israel who were affiliated or close to the Israeli Labor Party, winning the support of the mayor of Nazareth, Tawfik Zayyad, among other figures, and promoted a committee that responded directly to the people rather than to the mayors. The committee was established but was unable to prevent the land expropriations.

The Episcopal Rev. of Haifa, Na'im Ateek, and other Christian religious figures also endorsed the movement. Palestinian Christians who became some of the main organizers of the movement included Advocate Hanna Nakara, Emil Habibi, Saliba Khamis, and Nimer Morkos. Even personalities such as Massad Kassis, former member of the Israeli parliament and mayor of Mi'iliya who had been criticized by the national movement for his relationship with Zionist parties, endorsed the demonstrations and joined the Committee for Land Defence.

A large demonstration was called for Tuesday March 30. One day earlier, on Monday March 29, the Israeli authorities imposed a curfew on the villages of Kabul, Tamra, Deir Hanna, Tur'an, Arrabeh, and Sakhnin. Threats against teachers and other Arab public servants not to join the demonstration were ignored. People violated the curfew and the demonstrations were accompanied by a general strike that was joined by close to 100 percent of the Palestinian citizens of Israel. The Israeli government sent the army to attack its Arab Palestinian citizens and the confrontations intensified, including the use of Molotov cocktails against the armoured vehicles. By the end of the day, Israel had killed six of the demonstrators.

Israeli Prime Minister Yitzhak Rabin did not apologize and declared that the expropriations would take place. There was incitement against Palestinian citizens, including Israel's Education Minister Zevulum Hammer declaring that the *"Arabs are a cancer in the heart of the nation"*.[300] Land Day weakened the Arab elite close to the Labor Party and regenerated Palestinian national identity. It strengthened the *yabha,* gave an impulse to *Abnaa Al Balad* (the Sons of the Land movement that supported a one democratic state solution) and consolidated the figure of Nazareth mayor Tawfik Zayyad as the main leader of Palestinian citizens. Zayyad, a prominent Palestinian poet, wrote: *"In al-Lydd, in Ramleh, in the Galilee, we shall remain, like a wall upon your chest, and in your throat like a shred of glass, a cactus throne, and in your eyes a sandstorm"*.

Entebbe, the Ramleh-Rome Trip and the PLO at the Holy See for the First Time

For a few years, the PFLP decided to stop conducting international operations. Their internal analysis suggested that the goal of raising the visibility of the Palestinian cause had been achieved. The man behind these operations, Wadie Haddad, disagreed with this assessment and was unwilling to give up his extensive list of international contacts. Under his command, the PFLP had been able to operate through movements and individuals from dozens of countries. There was no agreement within the organization and a drastic decision was taken: Wadie Haddad, the AUB doctor and son of a Melkite family from Safad, was expelled from the organization he co-founded.

But Haddad, known as Abu Hani, remained active. In 1976 some of his commandoes, composed of two Palestinians and two German members of the German Revolutionary Cells, hijacked Air France flight 139 en route from Paris to Tel Aviv. It was taken to Uganda where Israeli operatives conducted a massive rescue operation known as the Entebbe Operation, killing the four hijackers as well as two operatives dispatched to help with the negotiations. One of the operatives was Jael Al Arja, from Beit Jala, who had arrived from Baghdad after being sent directly by Wadie Haddad. Part of his instructions was to request that the group would be taken from Entebbe to Kampala as they *"knew that the airport had been built by the Israelis and did not trust Idi Amin (the Ugandan president)"*.[301] The forces of Idi Amin declined the Palestinian request.

One of the requests made by the Palestinian group was to free Melkite Archbishop Hilarion Capucci. This was not a new request and other operations against Israel by various organizations had put the issue of Capucci at the top of their priorities. Israel did not cede to the demands made by Palestinian groups but it engaged the Holy See in political negotiations that ended with Capucci being freed from Ramleh prison on November 6, 1977, following a personal appeal by Pope Paul VI to President Ephraim Katzir of Israel. Israel's Prime Minister Menahem Begin had requested that letter.

Israel and the Holy See had not established diplomatic relations at that time and the negotiations to release Archbishop Capucci were intended to demonstrate goodwill on both sides. The accusations against the Melkite prelate were not a minor issue for Israel as they claimed that he was transporting 100 kilos of explosives, four rifles, two pistols and hand grenades at the moment of his detention.[302]

The release included a number of conditions, including a prohibition on Capucci engaging in politics ever again. This included not allowing the Melkite leader to take part in any "anti-Israeli propaganda" and that he would be sent away from the region.[303] The Holy See complied with the terms of the agreements and sent Capucci to serve Arab Christian communities in South America. However, Capucci was not willing to stay away for long and on January 16, 1979, the Bishop of Jerusalem arrived in Damascus to attend a PNC meeting. He was welcomed as a hero by Yasser Arafat and hundreds of delegates. That PNC meeting was particularly fraught and was about to cause a split in the PLO, particularly between Fatah and the factions close to Syria and Iraq who had tried to take over control. When Arafat realized that the Syrian government was trying to control the organization, he stood up and said, *"The Palestinians are going to leave"*[304]. The majority of the audience left, mainly to Beirut. Perhaps the only consensus in that PNC was the welcome given to Capucci. Despite the fact that the Capucci was Syrian and Damascus was putting pressure in favor of certain PLO opposition factions, Capucci remained close to Yasser Arafat.

From Damascus, Capucci travelled to Tehran to meet with the government established after the Islamic Revolution. After his meeting with the Ayatollah Ruhollah Khomeini, Archbishop Capucci remained a key figure in Western-Iranian relations. He intervened in cases of attacks against the Roman Catholic community, managed to reopen several Catholic schools that had been closed by the new authorities, and even served as an envoy during the American hostage crisis, advocating to Iranian authorities for the release of the hostages.

Archbishop Capucci also became an important figure in the establishment of PLO-Holy See relations. When the Vatican Secretary of State Cardinal Casaroli received Farouk Kaddoumi (Abu Lutof), the head of the PLO political department (foreign ministry), many thought that Capucci was the person behind this first public and official meeting between the PLO and the Holy See on March 13, 1981. Coordination from the PLO side went through Ambassador Zuhdi Tarazi, the permanent representative to the UN, and Capucci was not a factor in the meeting. On this occasion, Fr. Ibrahim Ayyad, who at that time served as the President of the Latin Ecclesiastical Court of Lebanon, was the main person involved.

A statement by the Holy See after the meeting said that they *"wished to know personally the points of view of the PLO on the situation in the Middle East and the solution to the Arab-Israeli crisis in all of its various aspects, as the Holy See has done and continues to do with all interested parties."*[305]

In fact, Palestinian-Vatican relations were much older. The Holy See was one of the first parties approached by the Palestinian leadership during the British Mandate and they had a lot of information via the Latin Patriarchate and the Franciscans (Custodia) about the situation on the ground. This information had determined much of their early humanitarian engagement, whether through the Pontifical Mission since 1948 or via Caritas since 1967. Pope Paul VI's visit to Jerusalem in 1964 was the first direct papal contact with the reality of Palestine, but at that time there were no formal political relations with the PLO. This was the strategic goal of the 1981 meeting.

Two key factors would advance relations. First, the PLO wished to advance its diplomatic relations through the symbolism offered by the Holy See umbrella. This is evident in the emphasis placed by Yasser Arafat on the engagement and involvement of Christian representatives in the national movement. Second, the Holy See was interested in the situation taking place in Lebanon. An undocumented meeting had already taken place with the PLO during the visit to Beirut of Cardinal Casaroli during the previous civil war when the Holy See was making efforts to prevent violent confrontation.

There was consensus among Palestinian leaders about the importance of advancing relations with the Holy See, which had taken significant steps internationally under Pope John Paul II and had been instrumental in preventing an imminent war between Argentina and Chile.[306] Pope John Paul II came from Poland, where the local church was instrumental in demanding an end to the Soviet occupation and control. Clearly, he was not unfamiliar with the struggle for self-determination and this was an advantage for Palestinian diplomatic outreach.

What is known is that Yasser Arafat never lacked people to open doors with the Holy See. Whether through Archbishop Capucci, Fr. Ibrahim Ayyad or their many friends, the first exchange of letters between Pope John Paul II and Palestinian leaders took place during 1979. This was followed by an audience with the Pope granted in 1980 to a young assistant of President Arafat: Afif Safieh, the son of a renowned Catholic family from Jerusalem who had been prevented from returning home since 1967 and a graduate of the Catholic University of Louvain. He carried a five-page letter from Arafat that read: *"Please permit me to have a dream that I am seeing you going to Palestine and Jerusalem, surrounded by returning Palestinian refugees, carrying olive branches and spreading them at your feet."*[307]

Pope John Paul II was not just interested in engaging with the Palestinians but also believed that they should not be excluded from any peace negotiations, a significant diplomatic achievement for the PLO. It is in this context that the Holy See allowed a "Palestinian violation" of the Lateran Treaty of 1929 between Italy and the Holy See. This Treaty highlighted the independence of the Vatican from Italy. As such, diplomatic credentials to the Holy See were not automatic for diplomats who were accredited to Italy. Yet, the Holy See accepted Nimr Hammad, the PLO representative in Rome, as an "informal" representative to the Holy See as well. These "informal relations" were part of the Palestinian diplomatic approach in the eighties as several countries accepted "offices of information" for the PLO short of any diplomatic representation. This informal arrangement served the interests of both sides as it is not clear whether the Holy See would have accepted back in 1980 to formalize relations with the PLO through an official Palestinian representative in the Vatican.

1978 as A Regional Turning Point

In November 1977, Egyptian President Anwar Sadat visited Jerusalem, addressed the Israeli Parliament, and prayed in Al Aqsa Mosque. It was the first time that an Arab head of state had visited Jerusalem after the 1967 occupation in what was seen as an act of betrayal by the PLO and many in the Arab world. In Egypt it prompted the resignation of foreign minister Ismail Fahmi. Pope Shenouda, the leader of the Coptic Church, refused to accompany Sadat to Jerusalem and became one of the most critical voices of Arab normalization with Israel. When the Camp David Agreement was signed a year later, he banned Egyptian Copts from pilgrimage to Jerusalem or any other area under Israeli occupation.

Sadat's Jerusalem visit was followed by the Camp David negotiations, which were seen by the Egyptian President as the way to capitalize on the gains obtained by the October 1973 war. The agreement included the return of all occupied Egyptian territory, mainly in exchange for a number of security arrangements.[308] This agreement set the principle for future regional negotiations based on UNSC Resolution 242: Land for Peace.[309] Nevertheless, it was still a dramatic departure from the overall Arab consensus and a major change in Egyptian policy vis-à-vis the rest of the Arab world. In effect Egypt was boycotted and the Arab League moved its headquarters from Cairo to Tunis.

By 1978 the Lebanese Civil War, or at least the chapter that began in 1976, had ended. A well-established Syrian force remained in the country and used its presence to influence both the situation in Lebanon and Palestinian affairs. An Israeli invasion managed to push Palestinian groups a few kilometers north of the border (north of the Litani River). Israel had gained a mercenary, mainly Christian Lebanese, militia to support them in southern Lebanon as General Saad Haddad took a whole division of the Lebanese army and put it at the service of the Israeli forces. Israel eventually withdrew following pressure from the US and the UN Security Council. International forces arrived in the form of the United Nations Interim Force in Lebanon (UNIFIL). The PLO did not suffer important military losses but hundreds of Lebanese and Palestinian civilians had been killed by the Israeli bombardments.

Terror in Ein Munjed

Ein Munjed was one of the most peaceful neighborhoods of Ramallah. It lies to the south of the Old City and to the west of Jaffa Street, the historic road leading from Al Manarah Square to Betunia, Ein Areeq, and then through several villages to Jaffa. It also served as a demarcation of the area known as "Ramallah Tahta" or downtown. In 1980 Ein Munjed had hundreds of old pine trees on agricultural plots, many of them abandoned when their owners immigrated to the US. Only a few families lived in the area. Overlooking the beautiful valley was a three-story villa built in the early 20th century of Karim Khalaf, the mayor of Ramallah. He lived there with his Italian-Egyptian wife Teresa, a devout Catholic, and two daughters, Viviana and Daniela.

He was the mayor of a town with fewer than 20,000 inhabitants and June 2, 1980, started as a normal summer's day in Palestine. That morning, the thermometers had reached almost 30 degrees Centigrade by 7:45 am. Khalaf went to his car to go to his office in the city council distant almost two kilometers away. Suddenly, everything changed with the sound of an explosion heard by many people across the city. A bomb planted under Khalaf's car had exploded and severely injured him. Almost at the same time, another bomb exploded in the car of Nablus mayor Bassam Shakaa, and another in the garage where Al Bireh mayor Ibrahim Tawil kept his car. That same day of terror had begun at 6:15 am when a hand grenade was thrown into the market in the Old City of Hebron, injuring seven people.[310]

The bombs were all connected to the same terrorist group. Another two attacks that were supposed to take place in Bethlehem and Jerusalem did not succeed due to logistical failures. Each attack was conducted by cells of three people who had acted overnight, receiving logistical support from people recruited by the Jewish underground in the Civil Administration (Israel's administration of the occupied Palestinian territory, with the exception of illegally annexed East Jerusalem). This was how they obtained information about the movements of the Palestinian mayors.[311] It was a terrorist network set up by Israeli settlers to create chaos and facilitate the transfer of the Palestinian population. The notorious leader was a Brooklyn-born rabbi called Meir Kahane and the organization was known as Gush Emunim.

Three hours after the attack, doctors in Ramallah Hospital had to amputate the right foot of Mayor Karim Khalaf. His colleague from Nablus was in a worse condition and lost both his legs. An Israeli-Druze police officer who checked the car of the Al Bireh mayor lost his sight. Most of the perpetrators were arrested but Israeli judges did not charge them with attempted murder, charging them instead with "grievous bodily harm".[312] Some of the terrorists such as journalist Haggai Segal served merely two years in prison.[313]

Israel finally removed Karim Khalaf from his office on March 25, 1982. Bassam Shakaa was also deposed on the same day. Both were accused of *"general agitation, non-recognition of the Israeli civil administration and repeated attempts to disrupt public order"*.[314] Israeli officials took over their places. A day later, the *Washington Post* wrote: *"Israel dismissed the two most prominent Arab mayors still holding office in the occupied West Bank"*.[315]

Israel's Annexation of Jerusalem

While Israel de facto annexed Jerusalem from the very beginning of its occupation, including the dissolution of the Palestinian municipality and the unilateral extension of the Israeli municipality boundaries, it was not until July 30, 1980, that Israel made a formal declaration of annexation aimed at making it irreversible. On that day, the Israeli Parliament approved the Basic Law which declared that *"Jerusalem, complete and united, is the capital of Israel"*.[316] The move was heavily criticized worldwide, leading to the approval of UNSC Resolution 478 which referred to the Israeli decision as *"null and void"* and *"Affirms that the enactment of the "basic law" by Israel constitutes a violation of international law and does not affect the continued application of the Geneva Convention relative to the Protection of Civilian Persons in Time of War, of 12 August 1949, in the Palestinian and other Arab territories occupied since June 1967, includingJerusalem"*.[317]

Israel's ambassador to the UN, Yehuda Blum, responded with a statement that made no references to Israel's obligations under international law but focused on being "singled out" by other countries. Jerusalem was described in the statement as "the capital of the Jewish people" and Blum focused on "freedom of access" to all holy sites.[318]

Making use of the context of the Camp David Agreement, the Israeli statement said that such resolutions were not useful to achieve peace, including Resolution 465, also passed in 1980. This Resolution: *"Determines that all measures taken by Israel to change the physical character, demographic composition, institutional structure or status of the Palestinian and other Arab territories occupied since 1967, including Jerusalem, or any part thereof, have no legal validity and that Israel's policy and practices of settling parts of its population and new immigrants in those territories constitute a flagrant violation of the Fourth Geneva Convention relative to the Protection of Civilian Persons in Time of War, and also constitute a serious obstruction to achieving a comprehensive, just and lasting peace in the Middle East (...) Strongly deplores the continuation and persistence of Israel in pursuing those policies and practices and calls upon the Government and people of Israel to rescind those measures, to dismantle the existing settlements and in particular to cease, on an urgent basis, the establishment, construction and planning of settlements in the Arab territories occupied since 1967, including Jerusalem (...) Calls upon all States not to provide Israel with any assistance to be used specifically in connection with settlements in the occupied territories."*[319]

The Holy See did not buy into Israel's argument of "free access" to holy sites. In fact, by June 1980 they had already circulated a communication to the members of the Security Council stating that *"the Jerusalem question cannot be reduced to mere 'free access for all to the Holy Places'"*.[320] The document emphasized the need for "equality" (clearly violated by the exclusive Jewish status that Israeli laws and practices had given to the city) and referred to the fact *that "the Question of Jerusalem during these very days attracts the attention of the world in a special way (...) any unilateral act tending to modify that status of the Holy City would be very serious"*.[321]

The PLO Executive Committee held an emergency meeting in Damascus on August 1, 1980, to discuss the matter of annexation and stated that: *"Jerusalem has been the capital of our homeland, Arab Palestine, since the time it was built by our ancestors the Canaanites. Thus the liberation of Jerusalem from its Zionist occupiers is an issue of destiny for our people, besides being the only means to secure freedom of worship for all believers"*.[322] The statement referred to the move as an *"aggression against the Islamic and Christian religions"*.

On the same day, the Egyptian National Assembly issued a strong statement of condemnation. But for Israel, relations with Egypt were already guaranteed through the Camp David Agreement. Egyptian diplomacy clarified that this agreement represented a step towards the implementation of UNSC Resolution 242, including East Jerusalem.

Israel's PM Menahem Begin reaffirmed his position just a few days before signing Camp David: *"Israel will never return to the pre-1967 lines (...) mark my words, united Jerusalem is the eternal capital of Israel. It will never be divided again"*.[323] It was against that background that the Israeli response to the Egyptian statement was simply and dismissive: *"Israel's stand regarding Jerusalem is well known and the decision of the Egyptian National Assembly (...) will not determine or alter anything on this matter. Our position, shared by all not only in Israel, but among the Jewish national abroad, is that Jerusalem is the eternal capital of Israel, and will never again be divided"*.[324] Pope Shenouda's response was a reaffirmation of forbidding all Coptic pilgrimage to Jerusalem and elsewhere in the occupied territory of Palestine.

The Churches of Jerusalem in 1980

The heads of churches in Jerusalem did not react as their faithful would have expected. Despite several acts of vandalism against Christian sites (including against the Basilica of the Dormition), as well as attacks against Christian communities (mainly linked to land expropriation, building permits, and ID revocations), the leaders of the Christian churches in Jerusalem had revived the divisions between foreign clergy and local congregations. The former remained silent or dealt with the Israeli authorities as if they were a sovereign state rather than an occupying power. In one extreme case, the Armenian Patriarchate even agreed to the Israelis demolishing the Armenian Church in Sheikh Bureik, the depopulated Armenian village near to Haifa in 1981.[325]

In 1980, the Greek Orthodox Patriarch was Benedict I. He had consistently bypassed the agreements reached with the Jordanian government to respect representation by the Arab population, including refusing to appoint an Arab to the Patriarchate's financial committee.

The Latin Patriarch was Giuseppe Beltretti, an Italian who arrived in Palestine at the age of 16 (in 1926) to study at the Patriarchate's Beit Jala Seminary. He was active in providing humanitarian support to Palestinians in both 1948 and in 1967, as well as using his position to call for international support. In a letter to the US Council of Catholic Bishops, he wrote: *"Continued injustice, discrimination and suppression of human rights in the Holy Land endangers the peace of the world"*.[326] As the leader of a Patriarchate where over two-thirds of the clergy were Arabs, notably Palestinians, his role was constantly challenged by the realities of the occupation and the refugees. While his position was firm, he did not play a major public role other than his public appearances for religious reasons. Unlike the Greek Orthodox heirarchy where Arabs were systematically excluded, Patriarch Beltretti had two Arab bishops in 1980: Hanna Kaldani and Ni'meh Simaan, who had close connections with the Royal Palace office in Amman.

Other heads of churches were not in a position to take action independently. For the first time, Palestinians had assumed some important posts, including Bishop Faik Haddad, the first Arab to head the Episcopal (Anglican) Church in the Middle East, while the Lutherans had their first Arab bishop in Daoud Haddad, born in Beirut. The Melkites had refused to officially appoint a replacement for Capucci, but they appointed Bishop Lufti Lahham as administrator. The Armenian Orthodox Patriarch was Yeghishe Derderian who, despite the importance of his church in Jerusalem both historically and materially, remained isolated from the political realities of his surroundings.

In the absence of a strong stance by the heads of churches in Jerusalem, a network of Palestinian Christian clergy and activists succeeded in turning the issue of Palestine into a political issue for multilateral Christian forums such as the Middle East Council of Churches (MCC) and the World Council of Churches (WCC). In August 22, 1980, the WCC Central Committee issued a statement from Geneva: *"The Central Committee calls the member churches to exert through their respective Governments all pressure on Israel to withhold all action on Jerusalem, the future of which should be included in the agenda of official negotiations involving Israel and the Palestinians on self-determination and on the solution of the Middle East Conflict".*[327] The WCC emphasized the importance of Jerusalem for the three monotheistic religions, making clear their opposition to *"Israeli unilateral action of annexing East Jerusalem and uniting the city as its 'eternal capital' under its exclusive sovereignty".*[328]

The MCC issued a stronger statement that went beyond the issue of the city to address broadly the consequences of the Israeli occupation. Their engagement in the discussion was not taken seriously by Western powers in yet another demonstration of how Arab or Middle Eastern Christian voices had been marginalized. The main people affected by the lack of access to Palestine, particularly Jerusalem, were the citizens of Arab countries. The MCC referred to Israeli intentions: *"For the Israeli occupation, with its denial of the Arab character of the City and its bid to settler Jews alone in Palestine, is bound to render, on the basis of such political logics, the lives of the Arab Palestinians impossible and void of all national expression (...) The City is inseparably tied to the Palestinian people. No resolution on the issue of Jerusalem can be accepted unless the Palestinian people are reassured of their freedom and prosperity, and their deliverance from subjugation and bondage."[329]*

Although Palestinian Christian activism via these organizations was not rare, it was in the 1980s that a fair resolution to the question of Palestine become a central issue for inter-church relations. Christian Zionism was still an important aspect in the tradition of several, mainly Western churches, from Evangelicals to Catholics, but Palestinians had obtained important posts and their case began to be explained from a Christian perspective, including the work of Palestinian theologians and clergy.

Abu Nidal

Sabri Al Banna was born in Jaffa. At 11 years of age he was forcibly displaced during the Nakba, beginning a path similar to that of many others of his generation, finishing high school, becoming close to the Baath Party, studying in Egypt, and moving to Saudi Arabia for work. There, he was fired by his employer (ARAMCO) for his political activities and then moved to Jordan where he became a member of Fatah. He became known as Abu Nidal. In 1974 he split from Fatah, taking a good number of members with him. They received funding and logistical support from the Iraqi regime, where Abu Nidal was representing Fatah. It was seen as a move by the Iraqi intelligence to gain more influence in the Palestinian arena. The Iraqi government provided the properties, camps and weapons owned by Fatah in Iraq to Abu Nidal, who began an aggressive campaign of operations. The new organization was known as the Fatah Revolutionary Council.[330]

At the time of the split, there were several ideological disputes within Fatah. Another person who left the organization around the same period was Naji Alloush, a Palestinian Christian from Birzeit and one of the organization's key intellectuals. It soon became clear that Abu Nidal's split was less about ideological differences over the liberation of Palestine and more about becoming a mercenary entity in the service of the Iraqi government. Later, he provided similar services to the governments of Syria and Libya.

At 9:00 am on June 1, 1981, Naim Khader left his home in Brussels to go to his office as the PLO representative in Belgium. Suddenly, a gunman appeared and fatally shot him. Up until today, mystery remains about who was behind the assassination. Some claimed that it was the Mossad as part of their assassination campaign of Palestinian representatives (including Wael Zwaiter in Rome, Mahmoud Hamshari in Paris, and Hussein al Bashir in Nicosia), while others pointed the finger at Abu Nidal.

Naim Khader was born in Zababdeh and studied in the Beit Jala Seminary. He completed his studies but instead of moving into the priesthood, he joined the PLO and left for the Catholic University of Louvain to continue his studies. In 1976 was appointed as the first Palestinian representative to Belgium and the European institutions.

An intellectual, Khader had been engaged in dialogue with left-wing Israelis, which could have been enough for Abu Nidal to attack him. He was a proponent of dialogue and fervent advocate of a one state solution.

In an article published in 1976, Khader defended the idea of a "democratic state" that *"transcends the Zionist enemy as an enemy that must be fought, in order to reach out to the Israeli Jewish person with whom it is incumbent upon us to live together in brotherhood and peace (...) We do not fight the Jews because they are Jews in order to kill them or expel them or throw them into the sea. We fight the occupied viciously, whatever his religion, race or country of origin might be. We have in the past fought against the occupying Catholic Crusaders and we have fought the occupying Muslim Ottomans, and we have fought the occupying Protestant British, and we are currently fighting the Jewish Zionist in his capacity as occupier.*[331]*"* Israel did not allow Khader's body to be buried in his hometown Zababdeh but it was received by thousands in Beirut in a ceremony led by Yasser Arafat. The body was then taken to Amman, where the funeral took place.

The reality on the ground was shaped by funerals and threats of a large Israeli invasion of Lebanon. Israel's right-wing government headed by Menahem Begin, had appointed Ariel Sharon, himself responsible for the Qibya massacre, as defense minister. Sharon had developed an obsession with eliminating the PLO and based on that logic, he began preparing to invade Lebanon. The preparations took several months. Between July 1981 and March 1982, the UNIFIL reported 193 violations of the ceasefire since the previous invasion that were Israel's responsibility.[332] From then on, the preparations were complete to implement Sharon's plan and any event could have triggered it.

Iraq Orders, Abu Nidal Executes,
the PLO is Blamed

The PLO was aware of the Israeli plans and took great care during early 1982. In fact no attacks against Israeli positions took place from Lebanese soil. The information had arrived through several sources in the diplomatic and intelligence community, with Salah Khalaf (Abu Iyad) playing a prominent role. Palestinians knew through several intelligence services that Israel was preparing in advance yet their analysis of the situation underestimated how far Israel was willing to go. The PLO and its forces did not think that Israeli forces would attack Beirut but would focus on large areas to the south.

Everything changed on June 3, when at 11:00 pm a group of three agents shot Israel's ambassador in London. Ambassador Shlomo Argov was shot in the head as he was leaving a reception at the Dorchester Hotel in London. He survived the attack but stayed unconscious for months. The rapid response of British police led to the detention of the shooter, Hussein Ghassan Said, and the revelation that the orders had come from Baghdad. It was later speculated that one of the three men involved was actually an Iraqi intelligence officer. This attack had Abu Nidal's signature on it.

For Sharon, this was the excuse he needed to launch his long-awaited operation, accusing the PLO of committing the attack[333] despite solid evidence otherwise. The invasion plan had already been presented one month earlier to US Secretary of Defence Caspar Weinberger.[334] According to the plans, Israel would impose a new political reality in Lebanon. The US had quietly endorsed the action[335] but later it became clear that the Americans did not realize the magnitude of the offensive embarked upon by Sharon.

Beirut and the 88-Day Siege

According to the explanation given by Ariel Sharon to the Israeli cabinet, the invasion would last 48 hours. This was an average between Menahem Begin's initial statements of about 24 hours and a maximum of 72 hours. This estimate proved to be completely inaccurate and the offensive was the beginning of one of the greatest acts of carnage in the region since 1948. Israel carefully calling the operation "Peace for Galilee", alluding to Palestinian attacks from Lebanon. In reality, the shooting of Ambassador Argov was not related to the PLO, nor had Israel undergone attacks from southern Lebanon from several months. The interest was to finish the PLO.

On June 6 around 100,000 Israeli soldiers were mobilized to the north, including Israel's powerful Air Force and their naval contingents. The ground invasion came from areas controlled by the UNIFIL mission. Israel had mobilized over 1,200 tanks while the PLO forces had only 60 tanks and around 6,000 soldiers deployed in the south. There was confusion involving scenes of fierce resistance while several Palestinian groups were ordering withdrawal given the disparity of forces. The following day, the first refugee camps began to fall under Israeli fire, beginning with the unrecognized camp of Al Bassa, home to hundreds of Palestinian Christians.

The PLO had approximately 10,000 soldiers, including regular combat units and reservists such as the Student Batallion, but even combined with the allied Lebanese forces, their numbers were much fewer than the Israelis put into combat. Without an air force and very limited naval units, the Palestinian forces had only artillery and anti-air defense systems. With almost no possibility of defeating the invading Israeli forces, the PLO and allied forces began a progressive withdrawal. On June 7, President Reagan met Pope John Paul II for first time. While both had a private audience in the Vatican, a parallel meeting was taking place between Cardinal Casaroli and Archbishop Silvestrini, the secretary for relations with states at the Vatican, with US Secretary of State Alexander Haig and National Security Adviser William Clark. Their discussions were mainly about Lebanon and the concerns of the Holy See about the Israeli attack. Secretary of State Haig said they had received assurances from Israeli PM Menahem Begin that the invasion *"would not go farther than 25 miles inside Lebanon"*.[336]

Contrary to Israeli calculations, the Palestinian resistance did not vanish after 72 hours. Having withdrawn to Beirut, while keeping some units in the south, the Palestinians and their Lebanese allies were offering unexpected resistance. Ariel Sharon, who was leading the invasion, had shown no mercy to Arab civilians in his previous military experiences, including by killings and blowing up Palestinian homes such as in Qibya, 1953.[337] The Israeli forces took an unexpected step and despite the US assurances to the Holy See, the invasion went beyond southern Lebanon. Israeli tanks were besieging Beirut just one week after the invasion had started.

The siege of Beirut lasted for months until an agreement that included PLO military withdrawal from Lebanon was achieved. The negotiations involved the United States and several European countries. At this stage the PLO leadership had three main goals regarding a cease-fire: international recognition, withdrawal with their weapons, and securing international protection for the refugees left behind. The PLO acceptance of withdrawal was also the result of dialogue with the allied Lebanese groups, including George Hawi's Communist Party and the Druze Socialists of Kamal Jumblatt.

Under the agreement, the military groups allied under the PLO, including the Palestine Liberation Army, left to several different locations such as Syria, Iraq, Yemen, Sudan, and Algeria. Some PLO officials were allowed back to Jordan while the PLO headquarters were moved to Tunisia. Palestinian soldiers left with their light weapons but were not allowed to carry their heavier weaponry. A few tanks, Katyusha rockets, RPGs and explosives were distributed either to the Lebanese Army or to allied Lebanese groups. An international force that included Italian and US forces entered Lebanon to oversee the Palestinian withdrawal, and commitments on the safety of Palestinian refugees were reiterated to Palestinian officials by international representatives.

Yasser Arafat left surrounded by the 17-Force (the first Palestinian presidential guard created by Ali Hassan Salameh) and under Greek naval protection. Both Greece and Cyprus played a prominent role in the Palestinian departure as they had maintained close relations with the Palestinian struggle. Asked where he would be going, Arafat said, *"To Jerusalem"*. In reality he went first to Athens to meet with his close friend, Greek PM Andreas Papandreu. He was received with military honors and thousands of Greek demonstrators waving Palestinian and Greek flags. Despite the strong show of solidarity, the most historically relevant moment of this journey was not Athens but Rome, where he attended a meeting of the Inter-Parliamentarian Union after a brief stop in the PLO's new home, Tunisia.

The key moment of the visit to Rome came when Yasser Arafat was granted his first audience in the Vatican on September 15 and was received by Pope Jean Paul II. Arafat was accompanied by Afif Safieh, the young Palestinian diplomat from a traditional Catholic family in Jerusalem and tasked by the Palestinian leader to strengthen relations with the Holy See.

The meeting between Pope Jean Paul II and Yasser Arafat was one of the most important Palestinian diplomatic victories. Arafat had opened up several channels with various Christian churches but the Catholic

Church represented an entry point to several Western countries. Vatican diplomacy had already succeeded in 1978 in stopping an imminent war between Argentina and Chile (the Beagle crisis) and Pope Jean Paul II appeared to have an interest in contributing to world peace, including the Middle East. Yasser Arafat obtained the result he sought after a regular 20-minute meeting. The Vatican issued a statement that was seen as an endorsement of Palestinian demands and which stressed: *"The recognition of the rights of all peoples, and in particular of the Palestinian people to their own homeland and Israel to its security".*[338] As part of his weekly audience, Pope Jean Paul II explained that: *"The Holy See is convinced that true peace cannot exist without justice and that there will be no justice if the rights of all the interested peoples are not recognized in a stable, adequate and equal way".*[339]

The Israeli government understood the legitimacy won by the PLO after this meeting and bitterly condemned it, only to face strong Vatican support for the meeting in what became one of the most important diplomatic landmarks of Yasser Arafat's political career.

September 15 also marked the assassination of the recently elected Lebanese president Bachir Gamayel. A right-wing politician who had established strong military connections with Israel had been eliminated by a bomb that Yasser Arafat declared was *"a provocation by the Americans and Israel so that the Israelis could enter Beirut".*[340] The Palestinian leader had stressed the importance of fulfilling international commitments regarding the security of Palestinian refugees left in Lebanon during his meetings with Italian officials, but the worst scenario was about to materialize. Using the assassination as a pretext, the Israeli Army commanded by Ariel Sharon violated the principles of the ceasefire agreement and invaded West Beirut, where most Palestinians were located. Sharon had legally become the officer in charge of the occupying power troops and was entrusted with providing security for civilians. He claimed that "2000 terrorists" had been left by the PLO in refugee camps,[341] and provided logistical support to Lebanese Falangist troops, allowing them to enter the refugee camps of Sabra and Shatila. This was the beginning of the infamous massacre committed for three days in the refugee camps.

A furious Yasser Arafat quickly blamed the early withdrawal of the international force (mainly composed of the US, France and Italy). He was still in Rome when news of the massacre began to arrive. French, Italian and US diplomats were also furious yet the Israeli government did not feel enough pressure to stop what was taking place. While urgent talks took place to reconstitute the international forces in Lebanon, US Secretary of State George Shultz concluded: *"The brutal fact is that we are partially responsible (…). We took the Israelis and the Lebanese at their word".*[342]

The reports by the International Committee of the Red Cross were undisputable. A massacre had taken place in Beirut. The analysis of most international parties was unanimous, that Israel was the responsible power and had cooperated with the Falangist militias. The US had violated its own commitments in the first agreement ever achieved with the PLO. It was almost impossible to accurately count the deaths as there were mass graves and some people had been taken in trucks and executed outside the camps under the authority of Ariel Sharon. Around 400,000 Israelis took to the streets of Tel Aviv urging the government to investigate what had happened, ending with the formation of the Kahan Commission. This avoided any mention of direct responsibility by Israeli but stated that Sharon held *"personal responsibility"* for what had happened. No real accountability was accepted and less than two decades later, Sharon became Israel's Prime Minister.

4.

Palestine and the Peace Process

Grassroots Organization and Resistance by Churches in Palestine

The PLO withdrawal from Lebanon did not trigger a major change in the activities of the national forces in Palestine. The main organizations, Fatah and the PFLP, committed a number of attacks and acts of sabotage on a local level, but at a high cost, including thousands of members becoming prisoners in Israeli jails. They also set up several grassroots organizations to provide services to the people under occupation.

In Beit Jala the left-wing forces were particularly strong. While the Communist Party took control of the traditional Orthodox Club, the PFLP established a Beit Jala Youth Club that offered a library, courses and educational support for Palestinian students, and a folkloric group. With the Israeli occupation banning even the Palestinian flag, these organizations took on the challenge of raising flags in the streets, particularly in strategic places such as the market. Their activities included writing slogans on the walls of the streets, distributing hand-made copies of political statements, and carrying out operations ordered by their leadership. In April 1982 one such operation took place when Molotov cocktails were thrown at an Israeli military convoy passing through the middle of Beit Jala (between the Orthodox and the Latin churches). The bombs did not explode but

Israeli forces captured those involved a few days later. One of them was Johnny Abu Eid who spent the next six years of his life in jail: *"We spent a lot of time on strikes to gain basic rights such as a bed, a radio or a TV (...) One Christmas we (the Christian prisoners) were allowed to receive sweets, but we refused. It was either sweets for everyone or nobody would enjoy them. So we all got sweets... you don't know what it was to get chocolates or halva (Halawe) under suchconditions!"*[343]

Palestinian prisoners have historically been at the core of the national agenda. Dozens were arrested in each village in military raids and the experience of imprisonment and torture became familiar to almost every Palestinian home. In 1985 the PFLP-GC, headed by Ahmad Jibril, succeeded in achieving an agreement to exchange three Israeli prisoners from the Lebanon war for 1,150 prisoners in Israeli jails. The PFLP of George Habash was one of the main beneficiaries of the agreement and anticipated the release of many of their prisoners, including the arrested Beit Jala cell. However, those prisoners declined on the grounds that their sentences were insignificant compared to others with 15-year jail terms or prisoners who were sick and elderly.[344]

Organizations like the one set up by the PFLP in Beit Jala were multiplied all over the occupied territory. Their work was key in preventing the normalization Israel sought to control Palestinian lives, and represented yet another setback for the strategic planning of the Israeli occupation, as had been the case during the municipal elections. The economic situation was relatively stable, prompting Israel to believe that Palestinians would ultimately accept their rule. However, ordinary Palestinians played a major role in challenging Israeli rule, although there were some who contributed to Israeli policy. A symbol of the struggle became the Notre Dame building opposite New Gate in Jerusalem. Built in the 19th century as a center to welcome French pilgrims, it was severely damaged during the 1948 war and was separated from the Old City from that year until 1967. The building overlooks the Christian Quarter in a strategic spot in the city.

The French religious order in charge of the building, the Assumptionists, tried to sell the building to the Hebrew University in the late sixties, prompting the local community to take strong action to return the building, reaching up to the highest spheres in the Vatican. The Holy See intervened, refused the transaction, and returned the building to the Church. Notre Dame was reopened in 1980 as a guest house.

The Notre Dame case revived the issue of churches selling and leasing property to Zionist organizations, a process begun with the Greek Orthodox Patriarchate in the early 20th century. The crisis between foreign religious orders and their staff in relation to the indigenous Palestinian communities tended to increase after the Nakba, though in some cases the churches understood the demands of their communities and promoted a number of Palestinian clergy. For the Roman Catholic institutions, whether the Latin Patriarchate or the Franciscans, their work under Vatican guidance had to take into consideration basic norms of Vatican diplomacy, including respect for international law. The Notre Dame case became a turning point at which strict guidelines were established with regard to church property. The main issue for the national movement remained the Greek Orthodox Church, which leased and sold land for the building of some of Israel's most iconic landmarks, including the Israeli Parliament (Knesset) near to the San Simon monastery and the Prime Minister's residence in Talbiya, close to Salameh Square.

Just as during the British Mandate, Palestinian Orthodox organizations such as the Jerusalem Orthodox Club took over the burden of a difficult struggle. With Israel as the sole power in control of Jerusalem, the

Greek Orthodox Patriarchate could continue real estate deals without fear of accountability, while pressure from the Palestinian community mainly aimed at provoking a reaction from Jordan. The PLO had few tools to deal with this issue, yet the fact that it did not make use of its friendly ties with Greece to attempt to resolve this case shows the absence of a national agenda with regard to church properties. In other words, while there was concern and awareness of what had taken place with the properties, the Palestinian response did not go beyond letters and improvised demonstrations. There was a lack of a consistent diplomatic approach that would exert pressure on the Patriarchate to stop such practices. Several documents show that church property continued to be leased to illegal Israeli settlements during the seventies and eighties.

It is in this context that the work of grassroots church groups contributed to creating awareness among larger churches and Christian groups worldwide, and put pressure on the international community to take action on Palestine. This can be seen as complimentary to the advanced relations the PLO had established with the Holy See, despite Israel's anger at the meetings, and went beyond previous efforts like the office for church relations established during the Beirut period and headed by Nabil Shaath.

This is how Palestinians silently began to overcome their initial fears and systematically started to share their experiences with foreign pilgrims, including priests. The World Council of Churches (WCC) took the case seriously and in 1983 issued a statement calling upon Israel to withdraw from the 1967 occupied territory, to implement the rights of the Palestinian people to self-determination, including through a sovereign state, and even expressed some criticism of the permissive attitude taken by churches in the West with regard to Israel: *"To remind Christians in the Western world to recognize that their guilt over the fate of the Jews in their countries may have influenced their views of the conflict in the Middle East and has often led to uncritical support of the policies of the state of Israel, thereby ignoring the plight of the Palestinian people and their rights."[345]*

Many such testimonies were being delivered by clergy in Palestine, several of whom played a prominent role not only in providing services to the community, particularly in education, but also in supporting the resistance. While all the clergy interviewed for this book made clear that they did not support armed struggle, some emphasized that resisting injustice is a must and that they did *"what we had to do"*. Other personalities who were close to the churches, from regular workers to businesspeople, made use of their connections with the churches to establish contacts with foreign delegations.

Christian Clergy as Palestine Envoys:
Fr. Ibrahim Ayyad and Bishop Elia Khoury

The aftermath of Lebanon resulted in a deep crisis in the Palestinian national movement. Internal investigations, commissions of inquiry, and even martial courts took place to analyze what had happened. While the PLO had succeeded in being recognized as an international player, even by the US that had engaged in indirect talks to achieve a ceasefire, the departure from Beirut fueled internal divisions. The Syrian and Libyan governments backed splits in the PLO, including that of Colonel Said al-Muragha, known as Abu Musa and one of the most prominent Fatah military leaders, who left the organization with an important number of its combatants and based himself in Syria under the name Fatah Al Intifada.

But the most challenging obstacle that for the first time since its creation, the PLO had no borders with the homeland. Syria had banned military operations from its territory since the late sixties, Egypt had signed a peace agreement with Israel, and both Jordan and Lebanon no longer had any active PLO forces. In addition, an economic crisis hit the organization while Israel was enjoying a process that appeared to normalize its control over the occupied Palestinian territory. Although the 1980 municipal elections were cancelled due to fear of a new PLO victory, Israel had managed to achieve unprecedented control over Palestine.

The PLO continued its activities and some civil disobedience events took place in the occupied territory. Israel's repression was harsh and thousands of people were imprisoned, increasing the need for economic support not only for PLO structures but for ordinary citizens affected by Israeli policies, including relatives of prisoners and martyrs.

One step taken by Yasser Arafat was the appointment of Fr. Ibrahim Ayyad as his personal envoy to Latin America. The political situation in the subcontinent was certainly not conducive to expanding Palestinian relations. The PLO had succeeded in opening diplomatic representations in Mexico, whose PRI-led government had pushed for an independent foreign policy regardless of neighboring relations with the US. At the same time the PLO opened offices in Cuba and Nicaragua. In Brazil the PLO was working as part of the Arab League delegation but in other countries it succeeded in opening Information Offices tied to local Palestinian communities. Most countries in the region were living under dictatorships that had close military relations with Israel or under newly elected civilian governments that were still relatively weak. Fr. Ibrahim Ayyad's appointment had a far larger strategic meaning for the PLO as he was there to re-articulate the largely Christian Palestinian communities and fundamentally, to source funds for the PLO from the wealthy Palestinian businessmen in the area.

Fr. Ayyad represented a significant part of what Yasser Arafat wanted to portray to the Western world: the prominence of Palestinian Christians in the national movement as part of the defense of the "Holy Land". He was the priest chosen by Yasser Arafat to bless the beginning of the military struggle back in 1964, had close connections with the Holy See, and had proved his commitment to the national movement throughout his career. His origins from the Bethlehem area was a further plus as the region was known as the birthplace of Jesus.

During his trips, Fr. Ayyad impressed people with his humble stance. When wealthy Palestinians invited him to luxury hotels, he asked instead to donate that money to the national cause. He preferred to sleep in the residences of few Palestinian diplomats in the region or in the private homes of Palestinian expatriates. When a Palestinian diplomat in Peru drove him from the airport to the Sheraton Hotel, Fr. Ayyad *"made a scandal"* and asked to be sent to the residence of the Palestinian ambassador. *"His requests were simple; we always had to have olives and cheese,"* said one of his hosts.

But beyond the anecdotes, Fr. Ayyad played a major role in fundraising for the PLO in Latin America and strengthened Palestinian structures, including the election of the first representatives of the Latin American diaspora to the Palestine National Council (PNC). Fr. Ayyad had a meeting with the Chilean government authorities, who were supported by some of the Palestinian community, and received an offer to open a PLO mission in Chile. The offer was declined by the PLO until the fall of the Pinochet dictatorship. On another occasion, Fr. Ayyad managed to obtain a building permit for the first mosque in Caracas, Venezuela. He effectively raised considerable funds for the PLO.

Meanwhile, Episcopal (Anglican) Bishop Elia Khoury had become a member of the PLO Executive Committee. Originally from Zababdeh and a refugee from West Jerusalem in 1948, he studied theology in

London and at the University of Colorado and was deported from Palestine in 1969. Bishop Khoury became the first Christian clergy to serve in the highest PLO executive body. His election was part of a strategy by the PLO to empower figures from the occupied territory, but also served as a message of mobilization in which all, even a religious clergy, had a role to play. In Khoury's words, *"a church leader is not here to sit all the time in church folding his hands like this, closing his eyes, praying (...) I believe the church has to live within its own people... and not put itself aside."*[346]

It did not take much for Bishop Khoury to use his connections to raise awareness of his people's cause. British PM Margaret Thatcher invited him to London as part of a joint Palestinian-Jordanian delegation of four members. The extremist group led by Sabri Banna (Abu Nidal) issued death threats against the delegation, which included Muhammad Mulhim, the exiled mayor of Halhoul and also a PLO Executive Committee member. From his base in Amman, Bishop Khoury oversaw an agreement to increase cooperation between King Hussein and Yasser Arafat.

Based in Tunisia and with fewer means to apply pressure, the PLO was forced to reshape its foreign relations approach and include more figures able to approach Western capitals. This included a generation of fresh graduates from Western universities who were quickly turned into diplomats, mainly leaders from the General Union of Palestine Students as well as more senior figures such as Bishop Khoury.

Between Intra-Palestinian Divisions and the Intifada

The eighties marked some of the most vicious attempts by Arab governments to control the PLO. Iraq had already played its cards with Abu Nidal's gang, while the governments of Syria and Libya got heavily involved in funding factions and promoting divisions. The most difficult moment for the PLO was the secession of Abu Musa from Fatah. This was funded by the Syrian government with some Libyan support and provoked a crisis that led to the War of the Camps. These events prompted the return of Yasser Arafat to Lebanon to raise the morale of the forces defending the camps from the attacks.

The groups fighting in the pro-Syrian camp mainly included the Abu Musa forces, the PFLP-CG of Ahmad Jibril, and Al Saiqa. They had already suffered a major blow a few years earlier when Hanna Bathish, a Palestinian Christian refugee who was the deputy leader of Al Saiqa, split from the movement and took a significant number of well-trained fighters to Fatah. The main reason for the split was the decision by Bathish to pursue Palestinian national interests rather than become a tool of the Syrian government.[347]

Despite the turbulent first half of the decade, the 1980s represented a period of strategic planning for the PLO, including greater diplomatic outreach, and strengthening support and the balance of power inside Palestine. Yasser Arafat pushed for new figures to join the PNC and representation of a broader spectrum of Palestinians. Soon, those factions who had split began to see the results when their boycott of the 17th PNC held in 1984 did not influence the quorum of the meeting. The PNC meeting took place in Amman and strengthened relations with Jordan. The final communique made a gesture towards Egypt (*"as for fraternal Egypt, we highly appreciate and value its place and role"[348]*) and emphasized the need for national unity.

The subsequent session took place in April 1987 in Algeria in a context of broader dialogue between Palestinian factions and the Arab world. The final communique made positive references to a number of Arab states, including Libya which had funded some of the Palestinian divisions. Syria was not mentioned directly but this was not necessarily part of the calculations of the PLO leadership. Years of Syrian interference in internal Palestinian affairs had ended in violent attacks and raids, wounds that were still open for many. While a few Palestinian leaders still resided in Damascus, notably George Habash, Nayef Hawatmeh, and a number of communist leaders, the process of Palestinian-Syrian reconciliation was still not on the agenda.

The PLO had undoubtedly made pace in international relations and expanded its diplomatic presence. Several strong statements were issued in 1987 by Arab and Islamic leaders calling for the inclusion of the PLO in any solution, including a statement by the Jordanian Prime Minister Zaid Rifai calling for an international peace conference *"to be called by the UN Secretary General and attended by all interested parties in the conflict, including the PLO."*[349] This could be considered a symbol of the moderate success brought about by Palestinian-Jordanian dialogue in the eighties. At the same time, the PLO had found a coherent policy of support for the cells and organizations located in the occupied territory, including lobbying for generous financial support for universities and hospitals while supporting networks of civil society organizations that had successfully managed to identify, represent, and provide services to thousands of Palestinians under Israeli occupation.

This is how the second half of the eighties became a turning point for the Palestinian national movement. The most important Palestinian factions, including Fatah, the PFLP, and the DFLP had achieved unity. The Communist Party, whose PLO membership had been rejected for reasons that included their refusal to adopt armed struggle, finally became a full member of the organization. Funding for the PLO continued to flow from Palestinians in the diaspora, as well as from Saudi Arabia and Kuwait among other Arab countries. This provided a feeling of institutional strength that few thought could have been achieved after the departure from Beirut in 1982.

A Winter Morning in Gaza

For many Israelis it was a car accident. For many Palestinians it was a symbol of Israeli disregard for Palestinian rights, let alone lives. On December 9, 1987, a vehicle driven by an Israeli settler rammed a Palestinian car carrying workers close to the Beit Hanoun junction in Gaza, resulting in the killing of four Palestinians. This incident is recognized as the beginning of the First Intifada, which soon spread into all the occupied Palestinian territory.

The Israeli establishment was taken by surprise at the mass demonstrations that began in Gaza. Israeli political scientist Neve Gordon referred to it as the end of the *"colonial fantasy"* constructed by *"the political and military establishments (...) convincing themselves that the indigenous Palestinians were grateful to the Israeli military government for improving their living conditions."*[350] All attempts to that date to create either an alternative leadership to the PLO, including the infamous "Village Leagues" or support for Islamist organizations, had failed. Soon a Unified Command for the Intifada had been created including all PLO factions and a strong network of civil society organizations contributed to the organization of the resistance from the national dimension to even small neighborhoods. As one of the organizers in Bethlehem said: *"If a Palestinian was killed in Jenin, all of Palestine would go on strike, but we also had local issues like how to deal with Israeli closures, and then the neighborhoods were organized in a way that everyone would participate and assume a responsibility. So, for example, we secured flour, eggs and milk for everyone."*[351]

The astonishment with which Israelis viewed the rapid mobilization of Palestinian organizations was probably similar to that felt by the heads of churches in Jerusalem, but the latter failed to realize that they had indirectly contributed to the successful popular movement. Over the years, the Latin Patriarchate, the Franciscans, the Lutherans, Episcopals, and Greek Catholics had all invested in developing institutions that became strongholds of popular organization and support for the resistance, including schools, hospitals, community centers, and cultural organizations. The Greek Orthodox Patriarchate had smaller involvement in providing services to the community but the Palestinian Orthodox communities had already set up their own network of organizations.

Parish priests understood what was taking place and churches were involved in the Palestinian uprising from outset. For example, Fr. Manuel Musallam, a native of Birzeit and at that time parish priest of Zababdeh, was in charge of organizing classes for students when the schools were closed by the Israeli authorities. The political involvement of Fr. Musallam had deeper roots than the popular movement of the Intifada and included close connections with Fatah and support for Palestinian fighters when he was serving as a young priest nearby the Zarqa refugee camp in Jordan.

It was during this period that a young priest called Faysal Hijazeen, a Jordanian serving as an assistant priest in Ramallah, was severely beaten by Israeli forces. *"That Sunday when we left mass, everyone in town had known about what happened and many people were waiting outside the convent in order to demonstrate. So we went with them only to be met with deeper repression by Israeli forces,"* said Fr. Hijazeen.[352] A similar situation took place in Birzeit. With the Palestinian flag banned by the occupation, every night Palestinian youth would raise a Palestinian flag on top of a tree at the entrance to the Latin Convent. One morning a jeep with Israeli soldiers arrived and the officer asked the priests, *"I want to know how this flag got up the tree."* A young priest responded, *"Easy, at night we water the tree and in the morning the flag is raised."* The soldier was furious with the answer and beat the priest up with his weapon, causing the priest to collapse on the floor in front of the students of the local Latin Patriarchate School. But perhaps the most intrepid action taken by religious officials in the early days of the Intifada took place in Beit Jala. An Israeli military convoy was traveling up the hills around midnight and just below the Latin cemetery, it came under a rain of stones thrown by a group of young seminarians. When Israeli forces tried to raid the Latin Patriarchate Seminary, the perpetrators were all in their beds and the superiors pushed the forces out. The story of the attack became an anecdote that reflected the feelings of the Palestinian street, the strong refusal to live under Israeli control, and the inclusivity of the Intifada.

This was not the only act of "resistance" taken by the Seminary. The Military Governor of Bethlehem once made a tour of the building and stopped in front of a prominent map that showed the topography of the country under the name "Palestine". He asked for the name to be changed but the Rector of the Seminary, Fr. Boulos Marcuzzo, insisted that this map had been there from before 1948.[353] At that period it was rare to find the word "Palestine" displayed in public. In the case of the Armenian Balian family ceramics company on Nablus Street, opposite the US Consulate, the factory was destroyed in 1967 but was rebuilt with the same name of "Palestinian Pottery" on the outside of the building as it had been since it opened in 1922.

By the end of 1987 the Latin Patriarchate of Jerusalem was still headed by Patriarch Giacomo Beltritti, an Italian who had spent most of his life in Palestine helping refugees in 1948 and notably, expanding the school system for Palestinians since becoming Patriarch in 1970. Several Priests ordained under his mandate remember his quiet support for Palestinian rights. In 1987 he had reached the retirement age of 75 for a bishop and Pope John Paul II had to appoint the person to take over. Pope John Paul II took the historic decision to appoint a Palestinian as Latin Patriarch of Jerusalem.

Born in Nazareth in 1933 and ordained priest in 1955, Patriarch Sabbah had a long experience in charge of youth movements, schools and Bethlehem University, as well as a strong educational background that included a PhD from the Sorbonne in Arabic Philology. He was not even a bishop at the time of his appointment but had strong backing from the Arab clergy. Most importantly, it had become clear that the Holy See was making a strategic decision to appoint an Arab Palestinian as Patriarch. There were rumors that when Pope John Paul II was presented with two files for the position of Patriarch of Jerusalem, an Italian and a Palestinian, he told his confidents, "il palestinese" (the Palestinian) without any hesitation.[354]

Although shocking to many, the decision was particularly welcomed in Nazareth where the Patriarch's family resided and the communist mayor Tawfik Zayyad, the renowned Palestinian poet and author of *"Here we shall stay, sing our songs, take to the angry streets, fill prisons with dignity"*, issued a proud statement welcoming the son of their city. Zayyad was not the only one to welcome the news with excitement. From his headquarters in Tunisia, Yasser Arafat had followed the news with particular enthusiasm and tried to establish direct contact with Sabbah through an emissary who delivered a financial contribution to the Latin Patriarchate, a gift that was immediately declined by Patriarch Sabbah who knew that being the first Palestinian in this position would lead to more than one controversy. As soon as the ceremony for his appointment was finalized in the Vatican, a picture of Patriarch Sabbah kissing a cross carried by Bishop Capucci was altered by an Israeli news outlet that changed the cross for a rifle and a hand-grenade, and referred to Sabbah as "the Patriarch of Terror".[355]

At the time that Patriarch Sabbah officially entered the Old City of Jerusalem through Jaffa Gate, things were no longer the same in Jerusalem. It was January 12, 1988, less than a month into the First Intifada and there was a general strike after settlers had killed Raba Hussein Ghanem, a 16-year-old Palestinian teenager. The army commander for the occupation forces in the West Bank, Amran Mitzna, said the settlers had acted *"in self-defense"*[356] but Palestinian human rights groups were noting the acts of an army ordered to act with extreme severity against Palestinian demonstrations for freedom. That day a list of names was published by the Israeli authorities of people facing deportation from the country, including some who became prominent leaders such as Fateh members Jibril Rajoub and Hussam Khader.[357]

One of the main challenges faced by Patriarch Sabbah was how to make use of his national identity to be closer to the people while not neglecting his responsibilities as the most senior Catholic figure in the region. His approach was soon made clear in part of his first pastoral message released in 1988: *"It is the duty of the Church to deal with each injustice and each aggression against the dignity of man, regardless of who is committing them. Its duty is to defend the rights of man against all injustice (...) The Church appeals to all men and women to become conscious of their own dignity and to take up their role in society, whatever the situation, be it one of peace or one of struggle."*[358] Very soon he had to articulate a whole new policy for the Patriarch, make efforts to take joint actions with the other heads of churches in Jerusalem, and take steps to protect his congregation. In particular, the town of Beit Sahour with the biblical "shepherd's field" became the center of one of the most revolutionary models of resistance to take place against the Israeli occupation.

Popular organization by local committees went beyond what Israeli officials could have imagined. Popular pressure in the first few months forced several figures who had collaborated with the occupation either to leave their homes, appear in local courts or to apologize. In Beit Sahour during Sunday mass, a senior figure of the "Village Leagues" set up by the occupation apologized to the people. It did not end there as more and more Palestinian civil servants and police officers working in the Israeli Civil Administration presented their resignations as requested by the Unified Command of the Intifada. In other words, the target was to destabilize the system of management imposed by the Israeli occupation upon Palestinians. Beit Sahour went a step further than other Palestinian towns and adopted the slogan of *"no taxation without representation"*. The town stopped paying taxes to the Israeli occupation. As in other towns, people were organized to resist a blockade by moving into models of popular economy with labor divided between neighbors. Beit Sahour adopted the novel step of buying 18 cows to provide the town with milk and enable the boycott of Israeli dairy products.

These activities were strongly repressed by the Israeli authorities which did not want other towns to adopt the same model of civil disobedience as in Beit Sahour. Furniture was confiscated and elders were taken to jail. When people burnt IDs in protest, they were detained for deportation and accused of illegally residing (in their own towns). Organizations were closed. The occupation authorities also attempted to confiscate the cows[359] and most damaging of all, imposed a complete siege on the city. The issue of Beit Sahour went to the United Nations Security Council, where the US vetoed a draft resolution calling upon Israel to return confiscated properties and respect its obligations under the IV Geneva Convention.[360]

For his part, Patriarch Sabbah gathered the other heads of churches, brought trucks with humanitarian aid, and traveled from Jerusalem to the Nativity Church in Bethlehem where prayers were to take place before going to Beit Sahour with the intention of breaking the siege. *"When I left the church, I found the Israeli officer telling me that we could not continue. I said that we will deliver the food and that we shall continue,"*[361] clarified Patriarch Sabbah. Israel did not want anyone, let alone religious leaders, to be seen breaking the siege in front of the large group of journalists that had gathered. Ultimately, the Patriarch agreed not to go into Beit Sahour as long as the humanitarian aid was delivered. Patriarch Sabbah had effectively managed to break, even if symbolically, the siege of Beit Sahour.

This effervescence of the Intifada focused attention on Palestine and daily images of a powerful army attacking unarmed demonstrators were broadcast worldwide. While several meetings were taking place in Europe, the big moment for Palestinian diplomacy to extract a new political reality from the Intifada was seized with the 19th session of the PNC in Algeria. On November 15, 1988, a text written by Palestine's national poet, Mahmoud Darwish, was read by Yasser Arafat in what was presented as "Palestine's Declaration of Independence":

> *"The Palestine National Council hereby declares, in the Name of God and on behalf of the Palestinian Arab people, the establishment of the State of Palestine in the land of Palestine with its capital at Jerusalem (...) The State of Palestine shall be for Palestinians, wherever they may be therein to develop their national and cultural identity and therein to enjoy full equality of rights. Their religious and political beliefs and human dignity shall therein be safeguarded under a democratic parliamentary system based on freedom of opinion and the freedom to form parties, on the heed of the majority for*

minority rights and the respect of minorities for majority decisions, on social justice and equality, and on non-discrimination in civil rights on grounds of race, religion or colour or as between men and women, under a Constitution ensuring the rule of law and an independent judiciary and on the basis of true fidelity to the age-old spiritual and cultural heritage of Palestine with respect for mutual tolerance, coexistence and magnanimity among religions."[362]

The Palestinian declaration of independence confirmed Palestinian recognition of all UN resolutions, including some that had been rejected in the past, in what was also known as the Palestinian historic compromise that recognized the 1967 border as the border of the State of Palestine. For the first time, the PLO was limiting its territorial space to the occupied territory of 1967, while providing de facto recognition of Israel over 78% of historic Palestine. The international formula for a two-state solution opened the doors for the establishment of a formal channel between Washington and the PLO, and changed the name of the Palestinian representation to the United Nations from PLO to Palestine.

On the popular level, the declaration was warmly welcomed in the occupied territory, with thousands of people who had followed the PNC session via Radio Monte Carlo taking to the streets and celebrating by raising the banned flag of Palestine. Celebrations were so intense that Israel imposed a curfew on November 16 to avoid mass demonstrations. The *Guardian* correspondent Ian Black saw the curfew from a different perspective in his report from Ramallah: *"Brute force was the order of Independence Day, and the sheer scale of it worked. Yet staying at home was an appropriate answer, too: if it took more than 300 dead, thousands of Palestinians beaten or imprisoned to create the Algiers declaration, the people of the Occupied Territories deserved a rest, even if it was enforced by the army."*[363]

After the Palestinian declaration of independence there was an escalation of diplomatic activity, including a Washington announcement of relations with the PLO and the engagement of several European leaders. A month after the declaration of independence, Yasser Arafat addressed the United Nations, this time in Geneva as the US, despite the latest developments, had refused to grant him a visa. His address to the General Assembly was a combination of praise for the people of Palestine for the Intifada, while setting the framework for engagement in negotiations. He responded directly to Israel's description of Palestinians as always *"missing an opportunity to miss an opportunity"*: *"Were we not the ones who took the initiative of relying on the Charter and resolutions of the United Nations, the Declaration of Human Rights and international legitimacy as the basis for the settlement of the Arab-Israeli conflict?; Did we not welcome the Vance-Gromyko communiqué of 1977 as a move that could form the basis of a proposed solution to this conflict?; Did we not agree to participate in the Geneva Conference on the basis of the American-Egyptian statement of 1977 in order to promote the prospects of a settlement and peace in our region?; Did we not endorse the Fez Arab peace plan in 1982 and later the call for an international peace conference under the auspices of the United Nations in conformity with its resolutions?; Did we not support the Brezhnev plan for peace in the Middle East?; Did we not welcome and support the Venice Declaration by the European Community on the basics of a just peace in the area?; Did we not welcome and support the joint initiative of Presidents Gorbachev and Mitterrand on a preparatory committee for the international conference?; Did we not welcome scores of political statements and initiatives by African, Islamic, non-aligned, socialist, European States and groups of states which aimed at finding a settlement based on the principles of international legitimacy that would safeguard peace and end the conflict?; And what was Israel's posture in relation to all this? When we put this question, we must keep in mind that not a single one of those initiatives, plans or communiqués lacked political balance or overlooked the claims and interests of any of the parties to the Arab-Israeli conflict."*[364]

Bishop Elia Khoury was accompanying Yasser Arafat on this Geneva visit. Arafat, keen to send visual messages, sat him to his right during the official press conference. It was a pivotal moment for the Palestinian cause and Arafat knew it. The year of 1988 even concluded with a symbolic audience on Christmas Eve with Pope John Paul II in the Vatican. This time Arafat took with him a nativity scene carved in olive wood and mother of pearl brought from Bethlehem as a gift for the Pope. After the audience Yasser Arafat said: *"I have explained to His Holiness the suffering my people are facing under occupation. I have asked His Holiness to pray for them; and that peace may prevail in the Holy Land."*[365]

The Human Cost of the Intifada

A group of Palestinian lawyers, including Raja Shehadeh and Jonathan Kuttab, wanted to fill a vacuum in the documentation of Israeli violations of Palestinian human rights by establishing the human rights organization Al Haq. Their reports during the Intifada document widespread cases of torture and extrajudicial killings. The organization reported that 281 Palestinians were killed between December 9, 1987, and December 9, 1989. Of these, 11 were killed by beatings (the main source of killing was live and plastic bullets).[366] The beatings were part of a denounced policy of breaking the bones of Palestinian demonstrators suspected of throwing stones.

The 1989 Al Haq report documents several cases of abuses and violations that describe the situation in the streets of Palestine during the Intifada. *"At around 3:00 pm on 11 October 1989, Bishara Issa Elias Kheir, 24, a resident of Beit Sahour in the Bethlehem district, was stopped at a military checkpoint. His identity card was confiscated by a soldier who told him that he was wanted by the authorities. Another military jeep arrived. An officer stepped out, checked the identity card, and told the soldier that Mr. Kheir was not wanted. The first soldier then tore up Mr. Kheir's identity card, saying to the officer that this would cause problems for Mr. Kheir. Mr. Kheir was subsequently blindfolded, handcuffed, and beaten; he was then transferred to the military government compound in Bethlehem, where he was detained for five days."*[367]

Al-Haq's co-founder Jonathan Kuttab was the son of an Evangelical pastor and a US citizen, which enabled him to maintain strong contacts with Christian communities in the US. He partnered with his cousin Mubarak Awad to establish another organization promoting non-violent means of resistance. Awad, a US citizen whose Jerusalem ID had been revoked by Israel, was deported due to his activities. The deportation order was signed personally by Israel's PM Yitzhak Shamir. The White House refused to accept the Israeli arguments and said: *"We think it is unjustifiable to deny Mr. Awad the right to stay and live in Jerusalem where he was born."*[368] Once in the US, Awad continued his advocacy for Palestinian rights but it had become clear that Israel would not tolerate any form of resistance, including the peaceful methods promoted by Awad's organization.

In Bethlehem, Julia Dabdoub led the Arab Women's Union in extensive work with the families of Palestinian prisoners. The organization also initiated a museum to preserve the traditions of Palestine. In Ramallah, a group of women from the Greek Catholic parish created their own association to produce and sell Palestinian embroidery as a means of supporting families affected by Israeli policies against the Intifada. Similar initiaitives took place around parishes in Jerusalem.

These examples of popular mobilization received international support. In December 1989 Palestine welcomed South African Archbishop Desmond Tutu in a Christmas pilgrimage that marked his solidarity with the Palestinian people. Tutu was a symbol of the South African struggle against apartheid and a Nobel Peace Prize winner. As such, his visit was particularly significant. Tutu celebrated religious services in several locations, including in Beit Sahour which had become an icon of the Intifada. During his visit to Al Aqsa Mosque in Jerusalem, he said, *"We hope our presence gives hope and encouragement to the victims of oppression. We support your struggle for justice, peace, statehood and independence."*[369]

It is in this context that Patriarch Sabbah began the formation of a human rights organization for the Latin Patriarchate, creating the Saint Yves Society in 1991. This was part of a natural process triggered by the Intifada in which prominent international churches were questioning the legality of Israeli actions and policies. When the permanent observer of the Holy See to the UN, Archbishop Renato Martino, had to address the question of Jerusalem in 1989, he presented a position that did not leave room for any interpretation: *"It must be understood that the declaration of 1980 that Jerusalem is the 'central and indivisible capital' of Israel is contrary to international law, based as it is on military occupation without the consent of the interested parties or the United Nations and condemned as it immediately was by the United Nations Security Council."*[370]

Such challenges to the Israeli position were seen as real victories by Palestinian diplomacy, media, and the public in general. Yet the situation on the ground continued to deteriorate with further killings and arrests. Khader Tarazi, 19, a member of one of the oldest Christian families in Gaza, was killed after being beaten by Israeli soldiers, with the Israeli army claiming he had "heart failure".[371] Other cases were repeated in every single Palestinian district with such impunity that the US eventually gave up on its veto power and allowed for Security Council discussions and resolutions that included explicit calls upon Israel to implement its obligations as an occupying power under the IV Geneva Convention.

The US also allowed Resolution 611[372] to pass when Israeli forces violated Tunisian sovereignty to assassinate Khalil Al Wazir (Abu Jihad), the head of the western sector who was in charge of the Intifada for Fatah. His loss was deeply felt, triggered further demonstrations in the occupied territory, and a large funeral took place in the cemetery of martyrs in Yarmouk refugee camp, Syria.

While maintaining Palestinian pressure on Israel, the resistance tried to find ways for demonstrators not to fall into the hands of Israeli forces, especially given the documented cases of torture or "moderate physical pressure" as it was termed by the Israeli government.[373] In Beit Sahour a wanted man wished to get married. Fr. Peter Madros agreed to shorten the ceremony, opened all the doors of the church, and prepared a plan for the groom to escape through the altar should Israeli forces arrive. Ultimately the wedding took place.[374]

Birzeit as a Symbol

The Orthodox Church in Birzeit's old city rang its bells more than once a day, and it was not because of a change in the schedule of religious services. Rather, the bells rang whenever Israeli soldiers were spotted moving towards the town. The same bells used to announce weddings and funerals were used to protect the people of Birzeit from arrest by the Israeli occupation forces. The importance of this warning was appreciated not only by the approximately 3200 inhabitants of Birzeit in 1989 but by hundreds of students at Birzeit University, an institution that became a symbol of those days.

On January 10, 1988, Israel imposed a closure of the university. It was not the first time but it was the longest period of closure and lasted for 51 months. Classes did not cease; just as with schools and other universities all over the occupied Palestinian territory, Birzeit found creative ways to continue teaching, including by renting other buildings and even by teaching in homes. Education became a form of resistance for hundreds of students who refused to give up on their studies due to an Israeli military order.

The university had already been under attack, including the deportation of its President, Hanna Nasser. A decision was taken not to appoint another president in order to deny the Israeli decision and Vice-President Gabi Baramki became the acting head. Born in Jerusalem in 1929, his home was occupied by Israel in 1948 in what became a border area between East and West Jerusalem close to the Mandelbaum Gate. A chemist from the American University of Beirut with a PhD from McGill, Dr. Baramki had experience working for Palestinian refugees as part of the Middle East Council of Churches. He also had a known commitment to culture, particularly music. He played a prominent role in keeping the university functioning through this difficult period, as well as channeling resources brought from abroad, including indirectly from the PLO.

While Dr. Baramki was considered by many as the person who kept Birzeit University functioning, other figures identified with the institution began to appear in various national and international forums, notably Dr. Hanan Ashrawi who became the most prominent female figure in the national movement for foreign audiences. She was the head of the English Department at Birzeit University and organized legal support for students persecuted by the Israeli occupation. Her articulate speeches were recognized by diplomats and foreign journalists alike, and represented part of the identity of a university that was an integral part of the liberation effort. Between the exile of Hanna Nasser and the presence of Hanan Ashrawi, in addition to a number of students and young staff who would later become important national figures such as Marwan Barghouthi, Khalida Jarrar, Muhammad Shtayyeh and Bassam Salhi, Birzeit formed a strong institution that constantly challenged the Israeli authorities.

Patriarch Sabbah as a Transformational Figure in the Palestinian Struggle

Sitting in his retirement in Taybeh, the biblical "Ephraim" located between Ramallah and the Jordan Valley, Patriarch Michael Sabbah remembers details of the First Intifada but tends to, whether intentionally or unintentionally, underestimate his role. *"We did what we had to do,"* he says. Yet the fact that he was referred to by a right-wing Israeli magazine as the Patriarch of Terror indicates how disgruntled some Israelis felt with the mere fact that a Palestinian had been appointed as Patriarch of Jerusalem.

Less than a year into the Intifada, the WCC issued an appeal to the UN Secretary General calling for the withdrawal of Israel from the 1967 occupied territories and the realization of the rights of the Palestinian people. *"The World Council of Churches has affirmed its conviction that the mutual recognition of the Israeli and Palestinian people on the bases of equality is the only guarantee for peace and security in the region."*[375] The element of equality was one of the central elements of Patriarch Sabbah's discourse. As a Palestinian citizen of Israel, he knew well the consequences of promoting any approach that would not grant equal rights to all Palestinians and this was part of his diplomatic efforts with church leaders worldwide. Though not a member of the WCC, Patriarch Sabbah coordinated the efforts of the Latin Patriarchate with the Geneva-based organization and soon replicated their model by uniting the Jerusalem heads of churches to break the Israeli siege of Beit Sahour.

The First Intifada was not only a challenge to the work of the churches regarding the attacks of the Israeli occupation on the Palestinian people but also posed theological questions about a phenomena that would dramatically shape US policy on Palestine a few decades later: Christian Zionism. In 1988 the International Christian Embassy opened in Jerusalem as an institution to represent Christian Zionists. Aware of the Christian Zionist's interpretation of the Bible in support of the Israeli occupation, the heads of churches, led once again by the Palestinian patriarch, issued a strong statement against such an institution representing or replacing the local Christian community, and "categorically" refusing and rejecting *any political interpretation of the Holy Scripture (...) According to our Lord's commands, we seek peace and justice for all the people in the world, and especially in the region, without any kind of discrimination or violence.*[376]

It was around that same period that an Episcopal canon born in Beisan, internally displaced to Nazareth and at that time serving in Jerusalem, Rev. Naim Ateek, created the first Palestinian Christian organization dedicated to propagating the theology of liberation and countering Christian Zionist arguments. The Sabeel Ecumenical Liberation Theology Center opened its doors in Jerusalem and brought together Palestinian Christians from different denominations. Rev. Ateek managed to create a group of Palestinians from Israel and the occupied territories involved in the defense of human rights.

The group included Fr. Elias Chacour, a refugee from Kufr Bir'im who later became the Archbishop of the Greek Catholic Church in the

Galilee; Fr. Riah Abu El-Assal, an Episcopal canon from Nazareth who in the nineties became the Episcopal Bishop of Jerusalem; Jonathan Kuttab, the co-founder of Al-Haq; renowned musician Samia Khoury; and Cedar Dauybis, one of the most articulate speakers and human rights defenders in Palestine. She was from Haifa and became a refugee in 1948 when the family literally ran through a bombardment by Zionist organizations while British troops failed to protect people in April 1948. Her family was internally displaced in Nazareth. As most of her generation, she was deeply marked by the scenes of the Nakba and exile. The group also included Jean Mikhail Zaru, a Palestinian Quaker from Ramallah who was also the sister of Hanna Mikhail, popularly known as Abu Omar, the renowned intellectual and Fatah official killed in 1976.

The creation of Sabeel did not occur in a vacuum. The local Episcopal Church's report of 1987-1988 included a clear reference to the *"need to develop a Palestinian liberation theology as a peaceful 'weapon'."*[377] Yet it is no exaggeration to claim that Patriarch Sabbah brought a revolution to local churches and strengthened the voices that believed that they could make a contribution to the national liberation struggle from a Christian angle.

For example, while Patriarch Sabbah did not resolve the Greek-Arab disputes at the Orthodox Patriarchate, he succeeded in making Greek Orthodox Patriarch Diodoros I appear as part an ecumenical movement with other heads of churches supporting justice in Palestine. Patriarch Diodoros I also promoted a Palestinian monk who had found acceptance where Arabs were often rejected: Atallah Hanna was a Palestinian citizen of Israel born in Rameh, upper Galilee. In the early nineties he was given responsibility for the Arab section of the Patriarchate at a very young age. His patriotic inclinations were clear from the beginning and it appears as if Patriarch Diodorios I wanted to make use of his presence in an attempt to balance his lack of engagement in the Palestinian struggle.

Other churches also found in Patriarch Sabbah a lever for their activities in support of the rights of the Palestinian people. The Lutheran Church, although small in size, had consolidated an Arab clergy at that time led by Bishop Naim Nassar, a Palestinian who quickly understood the need to engage with other churches to develop a stronger voice. Something similar took place with the Episcopal (Anglican) church in Jerusalem, at that time led by Bishop Samir Kafiti, the second Palestinian to lead their church in Jerusalem and previously a professor at Birzeit University. The Syrian Orthodox Church also engaged with Patriarch Sabbah through Bishop Jijjawi, who was originally from Mosul in Iraq. The Greek Catholic Church (Melkite) in Jerusalem was still dealing with the aftermath of Archbishop Capucci's case, but Bishop Lufti Lahham, originally Syrian just like Bishop Capucci, maintained a close relationship with Patriarch Sabbah.

The narrative changed quickly and the heads of churches used their position to literally protest against Israeli oppression. One of their statements during the Intifada said: *"In Jerusalem, in the West Bank and in Gaza our people experience in their daily lives constant deprivations of their fundamental rights because of the arbitrary actions deliberately taken by the authorities. Our people are often subjected to unprovoked harassment and hardship (...) We are particularly concerned by the tragic and unnecessary loss of Palestinian lives, especially among young and minors (...) We affirm our human solidarity and sympathy with all who are suffering and oppressed; we pray for the return of peace based on justice to Jerusalem and the Holy Land; and we request the international community and the UN Organization to give urgent attention to the plight of the Palestinian people, and to work for a speedy and just resolution of the Palestinian problem."*[378]

Saint John's Hospice
and the Intifada in Jerusalem

The Holy Week of 1990 was disrupted by the occupation. On April 11, Holy Thursday, around 100 Israeli settlers occupied the Saint John' Hospice, located around 100 meters from the Church of the Holy Sepulcher, turning it into the largest illegal Israeli settlement in the Old City outside the Jewish Quarter. The building, with an approximate size of 3,000 square meters and 72 rooms, was the property of the Greek Orthodox Patriarchate and marked a new real estate scandal involving church property. In this case, it was claimed that a tenant of Armenian origin had sold his rights to the building to a settler organization although he did not have the rights to do so. Later, it was revealed that the Israeli government was officially involved in providing a large sum of the money to the settlers through the Ministry of Housing,[379] at that time led by Likud's David Levy. Ariel Sharon, then Minister of Commerce and Industry, supported the move as he ended up being involved in another takeover of Palestinian property in the Old City. The home of the Tams family, a Palestinian Christians from Jerusalem, was taken over by the Israeli minister. The building is located opposite the Third Station of the Via Dolorosa, close to the Armenian Catholic Patriarchal Exarchate of Jerusalem.

The settlers were visited by cabinet members and parliamentarians, further angering the heads of churches. The Israeli mayor of Jerusalem Teddy Kollek opposed the move. *"How would they (Jews) feel if singing and dancing Christians and Muslims moved into the Jewish quarter on Passover?"* he declared.[380] Prime Minister Yitzhak Shamir, a prosecuted terrorist who was also accused of being involved in the assassination of UN Envoy Folke Berdanotte in 1948, had taken an extremely provocative step in occupied Jerusalem that put Israel in open confrontation with the heads of churches. An attempt by Patriarch Deodorios to physically enter the building, accompanied by members of his congregation, was violently opposed by the Israeli police who used tear gas against the clergymen, while the Patriarch himself was pushed to the floor. It was in this context that the heads of churches announced an unprecedented measure. All Christian holy places in Jerusalem, Nazareth and Bethlehem would be closed between Friday, April 27 and Saturday, April 28. A statement from the heads of churches specified: *"On the same day, all church bells throughout the country will ring a funeral toll every hour on the hour from 9:00 am until noon."*[381] Al Aqsa Mosque closed for 24 hours to foreigners and tourists in solidarity with the heads of churches.

One of the first Palestinian killed in Jerusalem during the Intifada was a Christian. Nidal Rabadi, a 16-year-old student, was Palestinian number 199 to be killed by the Israeli occupation during the First Intifada. The killing took place on July 9, 1988, and was reported by Al-Haq: *"Settlers shot and killed Nidal Fou'ad al-Rabadi, 16. He was shot in the right leg and left side of his head with two live bullets."*[382] A resident of the Old City, Nidal was riding his bicycle at the time that settlers ended his life, shooting the Palestinian teenager from a car. Nobody was ever held accountable for his killing.

Nidal Rabadi's killing sparked outrage in the Old City and a demonstration after his funeral ended in clashes. Israeli settlers fueled tensions in the occupied city and the issue of Saint John's was the highlight of several provocative acts that were often condoned by the right-wing Israeli government. At that time, Jerusalem was still a center of Palestinian national organization and several of the decisions of the Unified Command of the Intifada were taken in the occupied city.

A few days later, national forces organized a demonstration after Sunday Mass in Beit Jala. While such demonstrations had been common since the beginning of the Intifada, on this occasion the organizers displayed the largest Palestinian flag ever raised in Beit Jala, stretching from Saint Nicholas' Church down to the street of the Lutheran cemetery. Hundreds of people, mainly families, joined the demonstration and were met with live fire from Israeli forces. Groups of youths confronted the soldiers with stones and came under heavy attack. Jiries Kunkar, 40,[383] a father of three and known member of the Communist Party, was killed. That night hundreds of mourners took over the streets of Beit Jala and were, once again, met with violence by Israeli forces.[384] Around the same period of time, another demonstration that started after mass resulted in one of the most iconic pictures of the Intifada as Micheline Awad took off her heels to run and throw stones at Israeli soldiers attacking demonstrators in Beit Sahour.

The Palestinian media were based in Jerusalem and some of the most prominent reporters were Christians. Hanna Siniora, editor of *Al Fajr* newspaper, was summoned several times by Israeli authorities and accused of *"sedition, plotting to cause damage to others and incitement to refrain from paying taxes."*[385] The editor of the English version was Daoud Kuttab, the son of an Evangelical pastor. Other prominent figures of that generation were Sama'an Khoury and Sami Aboudi, the latter from Ein Areeq village. Raymonda Tawil was a key figure who engaged in media efforts as a partner in the Palestinian Press Agency. *Al-Awdah*, another Jerusalem-based publication, had Elias Zananiri as one of its editors. He was arrested for being suspected of "organizing a demonstration".[386] Even the traditional *Al-Quds* newspaper, known for a more conservative editorial line, suffered the consequences of the censorship imposed on Palestinian media and was closed for a period of time. Restrictions on Palestinian media in the occupied territory were often circumvented by reports in the Haifa-based *Al Ittihad* newspaper that was affiliated with the mainly Palestinian

Israeli Communist Party, as well as through Jordanian radio and Radio Monte Carlo broadcasting from Paris.

Several Israeli military laws criminalized even the raising of the Palestinian flag and cultural activities were also targeted by the Israeli occupation. This did not prevent several Palestinian artists from putting their talents to the service of the Intifada. A Palestinian Syrian (Syriac) from Jerusalem called George Kirmiz wrote many songs referring to prisons ("Ansar") as well as his classic "My Name is the People of Palestine". This included the lyrics, *"My name is the people of Palestine, today I die, today I struggle, today I live (...) I will have no other name (...) , I'm the son of Arab Jerusalem, I'm your son, Palestine"*.

Changing Context:
The Fall of the Soviet Union and the Gulf War

While Palestine had strategically expanded its diplomatic capacity with Western countries and through the non-aligned movement, it is undisputable that the Soviet Bloc represented a major source of political, logistical and economic support for the Palestinian national movement. In parallel, Moscow was playing a similar role in the struggle against apartheid in South Africa and Namibia, in the situation in Angola, and with several anti-dictatorship movements in Latin America. However, the Soviet Bloc began to collapse. Large demonstrations took place in Poland, Pope John Paul's homeland, and the destruction of the Berlin Wall was the most striking symbol of the changing situation. This, in addition to the consequences of the Iraqi aggression against Kuwait that led to the Gulf War and included the displacement of hundreds of thousands of Palestinians and the end of economic support, ended up playing a significant role in a changing context that affected the Intifada.

The New Middle East and the Madrid Peace Conference

Patriarch Sabbah made use of the Feast of Pentecost to remind Christians worldwide of their "duties" in Palestine: *"Pray for the peace of Jerusalem"* (Ps 122, 6.8) was the highlight of his pastoral letter, which turned into a masterpiece of advocacy for his people. In contrast to the letters and discourses largely disconnected from the day-to-day issues facing Palestine delivered by foreign clergy, the Palestinian patriarch made use of the occasion to summarize the effects of the Intifada. His message to the Palestinian Christian community was concrete: *"Your duty is to have a clear and precise idea of your rights and obligations in order to carry them out or to demand them all without neglecting any of them yourself, whatever the sacrifices involved."*[387]

If the Intifada achieved any goal, it was the awareness of Palestinian rights. Politically speaking, the First Intifada had become for Palestinians what the 1973 war had meant for Egypt: the possibility of changing the context and making clear to Israel that the status quo could not remain. The PLO had already taken a step towards seizing the momentum with the Declaration of the State of Palestine in 1988, but by the end of 1990, the situation had changed dramatically with the Gulf War. When Egypt attended the Camp David negotiations in 1978 it did so in a context of international support, while the PLO appeared isolated after the Gulf War.

On the other hand, the Gulf War created an unexpected diplomatic context in which the strongest Arab army of Iraq had been defeated and besieged, and Israel could not claim its security was threatened. There was regional pressure for the US to make use of its victory to force Israel into peace talks. And while the PLO had been weakened and funds to the Intifada had decreased, the Palestinian people were still on the streets and the struggle had not been crushed.

Such factors were studied by Palestinian diplomats who had already been tasked with initiating a diplomatic offensive in Europe. A number of Israeli-Palestinian channels had quietly been established through social democratic parties. Meanwhile the idea of a Middle East Peace Conference began to be cheered by the Bush administration that would soon share its plans with the United Nations, the Soviet Union, the European community, Arab countries, and Israel. The format seemed to be close to that proposed close to a decade earlier at the failed Geneva talks and the location chosen for the meeting was Madrid.

The Israeli government, under the hawkish figure of PM Shamir, was a combination of right-wing and Orthodox parties with traditional members of the Labor Party. Shimon Peres was the Minister of Finance and Yitzhak Rabin the Minister of "Defense", effectively in charge of repressing the Intifada. Rabin himself was accused of ordering the policy of breaking the bones of Palestinian demonstrators.[388] It was certainly not a government that was going to endorse any sort of withdrawal from occupied territory or any form of Palestinian sovereignty or rights, but the US government still grasped the opportunity and mobilized its diplomatic weight behind the peace conference.

The US Consulate in Jerusalem began talks with the Palestinian leaders gathered around Faysal Husseini. The official PLO-US talks had been interrupted on a few occasions since 1988 and, in any case, they had not reached the stage of a significant breakthrough for the peace process. In other words, the PLO was not being treated as a real partner by Washington, while the Israeli government had refused to hold any talks with PLO representatives, including the fact that meeting any of them was a violation of Israeli law.[389]

In reality, this refusal was part of the obstacles imposed by Israel to any meaningful peace process. In addition to not meeting any

PLO official, they had added other preconditions to attending the conference ever since the Bush administration had proposed the mere idea of a meeting. In 1989 Shamir had already communicated to the US *"our opposition to a Palestinian Arab state west of the River Jordan; our refusal to deal with the PLO; our commitment to interim arrangements and, once these were successfully tested, to a second stage of negotiation regarding permanent status; and (...) that Jerusalem, united would never be divided again."*[390]

The Palestinians understood that the US was committed to making the conference happen and that tactically they would have to attend no matter what the Israeli narrative. The group of Palestinians meeting the US representatives were "non-PLO officials", although they had strong connections with the Tunis-based leadership and rejected any kind of insinuation that they were a "moderate leadership" in the occupied territory as opposed to the PLO "radicals". The US understood their position and dealt with them in the understanding that any decision would have to be approved by the PLO itself. In effect, a letter of assurance from the US Secretary of State James Baker was negotiated with the Palestinian team while formulas were found to circumvent the conditions imposed by Shamir, including the absence of exiled Palestinians or representatives from Jerusalem in the delegation who eventually were part of the "joint" Jordanian-Palestinian delegation.

The Holy See realized the importance of the new situation and began to support the process discreetly through messages to various parties, including the PLO. At this stage, the Vatican had been involved in several peace processes and while they were not being directly approached to participate, they understood that peace in Palestine, "The Holy Land", was in their interests. Just as they had on previous occasions, they mobilized their diplomatic capacity to include their interests in the talks. Part of the Vatican interest, expressed publicly, was the full representation of the Palestinian people in any talks. This was also translated into more engagement from the local churches, which were being briefed by Faysal Husseini and Hanan Ashrawi, the Palestinian from an Episcopal family serving as the main address for foreign media in Palestine. The Orient House, the historic hotel owned by the Husseini family, soon became the center for the Palestinian teams, and they were joined by the renowned historian and intellectual, Palestinian Armenian Albert Aghazarian, who at that time was a professor at Birzeit University.

To Madrid

On October 18, 1991, a letter of invitation to the Madrid Peace Conference was extended by the US and the USSR explaining the modality and general terms of reference of the conference. The invitation clearly clarified that there would be discussions on Palestinian interim self-government for a period of five years. *"Beginning from the third year of the period of interim self-government arrangements, negotiations will take place on permanent status. These permanent status negotiations, and the negotiations between Israel and the Arab states, will take place on the basis of Resolutions 242 and 338."*[391] The only thing left was to define who would be included in the "joint" Jordanian-Palestinian delegation.

The Palestinians had accepted to play by the rules of the game in terms of the delegation's composition (people with residence in the occupied territory, excluding Jerusalemites) and soon organized several teams that reflected the vast majority of Palestinians. This is how renowned lawyer Camille Mansour, a Palestinian Christian refugee from Haifa became a legal adviser to the delegation. Faysal Husseini was the head of the steering committee and Hanan

Ashrawi the spokesperson. The steering committee included several prominent names such as Professor Rashid Khalidi, Anis Qassem, Sari Nusseibeh, and Zuhaira Kamal.

The delegation was formally headed by Dr. Haidar Abdul Shafi, a prominent and well-respected communist leader who was also the head of the Red Crescent in Gaza. Other members included people who were either close to PLO factions or secretly part of their ranks. The delegation included Dr. Nabil Kassis, a member of a Christian family from Ramallah and vice-president for academic affairs at Birzeit University, and Elias Freij, the veteran mayor of Bethlehem. Freij's presence was challenged by several members of the delegation as he was considered to be part of the group of "traditionalist" mayors who had not engaged with the Palestinian resistance and had developed close ties with the Israeli authorities. *"I never saw Yasser Arafat upset as much as when we questioned Elias Freij's presence in the delegation,"* said one of the youngest members of the group and a member of a left-wing party. *"We questioned his presence and Faysal Husseini told us that he understood but it was Arafat's decision, who at that time was in Amman. We decided to talk to him about the issue but he became furious and told us, 'If you want to represent the Palestinian people, you also have to represent people like him'."*[392] Arafat also made sure to create a system of direct communication with the delegation through his personal envoy Nabil Shaath, who was present in Madrid.

Yasser Arafat's insistence on Elias Freij's presence did not prevent an argument taking place between Saeb Erekat, the youngest member of the delegation alongside Ghassan Khatib, who saw Freij sitting in the first seat next to Dr. Haidar Abdel Shafi on the day of the conference. *"Who do you think you are? I represent Fatah here. Get up,"* the 36-year-old professor of political science at An Najah University allegedly told the 71-year-old mayor of Bethlehem[393].

Freij understood and ceded the seat to members identified with PLO factions. This was not the most controversial stand taken by Erekat who, without informing the rest of the delegation, decided to wear a *kuffiyeh* over his suit, angering the Israeli delegation. *"I brought Yasser Arafat inside the room,"* he later told other members of the delegation.

The Israeli delegation had Benjamin Netanyahu as its spokesperson, a young American-educated Likud member, formerly ambassador to the United Nations and utterly opposed to a Palestinian state. His perfect English and right-wing Zionist talking points were no match for Hanan Ashrawi, the spokesperson of the Palestinian delegation who played a major role in drafting the speech delivered by Haidar Abdel Shafi. Hanan Ashrawi had become the key Palestinian delegate dealing with the international media and the speech included all the items that Israel had tried to ban from the conference, including Jerusalem, the right of return, and the PLO as the sole legitimate representative of the Palestinian people. It also included the quote by Yasser Arafat in his historic 1974 UN speech: *"Let not the olive branch of peace fall from the hands of the Palestinian people."* Ambassador Afif Safieh referred to the speech, in his particular style, as "unreasonably reasonable"[394] and Israeli historian Avi Shlaim referred to Hanan Ashrawi as "Woman of the Year".[395]

The Palestinian delegation to Madrid marked a turning point for Palestine internationally. From the weak position after the Gulf War and the collapse of the Soviet Bloc, the Palestinian cause was reintegrated into the international agenda through a combination of independent professionals and politically affiliated officials who experienced their first important international exposure. They prepared several technical teams as a follow up to the conference, including talks in Moscow and Washington. The process naturally opened up to greater participation and others joined the Palestinian delegation, including Eli Sambar, a Palestinian Christian refugee from Haifa who became head of the Palestinian delegation to the multilateral working group on refugees.

Sambar's opening remarks as Palestinian delegate included references to Palestinian citizens of Israel and the laws used to confiscate their property rather than merely talking about the Palestinian refugees outside the homeland. In conclusion, he said: *"The logic of racial, religious or ethnic homogeneity, or 'purity', often used to justify the denial of the Palestinian right of return, is repugnant to the ethics of our age. It mocks the very concept of coexistence which motivates our present endeavors. Peaceful coexistence among the people and states of the Middle East cannot be built on societies which find plurality intolerable or threatening (...) To the Israelis we also say, in order for us to offer you the solution of the two states, mutually recognized and accepted, the people of Palestine have had to inflict a great violence upon themselves. Indeed, for unlike war, peace is always a tormenting victory of one's own self. And the time has come for you to take this decisive step and recognize the rights of our people."*[396]

Between Dreams of Peace and Israeli Oppression

The quiet evening of Sunday August 11, 1991, in Ramallah was interrupted by gunfire. It had been an ordinary day, especially for Christians who had attended mass that day. Those who attempted to continue their traditional walk along the main street to the Rukab Ice Cream shop had to change their plans when they encountered Israeli forces chasing a group of Palestinian youths. All but one escaped: Harout Guluzian, a 17-year-old Palestinian Armenian, known as Artim by his family and friends, was fatally shot as he ran from Rukab Street in the direction of the then-closed Odeh Hotel. He became the first Palestinian Armenian martyr of the Intifada.

Despite the fact that the Palestinians were finally included in the peace talks, the Intifada and Israeli oppression were ongoing. The occupation remained and colonial settlements were expanding. Palestinian diplomat Afif Safieh said: *"I saw Mr. Shamir on television say in Madrid that Israel had a hunger for peace. And I believe today that we Palestinians can solemnly and publicly say we can satisfy Israel's hunger for peace if ever Mr. Shamir abandons his appetite for territory."*[397] However, PM Shamir's appetite was not to achieve the peace that the Palestinians were talking about. Soon after losing the 1992 elections, he clarified his tactics, which were almost like a prophecy: *"I would have conducted negotiations on autonomy for 10 years and in the meantime, we would have reached half a million people in Judea and Samaria."*[398]

The Madrid Conference did not produce any concrete Israeli withdrawal from occupied territory, but it opened several channels of communication that pressed both Israel and the international community on the need to find a solution. Talk of Palestinian "self-government" took place while the Palestinian delegation to the negotiations was aware of the realities on the ground and focused on the need to halt Israel's colonial settlements, and to transfer the Palestinian population registry to the Palestinian government created by the talks. Both these demands were non-starters for the Israeli delegation, which had no mandate to end the occupation, let alone accept an independent State of Palestine.

The international pressure that had emerged from the Intifada, and from regional and global developments, had dragged Israel into a peace process it had not envisioned and whose goals it did not share. An opportunity for change occurred when PM Shamir lost the 1992 elections. Yitzhak Rabin became Prime Minister in a move that would not have been possible without the support of parties representing the Palestinian citizens of Israel (Hadash/Yabha, the Arab Democratic List and the Progressive List for Peace).

The main effect of the new Israeli government was that a secret channel of negotiations between the PLO and the Israeli Labor Party could come to light. Known as the Oslo Agreement, negotiations took place under utmost secrecy; the Madrid delegation and the technical teams then involved in the Washington talks were not informed.

When Mahmoud Abbas (Abu Mazen), then a Fatah Central Committee member and confidant of Yasser Arafat in charge of pursuing the negotiations, asked the leaders of the Washington talks to look at the Oslo Agreement, an immediate split took place. Faysal Husseini and Hanan Ashrawi presented their resignation from the negotiations team; Nabil Shaath, another veteran Fatah member who remained in charge of coordinating the work of the teams with the PLO leadership, stayed but highlighted some of the problems with the text.[399] The key element was the acceptance of an interim phase of five years. For those who resigned, an interim agreement that did not include clear clauses preventing the expansion of colonial settlements was doomed to fail, and the interim would turn into permanent.[400]

According to Edward Said, the most prominent Palestinian voice at that time in the US, the interim agreements were simply giving up the gains of the Intifada. A few days after the agreement becoming public, he wrote in the *London Review of Books*: "*Let us call the agreement by its real name: an instrument of Palestinian surrender, a Palestinian Versailles. What makes it worse is that for at least the past fifteen years the PLO could have negotiated a better arrangement than this modified Allon Plan, one not requiring so many unilateral concessions to Israel. For reasons best known to the leadership, it refused all previous overtures. To take one example of which I have personal knowledge: in the late Seventies, Secretary of State Cyrus Vance asked me to persuade Arafat to accept Resolution 242 with a reservation (accepted by the US) to be added by the PLO which would insist on the national rights of the Palestinian people as well as Palestinian self-determination. Vance said that the US would immediately recognise the PLO and inaugurate negotiations between it and Israel. Arafat categorically turned the offer down, as he did similaroffers."*[401]

In his criticism, Edward Said presented a part of the story that has not always been told. He described how people like him and Ibrahim Abu Lughod created channels between the PLO and the US that, by accepting a two-state solution on the 1967 borders, would have secured international recognition of Palestine.

Technically speaking, the Oslo Agreement did little to redress the imbalances of power and relied heavily on the "goodwill" of the parties, without clear mechanisms of accountability.

"There was no other option" are the words often heard by those involved in the Palestinian side. For Yasser Arafat, the agreement was the opportunity he sought to create a new fact on the ground with the return of the PLO to the homeland, accompanied by thousands of officials and soldiers who would form the new administration. From that perspective, Palestine could finally set its terms leading to an irreversible path of Palestinian statehood. A close adviser to President Arafat stated: *"His belief was that if the agreements worked, there would be an independent state. If they didn't, we would have thousands of people back in Palestine, including many able to fight from within the country if needed, no longer from outside."*[402]

Prayers in Jail

One of the key issues brought up by the Palestinian side was the freedom of thousands of Palestinian prisoners. Among them were several Palestinian Christians charged, like other Palestinians, with membership in an "illegal organization", which comprised every PLO faction or organization, or taking part in demonstrations or operations. There were also several elders from Beit Sahour who had refused to pay taxes in a form of peaceful resistance to the Israeli occupation. A 1991 report by Israel's leading human rights organization Btselem estimated that the number of Palestinians arrested by Israeli forces during the first three years of the Intifada was at least 75,000 people.[403]

Visits to prisons were coordinated by the International Committee of the Red Cross and included arranging whether religious services could take place inside jail. In 1992 a historic event took place when Latin priest Bulos Marcusso was allowed to conduct a mass at Megiddo prison in the Galilee, which had been opened in 1988 for Palestinian prisoners. The permit was personally granted by Yitzhak Rabin.[404]

The Israeli jailers provided the clergy with a tent to conduct the service. The visit had been prepared for several days with the support of the seminarians of the Latin Patriarchate in Beit Jala, who took the opportunity to enter the jail with several kilos of sweets from the traditional Da'na bakery in Bethlehem, as well as cigarettes and notebooks. They were distributed to all prisoners and not just to the Christians.

The event faced two difficulties. Fr. Marcuzzo, an Italian who had lived in Palestine since his childhood and was then the Rector of the Latin Patriarchal Seminary, had brought two priests to accompany him: Fr. Eli Korzom, originally from Haifa and fluent in Hebrew, and Aziz Halaweh, a young seminarian from Ein Areeq. The reason to include Aziz was more personal since his brothers were detained in Megiddo, but this was the excuse used by the directors of the prison to exclude him from the event: "You can visit with the families," he was told.

The second difficulty was the logistics of the religious service, including the important sacrament of confession that the church recommends before communion. All the prisoners refused to confess out of fear that the Israeli authorities might listen to them. The mass still took place and a number of other visits were arranged individually by other clergy. These visits included one to Dr. Mai Kaila, a young medical doctor from Birzeit and one of the most prominent female Fatah leaders in the occupied territory. She had been arrested for membership in an "illegal organization".[405] Another visit took place in the Naqab desert by an Armenian delegation from Jerusalem visiting Armenian-Syrian commandoes imprisoned by Israel.[406]

Signing the Agreements

The presentation of the Oslo Agreement to the Fatah Central Committee was not an easy exercise for those involved in the talks. Some of the most senior members such as Mohammad Ghneim (Abu Maher) and Farouk Qaddoumi (Abu Lutof) vehemently opposed the Agreement. This created a real problem for the organization as Qaddoumi was the head of the PLO political department in charge of all PLO diplomatic missions worldwide. A third senior member and one of Palestine's military heroes, Mohammad Jihad, simply stood up and left the meeting, never to return.[407] He ended his days in Amman.

The Agreement was finally accepted after several hours of explanation and commitments led by Yasser Arafat and Mahmoud Abbas (Abu Mazen). The idea of creating Palestine's own "facts on the ground" with the return of hundreds of thousands of Palestinians to the homeland, and the possibility of an internationally supported process leading to a Palestinian state, was seen by some as a real opportunity. The divisions created by the Oslo Agreement caused collateral damage to Palestine's foreign relations as Qaddoumi retained administrative control over the PLO diplomatic missions, while the political work was diverted mainly to Yasser Arafat's office. The orbit of influence moved to Nabil Shaath as the President's envoy, plus a number of younger diplomats who were effectively seen as protégés of the Palestinian President.

Strategic postings included Nasser Al Qudwa in New York, Laila Chahid in Paris, and Afif Safieh in London, who also served as Palestine's envoy to the Holy See. In Brussels Ambassador Shawki Armali was an experienced lawyer who had served in the Palestinian embassy in Beirut under Ambassador Shafik Al Hout. Born to a Catholic family in Shafa Amr, a prominent town close to Haifa in 1936, Ambassador Armali was one of the most prominent Palestinian representatives in Europe, where he had served since the seventies. Another prominent Europe-based diplomat was Eugene Makhlouf in Stockolm, a Palestinian Christian born in Haifa and one of the founders of the Palestinian Red Crescent in Beirut. Sweden had been the location for the first talks that led to the Oslo Agreement and remained one of the most relevant places for Palestinian efforts. The majority of these diplomats had little to do with the secret talks in general and were largely mobilized to secure international support for a Palestinian state.

The ceremony to sign the Oslo Agreement took place on September 13, 1993, in Washington. Hundreds of guests witnessed Yasser Arafat make Palestinian recognition of Israel official and Israel's PM Yitzhak Rabin recognized the PLO as the representative of the Palestinian people. It was not mutual recognition as Israel did not agree to recognize the State of Palestine as declared by the PNC five years earlier. The Declaration of Principles, known as the Oslo Agreement, simply set a timeframe for final status negotiations while implementing an Israeli withdrawal from Palestinian civil affairs.

Within five years, they were to have concluded negotiations on all final status issues, including Jerusalem and refugees, but Israel still did not endorse the two-state solution as government policy.

The implementation of the agreement remained unclear and negotiations were to begin as soon as possible. Thus, a channel was inaugurated in Paris to determine economic relations for the interim period, while in Egypt, Palestinian and Israeli teams were to meet to follow on what was known as "Oslo 2" to implement the Oslo Agreement. The Palestinian team in Egypt was initially headed by Nabil Shaath and one of its first legal advisers was Jonathan Kuttab, the son of an Evangelical pastor and co-founder of Al-Haq. He soon found several problems with the agreement but there was little that could have been done at this stage. *"I was in a meeting in Cairo that had nothing to with the talks and Dr. Shaath briefed us about the negotiations. When I questioned the expertise of the team, he responded by asking me to immediately join the team. That's how I unexpectedly became the head of the legal team that negotiated the agreement."*[408] The most experienced member in the negotiations from the Palestinian delegation was Egyptian diplomat Ambassador Taher Shash, provided by the Egyptian government as a veteran and highly experienced negotiator to the Palestinian team. *"We found substantial issues that were wrong, but we were told that the Declaration of Principles had already been signed and we had to work under that framework, so we were not free to add other issues. In our own discussions, some would argue that these were interim agreements and that the real substantial issues such as Jerusalem, refugees, borders, settlements, and the security arrangements were all final status issues to be settled later within the next five years,"* said Kuttab.[409]

The Paris Protocol on Economic Relations was concluded in April but the first agreement to implement a Palestinian presence on the ground, worked on by Jonathan Kuttab, Taher Shash and Nabil Shaath among others, was signed in Cairo on May 4, 1994. The ceremony did not lack polemics as Yasser Arafat refused to sign the maps presented to him in front of an audience of hundreds of people. It had become clear that the negotiations would not be easy despite the flexibility of the interim nature of the agreements. Eventually, Arafat signed what was known as the Gaza-Jericho Agreement which established the basis for Palestinian self-rule in both areas, and started the clock for the beginning of the five years of interim self-rule prior to signing a final status agreement by May 4, 1999.

The agreements were largely followed with both enthusiasm and uncertainty. The lack of references to Jerusalem in the interim phase was seen by several officials as a threat to the rights of Palestinians in the city before a final status agreement could be reached. This was also a matter of concern for the local churches. Jerusalem was recognized by Israel as a final status issue and therefore, negotiations on its status (in a reversal of the original policy of not touching the issue) during final status negotiations was dealt with by Norwegian diplomacy and a communication known as the Peres-Holst letter, in which Israel's foreign minister Shimon Peres stated: *"I wish to confirm that the Palestinian institutions of East Jerusalem and the interests and well-being of the Palestinians of East Jerusalem are of great importance and will be preserved. Therefore all the Palestinian institutions of East Jerusalem, including the economic, social, education, and cultural, and the holy Christian and Muslim places, are performing an essential task for the Palestinian population (...) Needless to say, we will not hamper their activity; on the contrary, the fulfilment of this important mission is to be encouraged."[410]*

The most prominent Palestinian institution in East Jerusalem was Orient House, headed by the late Faysal Husseini. The work of the organization, including notably of Hanan Ashrawi, was to keep diplomatic missions briefed about the Palestinian identity of the city while building teams not merely to negotiate with Israel but to form the basis for institutions needed for a Palestinian state. Several Palestinian Christians took part in those preparatory groups, including young professionals such as George Sahhar on the education committee and Daoud Kuttab in the media, producing the first Palestinian news show as a pilot for what later became Palestine TV. Hanna Siniora, the prominent editor of *Al Fajr* newspaper, remained a key contact between the people inside and the leadership in Tunisia, and was identified with the work of the Orient House.

5.

Between Oslo and the Intifada

By December 1994 the city centers of Gaza and Jericho had been transferred to the recently created Palestinian Authority. The remaining cities in the occupied West Bank, including Bethlehem and Ramallah, were to be part of further Israeli withdrawals during 1995. Nabil Shaath, one of the first senior officials to return to Palestine in preparation for the new government, wanted to attend midnight mass in Bethlehem on December 24 and appeared in the Nativity Square alongside handful of PLO officials. Some people thought that this indicated that Yasser Arafat himself would attend, although this was not the case.

Shaath was received by Mayor Elias Freij and more people gathered with the excitement of the announced Israeli withdrawal, which did not take place in Bethlehem until Christmas 1995. The Israeli officers reminded Shaath with these precise words: *"We are here this year as according to the status quo we are the authorities of the ruling power that attend the mass."* This was a diplomatic way of saying that he was not welcome. His disappointment quickly changed to excitement when some young priests smuggled him and other Palestinian officials into the upper floors of Saint Catherine's Church, the Roman Catholic section of the Nativity Church. From there, they listened to the sermon delivered by Patriarch Michael Sabbah inside Bethlehem where despite the delayed Israeli withdrawal, Palestinian flags were already waving as part of the Christmas decorations. *"When the Israelis leave, there will be a really festive Christmas,"* Hanna Nasser, Bethlehem's deputy mayor told *The New York Times*.[411]

Dr. Shaath was not a Christian but he understood the importance of the occasion for the Palestinian identity in general. That same Christmas, Yasser Arafat was already in Gaza participating in a massive celebration at the local Latin Church with hundreds of children dressed as "Papa Noel". Unlike in Israel where Christmas is only observed by Christians, Christmas became a national holiday for Palestine. In 1994 the traditional Christmas carols sung by Lebanese star Fayrouz about *talj talj* (snow snow) and *laylet Eid* (the night of feast) were mixed with *"With our souls and blood we'll redeem you Palestine."*

That December the Nobel Peace Prize was awarded to Yitzhak Rabin, Shimon Peres and Yasser Arafat. In his remarks at the event, Yasser Arafat described the Palestinian perspective of Jerusalem as a city sacred for three religions, much in line with the international consensus, with the Palestinian people serving as protectors of that universal heritage: *"As for Jerusalem, it is the spiritual home of Christians, Muslims and Jews. To Palestinians, it is the city of cities. The Jewish shrines in the city are our shrines, the same as the Islamic and Christian shrines. So let us make Jerusalem an international symbol of this spiritual harmony, this cultural brightness, and this religious heritage of humanity as a whole."*[412]

In light of the new political developments, the heads of churches in Jerusalem declared their positions regarding the Holy City. Making references to the ongoing negotiations, the religious leaders called for respect of the rights of Christians in the city, as well as for Muslims and Jews. In a tone that was rather equidistant and tried to equate the Israeli and Palestinian positions, they revived the idea of a special statute for the city very similar to the corpus separatum presented by UN Partition Resolution 181. *"We call upon all parties concerned to comprehend and accept the nature and deep significance of Jerusalem, city of God. None can appropriate it in exclusivist ways.*

We invite each party to go beyond all exclusivist visions or actions, and without discrimination, to consider the religious and national aspirations of others, in order to give Jerusalem its true universal character and to make of the city a holy place of reconciliation for humankind, "[413] concluded their memorandum.

Opposition to the Agreement

Certainly, not all Palestinians supported the Olso Agreement. Among its strongest detractors were several Palestinian Christians, including George Habash who refused to return to the homeland under the terms of the Agreement. In Israel a group of Palestinian intellectuals, including several from Palestinian Christian backgrounds such as Azmi Bishara, Hanna Abu Hanna, Bassel Ghattas, Raeda Ghattas, Elia Zureik, Raef Zreik, and Episcopal Rev. Riah Abu El-Assal, developed the idea of a new movement in light of overall acceptance of the two-state solution. The National Democratic Assembly, known as *Tajamu* or *Balad*, took significant parts of the Palestinian Christian electorate from the Hadash party and pushed for recognition of Palestinian citizens of Israel as a national minority in the context of full citizenship for all citizens of Israel regardless of their religion. Despite the fact that Tajamu/ Balad officially endorsed the two-state solution, a significant part of its constituency historically supported the one-state solution. The party was created as a response to the new context to focus on the rights of Palestinian citizens of Israel rather than as an attempt to support the peace process.

As the Palestinian Authority was established on the ground, several Palestinian Christians who had been traditionally linked to left-wing parties, particularly the PFLP, felt that they were being displaced. *"The same comrades from Fatah who were in the barricades with us were now asking us to stop the demonstrations against the Israelis,"* said a former PFLP leader in the Bethlehem area.[414] Soon the concept of "security coordination" was known to Palestinians with all the contradictions this brought for a people under occupation in relation to the occupying power.

As people returned home, several former leftists joined the Palestinian Authority and opinion surveys showed majority support for the peace process in the occupied territory. The Oslo process also brought about the demobilization of Palestinian diaspora organizations, including some of the key PLO institutions such as the General Union of Palestine Students (GUPS). *"We saw an opportunity, a time frame of five years, and decided to focus on building the state,"* was the explanation delivered by a prominent official of Palestinian Christian background who served as Yasser Arafat's envoy to several Palestinian communities.[415] In effect, the peace process consolidated the shift made by the PLO from exile to the homeland. The political stance of countries that hosted refugees, including opposition by Syria which had considerable control over Lebanon where a significant number of Palestinian refugees lived, created a complex new scenario. Libya's leader Mouammar Qadhafi went as far as expelling thousands of Palestinians.[416]

Returning Home

In a convent in downtown Amman, Fr. Ibrahim Ayyad was following the news of the negotiations. He had been pardoned by the Hashemite Kingdom for his alleged involvement in the assassination of King Abdallah in 1951 and had settled in Jordan. His political opinions had not changed and his loyalty to the PLO remained intact. Young priests from the Latin Patriarchate of Jerusalem came to know this iconic figure and his strong convictions regarding his people's struggle. Fr. Ayyad became one of the thousands of Palestinians who managed to return from exile.

As part of the agreements Israel allowed thousands of Palestinians to return to Palestine in the occupied West Bank and Gaza. Many of them had had their IDs revoked by Israel; almost 240,000 IDs were revoked between 1967 and 1994.[417] Others had never had never been part of that population registry, including refugees from 1948, former citizens of Israel or Jerusalem ID holders. While the influx in the Palestinian population registry, still controlled by Israel, was considerable, Israel imposed several difficulties for people to regain their Jerusalem and Israeli IDs.

When the Palestinian ambassador to London and the Holy See, Afif Safieh, tried to return to Jerusalem, his birthplace where his mother and sister were still living, he received the response that his request for family reunification was denied. When members of the British Parliament inquired and protested, the Israeli response was that family reunification prioritized "children and spouses". Not even the excitement of the peace process could change the fact that under Israeli law any Jew in the world could become a settler in occupied East Jerusalem, but a Jerusalem-born Palestinian who contributed to the peace negotiations was not "eligible" to reunite with his mother in his own home.

It is estimated that only five Palestinian citizens of Israel of those who left with the PLO succeeded in recovering their Israeli-issued ID. One of them was Sabri Jiries from a Palestinian Greek Catholic family in the Galilee who left Israel in 1970, became the director of the Palestine Research Center in Beirut, and a member of the Palestinian National Council (PNC). He returned to his village as an Israeli citizen.

One of the few prominent figures to be expelled by Israel from the occupied territory after 1967 and who did not return home was the Episcopal Bishop Elia Khoury. He had resigned from his position on the PLO Executive Committee after the Achille Lauro attack of 1985.[418] He played a role in trying to build stronger relations with the United Kingdom and other Western countries, including an attempt at setting up an official meeting with PM Thatcher that ended up being thwarted by London.[419] His decision to stay in Amman did not prevent him from visiting Palestine on several occasions.

Many Palestinian Christians returned to the homeland, including military officials and political appointees. Among the military ranks were Raji Musleh from Beit Sahour, who worked closely with Khalil Al Wazir (Abu Jihad) and Fayez Saqqa from Bethlehem, and who had played a determining role in Spain and Latin America. The return of thousands of exiles, in addition to the release of almost all Palestinian prisoners in Israeli jails, were perhaps the most important images of initial success for the peace process.

Establishing Diplomatic Relations

The Holy See had been cautious about establishing diplomatic relations with the State of Palestine declared in Algeria in 1988 but under Pope John Paul II it had notoriously increased its diplomatic approach towards Palestinian representatives. It maintained a similar policy with Israel, which was not recognized by the Holy See until the recognition of the Palestinians and the beginning of the peace process. This did not prevent important meetings and exchanges from taking place.

For Yasser Arafat the establishment of formal relations with the Holy See was a priority that came into being in 1995 when Ambassador Afif

Safieh officially presented credentials as the concurrent Palestinian ambassador in the Vatican. Despite the fact that Palestine had no effective control over Jerusalem, its position on the Holy City was very much in line with international law and therefore close to the Vatican position. Archbishop Touran, the Vatican foreign minister, was close to Patriarch Michael Sabbah and keen to strengthen relations with the Palestinians as well as with the rest of the Arab world. He valued the Palestinian position on Jerusalem yet invited everyone to look at Jerusalem from a holistic perspective: *"The solution of a territorial dispute alone is not enough for Jerusalem, precisely because Jerusalem is an unparalleled reality: it is part of the whole world. And the whole world had shown that it is fully aware of this when, for example, through resolutions of the United Nations it has sought to defend that patrimony."*[420] Archbishop Touran made efforts to explain their position of support for Jerusalem being turned into a *"special internationally guaranteed statute"*, including the preservation of the historical characteristics of the city, its religious and cultural character, and equality for all inhabitants, freedom, including freedom of worship, and the right of people coming from abroad to pray at the holy sites.[421]

In addition to the agreements that defined specific mechanisms of implementation for the Oslo Agreement, 1994 brought another major diplomatic breakthrough with the July peace agreement between Israel and Jordan, known as *the Wadi Araba* agreement and signed by PM Rabin and PM Abdul Salam Majali respectively. The document recognized the borders between both states as those of the British Mandate *"without prejudice to the status of any territories that came under Israeli military government control in 1967,"*[422] and established a quadripartite committee including Egypt and the Palestinians for the issue of refugees, with a clear reference to the role of Jordan in Jerusalem: *"Israel respects the present special role of the Hashemite Kingdom of Jordan in Muslim holy shrines in Jerusalem. When negotiations on the permanent status will take place, Israel will give high priority to the Jordanian historic role in these shrines.*"[423] This wording was later reframed by Jordan to include a special role with regard to the Christian holy shrines in Jerusalem, something accepted by the Heads of Churches.

The Agreement included a reference to the exchange of ambassadors within one month. King Hussein of Jordan decided to appoint Marwan Muasher, one of the most skillful diplomats he had at his foreign ministry and the former spokesperson for the Jordanian delegation to the peace process. Muasher descended from a traditional Christian tribe in Jordan and also had Palestinian ancestry on his maternal side. For him the appointment represented a real challenge. *"You cannot make this decision on behalf of the Christian community in Jordan,"* he was told by a relative. Several issues were referred to, including the role of the Islamist opposition.[424] Muasher finally assumed his duties as a Jordanian diplomat and accepted the appointment, taking as one of his first steps a visit to the house of his mother in Jaffa. *"I considered knocking on the door, but then thought twice: as Jordan's first ambassador to Israel, I would be making an inopportune political statement."*[425] This did not prevent him from raising issues that Israel would have preferred to avoid such as the absentee status of property owned by Jordanian citizens of Palestinian descent. He created strong ties in Jerusalem with Faysal Husseini and among the Palestinian citizens of Israel. He even visited Birzeit University, where his mother had studied, and was welcomed by its President Hanna Nasser who had recently returned from exile and was also a cousin of his father-in-law. Ambassador Muasher's experience as Jordan's first ambassador to Israel reflected the complexities of Jordanian-Israeli relations and that the Palestinian issue could not be separated from their bilateral agenda.

A similar situation was taking place in the negotiations between the Holy See and both Israel and the PLO. By December 1993 the

Holy See had already concluded its Fundamental Agreement where Israel committed to freedom of religion and to the Status Quo of the Christian Holy Sites, as well as a number of items regarding Catholic property in Israel.[426] While the agreement did not make references to the 1967 border, it also avoided references to Jerusalem, which could be considered as a Holy See decision not to give legitimacy to Israeli claims over the city. At the same time, it refers to respect for the Status Quo. This works mainly in churches that are in the occupied territory of Palestine and not in Israel proper such as the Holy Sepulcher in East Jerusalem and the Nativity Church in Bethlehem.

The Holy See and Israel negotiated a follow-up agreement in 1997 while negotiations with the Palestinians for a fundamental agreement were just beginning. In January 1996 Pope John Paul II had already called upon the international community to support the peace process in an address to the diplomatic corps in the Vatican: *"The year 1996 should see the beginning of negotiations on the definitive status of the territories under the administration of the National Palestinian Authority, and also on the sensitive issue of the City of Jerusalem. it is my hope that the international community will offer the political partners most directly involved the juridical and diplomatic instruments capable of ensuring that Jerusalem, and one holy, may truly be a 'crossroads of peace' (...) ".*[427] The years 1996 and 1997 were in effect years of movement in the peace process, but not regarding the final status negotiations that Pope John Paul II was referring to.

Palestinian Elections and "Christian Quota"

In January 1996 the Palestinian Authority hosted its first national elections in accordance with the signed agreements, in addition to the changes that had already taken place in the municipalities. The Palestinian government considered a system of quotas was needed to give Christians representation in the parliament, particularly given the fact that their numbers had fallen considerably since 1948. *"It would have been difficult in certain regions to have any Christian elected, but it was a matter of national consensus to keep Palestinian Christians well represented. In some cases it was a matter of status quo. Could you imagine Bethlehem without a Christian mayor?"* said one of the government officials involved[428]. It had already been decided that several municipal councils would retain a Christian majority and a Christian mayor, particularly in Bethlehem, Beit Jala, Beit Sahour, Ramallah, Birzeit and Zababdeh, and in the village councils of Jifna, Ein Areeq, Taybeh and Aboud. In some cases, such as Gaza City and Jericho, a Christian would be part of the municipal council.

The mayors of Bethlehem, Beit Jala and Beit Sahour have direct participation in the celebration of Christmas and this was part of the considerations. The mayor of Beit Jala welcomes the relevant patriarch at Mar Elias monastery on the way to any mayoral celebration in Bethlehem. On Christmas Eve the mayor of Beit Sahour is included in welcoming the Patriarch after passing Rachel's Tomb/Bilal Bin Rabah mosque, while the mayor of Bethlehem receives the Patriarch at Nativity Square.

The Palestinian Legislative Council (PLC) of 88 members was elected, with its members becoming the representatives of Palestinians in the occupied territory to the PLO's National Council. In this distribution it was decided to appoint a quota granting Christians two of seven seats in Jerusalem, one of seven seats in Ramallah, two of four seats in Bethlehem, and one of twelve seats in Gaza City.[429] The only Christian elected to the PLC who would not have needed the quota system was Dr. Hanan Ashrawi who came second in Jerusalem. Bishara Daoud, the nationalist former mayor of Beit Jala, became the deputy speaker of the parliament.

The discussions over a quota for Christians were sometimes heated and some politicians and community leaders of Christian origin claimed that a quota was not needed as they were all Palestinians. One of the officials involved in making the quota system said: *"I received a lot of criticism from one of the elected Christian officials because of the quota, but I think that at the end the result was positive."*[430]

The End of the Peace Process

On November 4, 1995, Israel's PM Yithak Rabin was assassinated by an Israeli Jewish terrorist. His assassination followed an intensive campaign of incitement promoted by Israel's right-wing opposition which published pictures depicting Rabin as a Nazi or as a Palestinian. One of those leading the attacks against Rabin and the peace process was the leader of the opposition Benjamin Netanyahu, who was elected as Prime Minister in the elections that took place on May 29, 1996, with 50.5% of the votes and defeating Shimon Peres. This marked the beginning of several steps taken by the Israeli government to undermine the prospects of an agreement with the Palestinians and creating tensions around the holy places. Netanyahu's decision to open tunnels under Al Aqsa Mosque compound sparked popular demonstrations that resulted in around 100 Palestinians and 17 Israeli soldiers being killed. Palestinian security forces also took part in the confrontations that spread even to areas beyond the 1967 border such as Jaffa, Nazareth, and al-Lydd.

Ironically the end result of the open provocation by Benjamin Netanyahu was a US intervention that expedited part of the peace process that the Likud-led government was hoping to prevent. A summit in Washington was attended by President Arafat and Prime Minister Netanyahu, in addition to King Abdullah of Jordan and President Clinton (President Mubarak of Egypt declined the invitation due to lack of preparation for the meeting and the *"political inflexibility"* of Benjamin Netanyahu).[431] Little was agreed in the meeting but it set the basis for talks that had been blocked by the Israeli government and led to other issues such as the city of Hebron being tackled. By midway through his term in office, Netanyahu had succeeded in sabotaging the prospects of meaningful final status talks that had been constantly requested by Yasser Arafat.

Patriarch Michael Sabbah was harsh in his condemnation of the events and the poor results of the peace process for the Palestinian public. He stated: *"We believe that the direct reasons beyond the outbreak of this wave of violence triggered by the tunnel incident and which spread throughout Palestinian cities, are the deadlock of the peace process, along with all the accumulated injustices and sufferings of people in the Palestinian cities: the repeated closures, especially of Jerusalem, the continuous land confiscations to expand Jewish settlements, the effort to reduce the Palestinian Christian and Moslem presence in Jerusalem through confiscating IDs of Jerusalem residents who live, for any reason, outside the Holy City borders, whether in Palestinian areas or abroad, the demolition of houses, the detention of Palestinian prisoners, the continuous humiliation and harassment of Palestinians and finally, the deterioration of the situation of daily life to a miserable level."[432]* The heads of churches in Jerusalem made a *"call for peace and justice in the Holy Land,"* stating that *"what is required is the closure of the tunnel,"* as well as making an indirect appeal to find a political solution: *"When the closure of Jerusalem is lifted and the two parties share sovereignty over it, Jerusalem will become the city of peace. If Israel maintains an exclusive sovereignty over the city and continues its 'Judaization', Jerusalem will never feel secure and Palestinians will never submit to it. We therefore insist on an open Jerusalem, the capital of two states (...)."[433]*

From the beginning of the peace process, the churches had not issued such strong statements about the political developments and it was a reflection of the frustration many felt at that stage. Relations between various heads of churches and President Arafat were often affectionate and visits to the presidential compound in Ramallah had become regular. Episcopal Bishop Samir Kafity had compared the entry of Yasser Arafat to Bethlehem to that of Omar Ibn Khattab to Jerusalem,[434] a comparison that was certainly in line with the image Arafat portrayed of himself as the protector of all Palestinians. It was also full of symbolism in likening the Palestinian struggle to the wars against the Crusaders, something the PLO had been keen to promote since 1964 with the creation of the "Hattin" brigade of the Palestine Liberation Army. Bishop Kafity, born in Haifa in 1933 and ordained as Bishop in 1984, had become very close to the struggle of people on the streets during the Intifada and hired former detainees in church institutions, such as medical personnel at the Saint Luke's Hospital in Nablus.[435]

President Arafat was aware of the historic problems facing some of the churches, including the conflicts between the Arab Palestinian congregation and the Greek hierarchy at the Orthodox Patriarchate. The appointment of Ibrahim Qandalaft as deputy minister for Christian affairs, an Orthodox Jerusalemite, could be seen as a sign of indirect support for the Palestinian congregation. The issue of the Greek Orthodox Patriarchate remained a constant tension in relations between Palestinian officials and the Church, including accusations of discrimination against the Arab faithful as well as leases and sales of property to Israeli settlers. Arafat constantly tried to take a conciliatory approach and his ambassador in Athens, Dr. Abdullah Abdullah, retained cordial relations with the Church in Greece, including by accompanying Church authorities to receive the "Holy Fire" arriving at Athens airport from Jerusalem every Easter on "Holy Fire Saturday".

One of the most important demonstrations of how central the Christian component of Palestine was for the new Palestinian government was the Bethlehem 2000 Project. This aimed to link state-building efforts with the development of the Bethlehem area and tourism in particular. Dr. Nabil Kassis, a Palestinian Christian born in Ramallah and a well-known academic from Birzeit University who had participated in the Madrid Conference, was appointed as minister in charge of heading the efforts. Work was initiated in March 1997 upon the initiative of the Palestinian government to prepare Bethlehem for the celebrations of the new millennium when around two million tourists were expected between Christmas 1999 and Easter 2001.[436] UN Resolution 53/27 of November 18, 1998, reaffirmed *"the need for immediate change in the situation on the ground in the vicinity of Bethlehem, especially with regard to ensuring freedom of movement (...) stressing the need for ensuring free and unhindered access to the holy places in Bethlehem to the faithful and the citizens of all nationalities."*[437]

The Resolution started by presenting the positive aspects of an initiative aimed at celebrating the new millennium and presenting Palestine's heritage to the world, but ended by referring to the situation on the ground that was openly deteriorating. The Israeli government had proceeded with the construction of the first colonial-settlement after the signing the Oslo Agreement on the mountain of Jabal Abu Ghneim, on land mostly belonging to Beit Sahour and that included church properties. The protests led by Faysal Husseini included a protest tent erected on the land but these did not prevent the Israeli government from annexing additional areas around East Jerusalem.

The consequences for Bethlehem would be catastrophic, and Palestinian Christians in particular were deprived of one of the few spaces available for urban expansion. For Israel, it was about consolidating a network of colonial-settlements in the unilaterally expanded boundaries of Jerusalem, which deprived Bethlehem, Beit Jala, and Beit Sahour of some 20,000 dunums of land. The new settlement, named by Israel as Har Homa, would be linked to the existing colonial-settlement of Gilo, beginning a barrier of settlements to separate Bethlehed from Jerusalem.

Palestine's representative to the UN, Nasser Al Qudwa, was directly instructed by Yasser Arafat to take immediate action on the matter and to mobilize the Security Council. However, the US vetoed a resolution twice in one month. Despite the fact that Washington had condemned the settlement, a collateral consequence of the peace process were its attempts to prevent the UN from taking any action on Palestine. Despite criticizing the Israeli plans, the US representative argued that: *"Members have heard our views on the inappropriateness of outside interference in the direct negotiations between the parties. We never believed, despite the useful role the Council can and has played in working for Middle East peace, that it is an appropriate forum for debating the issues now under negotiation between the parties."*[438] Contrary to these arguments by the US representative, there were no discussions between any of the parties about Jerusalem, settlements or any other final status issues as the Netanyahu government had constantly refused to advance final status negotiations.

The Egyptian representative, Ambassador Nabil al-Arabi, responded by stating: *"To say that the Security Council's fulfilment of its mandate and duties under the Charter would have negative repercussions for peace in the Middle East is unjustified. In fact, the opposite is true. The silence of the Security Council and its failure to take up its duties would send an erroneous message, a dangerous message likely to encourage the current Israeli Government to continue to violate international law. It would also encourage it to disdain and not respect its contractual obligations. This could abort the peace process, which is truly at a very sensitive and dangerous juncture.*"[439] Despite the legal arguments made by virtually the whole of the Council, the US government blocked an international response and Israel went ahead with one of its most dangerous colonial-settlement projects.

The Jabal Abu Ghneim (Har Homa) case became a symbol of the failure of the peace process to move beyond limited steps within its interim phase while avoiding any talks on final status issues. A forested mountain with an archeological Christian site was turned into a new settlement: Bethlehem, the very city that was supposed to represent a symbol of Palestinian development, felt the impact of a ring of settlements around it that suffocated and severely limited its potential. During 1996 the construction of bypass Road 60 to the west of the city aimed to link Israel's settlements in the southern West Bank with Jerusalem. New roads to enable Israeli settlers to avoid passing through Palestinian cities required further land grabs.

Bypass Road 60 seized land from Beit Jala for major infrastructural projects such as tunnels and bridges that created a de facto western border for Bethlehem. For some like Mitri Ghneim, this new development was the beginning of a new nightmare. He married on the eve of the 1967 war and left on June 4 for his honeymoon in Jordan. After the war, he could not return to Palestine and remained in Jordan for over a decade. Once the Red Cross managed to facilitate his return, the money he had earned while working as a taxi driver in Jordan was used to buy over two dunums of land in "one of the quietest" areas of Beit Jala. The construction of the road took almost half of it and Beit Jala was no longer the quiet place it had once been.

"Christian Diplomacy" and Efforts
to Contribute to an Agreement

Patriarch Sabbah had started a revolution in the stance adopted by the heads of churches in Jerusalem in support of the inalienable rights of the Palestinian people, and a similar process was also taking place in churches worldwide. The networks created with bishops worldwide, and the deep connections and sympathy of several Vatican officials, including from the Vatican foreign minister Archbishop Jean-Louis Tauran, resulted in concrete messages of urgency being sent to the US and to several European actors. But Patriarch Sabbah symbolized the synergy of these efforts rather than all of them because several religious Christian leaders took part in them.

A good example is the work of the Episcopal (Anglican) church, whose US branch issued a statement in 1997 calling for Jerusalem to be the capital of two sovereign and independent states, for Israel to remove all movement restrictions preventing Palestinian access to Jerusalem, called for equal rights for Palestinians to build in the Holy City, and demanded a solution that includes *"self-determination, release of prisoners, right of return and eventual sovereignty (...) The Convention urges the government of the United States to use its diplomatic and economic influence in support of the above and to demonstrate a firm commitment to justice for Palestinians as it does for the security of the State of Israel..."*[440]

Similar statements were issued by the (WCC) and various other Christian organizations. The activities of Palestinian organizations such as Sabeel and figures linked to Protestant churches, namely Lutherans and Episcopals, contributed to sharing the concerns of Palestinian Christian leaders over the deadlock in the peace process. In 1998 the Holy See issued a particularly strong non-paper published by their observer mission to the UN. Recalling UN resolutions, it stated: *"In consideration of the special identity of the Holy City, an outstanding religious and cultural center in the history of humanity, the Holy See appeals to the international community to ensure the avoidance of irreversible solutions which could prejudice the very future of Jerusalem and cause it to lose the universal character which makes it a heritage of humanity."[441]*

It was at this time that the Israeli government began to fall apart. Benjamin Netanyahu had taken bold steps to prevent progress in the peace negotiations and to create facts on the ground that would prevent the realization of an independent Palestinian state. He had to face early elections in May 1999, the same month and year that was supposed to mark the end of the interim period of the Oslo Process with a final status agreement. Netanyahu had succeeded in preventing negotiations from taking place, despite the fact that a number of further agreements of an interim nature were signed under his leadership, notably the Hebron and Wye River agreements in 1998 that aimed to secure further Israeli withdrawals, plus other terms that could have created an environment conducive to final status negotiations taking place.

In May 1999 President Arafat stated that he would unilaterally announce the freedom of the State of Palestine at the end of the interim period. This announcement sparked vehement objections from international actors who asked the Palestinian leader to await the result of the Israeli elections. It was a recurrent theme with Western international actors that concerns were based more on Israeli public opinion and excuses to violate deadlines than on Palestine's freedom and independence. The obligations signed by the State of Israel became "subject to further negotiations", including delays and ongoing violations, depending on the domestic needs of the Israeli government.

Earlier in March of that year, the European Council had released a statement welcoming *"the decision by the Palestinian National Council and associated bodies to reaffirm the nullification of the provisions in the Palestinian National Charter which called for the destruction of Israel and to reaffirm their commitment to recognize and live in peace with Israel,"* but did not announce any concrete steps to make peace a reality. The statement called for negotiations to be concluded *"within a target period of one year,"*[442] probably as a response to the rumors of the announcement by Arafat in May. President Clinton sent his own letter of assurances to Yasser Arafat in an attempt to deter the Palestinian announcement and acknowledged that *"your people have faced great difficulties in the past several years (...) clearly the Oslo process has not made the kind of process we would have hoped to see."*[443]

International attention returned to the region. In the Israeli elections Benjamin Netanyahu was finally defeated by Labor's Ehud Barak, a former Israeli general who was said to be committed not just to concluding a peace agreement with the Palestinians, but had also announced the need to negotiate peace with Syria and to withdraw Israeli troops from southern Lebanon. This was seen as a positive development by the international community. Negotiations began with Syria and Israeli soldiers finally left most of southern Lebanon, unilaterally withdrawing by May 24, 2000.

Israel's withdrawal from Lebanon ended with images of thousands of Lebanese collaborators from the South Lebanon Army (SLA) and their families, an army composed mainly of Christians. With the Israeli withdrawal, the SLA quickly collapsed and thousands of members were at the border with Israel seeking protection as Hezbollah and the Lebanese Army regained control of southern Lebanon. Initially Israel thought that their Lebanese allies could be relocated into Palestinian Christian villages in the upper Galilee.

This option was rejected by Palestinian Christians who could not forget the role played by that militia. A priest from the Latin Patriarchate once said: *"The biggest challenge was to the Maronite Church in the Galilee. I remember a priest who eventually refused to continue serving the Lebanese and effectively the masses had to be divided between the Palestinian and the Lebanese communities."*[444]

The Visit of Pope John Paul II

In March 2000 Pope John Paul II visited Israel, Jordan, and Palestine. The Palestinian preparations for the visit were made under explicit instructions from Yasser Arafat who realized that the organization of the visit would demonstrate readiness for statehood. One rumor was that Yasser Arafat was adamant that the Pope visit the baptismal site (Al Maghtas) from the Palestinian side rather than from Jordan, even though the Palestinian government had no control over the location, as it would reaffirm that it was part of Palestine. In fact, this is what eventually took place. The Pope made a reference to Jericho (which was under limited Palestinian control) by stating: *"It is near here that we find the remains of the oldest city yet discovered,"*[445] thereby linking both locations in the occupied territory.

Jerusalem was a center of political activity during the visit. Vatican and Palestinian flags were raised in several parts of the Old City, mainly in the Christian Quarter. This was the result of an organizational team that functioned from Orient House under the direct instructions of Faysal Husseini. Emile Jarjoui, a medical doctor and prominent figure in Palestinian Orthodox circles, also played a major role. He had become an elected representative for Jerusalem in the Palestinian parliament and chief Palestinian negotiator in the fundamental agreement with the Holy See.

The Holy See-PLO Basic Agreement included on its committee Ambassador Afif Safieh, minister Nabil Kassis, Jad Isaac, Minister Mitri Abu Aita, and young officials such as Violette Raheb and Issa Kassissieh. The Agreement was signed on February 15, 2000, and Palestine saw it as an important diplomatic victory because it included references in the text to a solution for Jerusalem *"based on international resolutions,"* and stated that *"unilateral decisions and actions altering the specific character and status of Jerusalem are morally and legally unacceptable."*[446] In the text, the Holy See reaffirmed its stated position in support of *"peace and security for all peoples of the region on the basis of international law, relevant United Nations and its Security Council resolutions, justice and equity."*[447] The PLO agreed fundamentally to respect the privileges of the Church in accordance with what had been the practice in Palestine since the Ottoman period, as well as the Status Quo of the Holy Sites.

The schedule for the visit to Palestine included the baptismal site, mass in Manger Square, mass in the Holy Sepulcher, a visit to Al Aqsa with the Mufti of Jerusalem, and a visit to Yasser Arafat and to Dheisheh refugee camp. There, the Pope made a passionate statement of support for Palestinian rights, including direct recognition of the historical links of the Palestinian people with their land: *"Dear brothers and sisters, dear refugees, do not think that your present condition makes you any less important in God's eyes! Never forget your dignity as his children! Here at Bethlehem the Divine Child was laid in a manger in a stable; shepherds from the nearby fields were the first to receive the heavenly message of peace and hope for the world. God's design was fulfilled in the midst of humility and poverty. Probably the pastors and shepherds of Bethlehem were your predecessors, your ancestors."*[448]

International media highlighted the support for Palestinian statehood. The British newspaper *The Guardian* described the visit thus: *"Pope*

John Paul II has at last touched down in the Holy Land. He has fulfilled his life's ambition – but it has hardly been a mission of joy or serenity."[449] The Pope's support for Palestinian statehood was declared in his first words upon being welcomed in Bethlehem: *"The Holy See has always recognized that the Palestinian people have the natural right to a homeland, and the right to be able to live in peace and tranquility with the other peoples of this area."*[450]

Camp David: The End of an Era

That summer of 2000 witnessed the first real efforts to achieve a final status agreement between Israel and the PLO. President Clinton invited the parties to Camp David, the symbolic summer resort where almost twenty years earlier, President Carter had managed to achieve the first peace agreement between Israel and an Arab country, Egypt. This time the conditions were very different. Egypt had succeeded in negotiating with Israel after changing the rules of engagement with the October 1973 war and had prepared for that moment for years. The Palestinians had neither an "October 1973" moment after the Oslo Agreement, nor had the US prepared the ground for final status negotiations during the interim period. Yasser Arafat felt that this was not an opportune moment and he delivered several messages to the US and other relevant international parties explaining his stance. He did not fly straight to the US but sought coordination with Egypt, meeting President Mubarak in Alexandria and attending the African Summit in Togo. Here he delivered a passionate speech to remind the audience of the importance of Jerusalem, receiving loud ovation in return. In preparation for what would come, Yasser Arafat requested that Hanan Ashrawi, an effective and well-known communicator, attend Washington and be responsible for the media. External communications from the summer resort were restricted to one telephone per delegation.

The summit began on July 11, 2000, and Jerusalem quickly became the most important point of division. Ideas on borders presented by the Americans were denounced by Palestinian negotiators as ideas *"developed by the Israelis and presented by the Americans"*. For the Old City, proposals included handing the sovereignty of Al Aqsa Mosque compound to Israel (it was later suggested that Israel be given "underground" sovereignty), and giving the Armenian Quarter (next to the Jewish Quarter) to Israel while accepting that the Christian and Muslim Quarters of the Old City would be under some sort of Palestinian autonomy.

Arafat was aware of the sensitivity of his position. He asked his foreign minister Nabil Shaath to call a number of Arab and Muslim leaders, plus the Holy See and other Christian religious leaders, and found that none of them agreed with the Israeli and US proposals.[451] Suddenly, the sessions with President Clinton turned into history classes in which Yasser Arafat asked: *"Do you want me to sell the Christians to Israel and hand over the Armenians?"*[452] Back in Jerusalem, Patriarch Sabbah understood the critical situation taking place in Camp David and managed to get Patriarch Diodoros I of the Greek Orthodox Church and Patriarch Torkom of the Armenian Orthodox to sign a statement that was sent to the delegations, including the US. It suggested a system of international guarantees and tried to prevent the separation of the Armenian and Christian Quarters: *"We appeal to you foremost as political leaders and negotiators to ensure that the Christian communities within the walls of the Old City are not separated from each other. We regard the Christian and Armenian Quarters of the Old City as inseparable and contiguous entities that are firmly united by the same faith."*[453]

The Christian dimension of Jerusalem was undoubtedly a key consideration for Yasser Arafat in his negotiating position. *"What would my friend (the Coptic) Pope Shenouda say if I did this?",*[454]

Yasser Arafat told Gamal Hilal, a US State Department official of Egyptian and Coptic origin who was translating the meetings with President Bill Clinton. On a different occasion, when confronted with the proposal to give away the Armenian Quarter to Israel, the Palestinian leader came out with one of his most famous statements in the negotiations: *"How are you asking me to give up on the Armenians. Don't you know that my name is Yasser Arafatian?"*[455]

The Camp David summit ended without an agreement. As he drafted the official response of Yasser Arafat to President Clinton, Saeb Erekat started to weep. Arafat asked him what was wrong and Erekat responded: *"You are doing the right thing, but what I'm drafting is your death certificate. They are not going to forgive you."*[456] The final tripartite statement of the summit was released on July 25 and signed by President Clinton. PM Barak and President Arafat made a commitment to continue negotiations based on UN Security Council Resolutions 242 and 338[457] but a blame game was already taking place and the Palestinians were blamed for the failure to reach an agreement. Arafat understood the importance of defending the Palestinian narrative, the significance of the Christian and Muslim holy sites, and support for a solution based on international law that would end the occupation that began in 1967. *"When it came to interim agreements he was more flexible, but if it was about reaching a final status agreement it was about ending the occupation, and understanding that the 1967 border was already a painful compromise"* said a member of the delegation.[458]

The Palestinians had to deal with a massive smear campaign with phrases such as *"generous Israeli offer"* rejected by the Palestinians. While interpretations about what truly took place in Camp David differ, and beginning with the fact that the Israeli delegation did move beyond what previous administrations would have offered, the proposals were rarely written. In any case, they did not meet the minimum requirements that the Palestinians could have accepted in light of Israel's obligations under international law and relevant UN resolutions. The fact that the Palestinians had already compromised on 78% of historic Palestine by accepting the 1967 border was largely ignored by those who criticized them for the failure of the Camp David summit.

The Second Intifada

The environment changed after the return from Camp David. Meetings between negotiators from both sides could not hide Palestinian frustration over blame for the failure of the talks, while PM Barak in Israel attempted to use the line of his *"generous offer"* to boost himself internally as someone who supported peace, but not at any price.

The leader of the Israeli opposition, Likud MK Ariel Sharon, decided to take a further step of claiming sovereignty over the most sensitive site in occupied East Jerusalem, Al Aqsa Mosque compound. On September 28, 2000, he effectively stormed the site surrounded by hundreds of armed Israeli forces. Demonstrations broke out immediately and the images of Palestinian worshippers defending the site, even by throwing their shoes at the Israeli forces, quickly went around the country. The provocation led to demonstrations all over the occupied Palestinian territory, and spreading within a few days to Israel proper in places such as Nazareth, Jaffa, and Haifa.

Some remembered the events of 1996 as the *"Intifada of the tunnels"* and confrontations took place over a limited period of time. This time the context was different as the date stipulated in the Oslo Agreement for a final status agreement had passed and there was a clear campaign against the Palestinian leadership after the failure of the Camp David summit. The Old City of Jerusalem became a battlefield with thousands of Palestinians confronting Israeli forces. Diplomats informed their capitals of the need to take immediate action but it was too late. The Israeli government took a strong position against the demonstrations and dozens of Palestinian civilians were killed within one week. The image of Mohammad al-Durrah, a 12-year-old boy being killed while his father attempted to protect him from the bullets became a symbol that soon mobilized the Arab streets in support of Palestine. Lebanese singer Walid Tawfik's song "The Voice of the Stone" (*sawt il hajjar*) became a top hit within hours in a musical effort that gathered top Arab artists. The song "Arabic Dream", made in 1998 and performed by 23 Arab singers, became a hit in 2000. Millions sang *"Maybe the darkness of the night will keep us away for a day but the beam of light can reach the highest sky. That's our dream as long as we live, one lap that hugs us all."* Julia Boutros, the Lebanese Christian singer, was more straightforward in her lyrics calling for support: *"Where are the millions? Where are the Arab people?"*

It was the beginning of the Second Intifada, known also as the "Al Aqsa Intifada" after the location where it began. On October 7, and after several days of discussions due to threats of a US veto, the UN Security Council approved Resolution 1322 deploring the *"provocation carried at Al-Haram Al Sharif"*, calling for the immediate cessation of violence, and calling *"upon Israel, the occupying power, to abide scrupulously by its legal obligations and its responsibilities under the Fourth Geneva Convention."*[459]

Several statements were issued, including from churches concerned about the situation of their counterparts in Palestine. The National Council of Churches, Church World Service, and Witness from the US issued a statement on October 11 declaring that *"the fundamental source of the present violent confrontation lies in the continued failure to make real the national rights of the Palestinian people to a sovereign state in their own homeland and to create just security arrangements in the region.*[460] Pax Christi sent an appeal to European parliamentarians and foreign ministers on October 13 also emphasizing the rights of the Palestinian people. On October 14 the Presbyterian Church sent a letter to President Clinton urging him to *"use whatever influence is left to you in this situation, working with the United Nations and the whole international community, to find a resolution to this conflict that is marked by justice for the Palestinian people, without which there will never be peace in the region."*[461] Two days later, the chairman of the US Catholic Conference Committee on International Policy, Cardinal Bernard Law, stated that: *"Support must be given to those who, in the midst of conflict, stand against violence and for the peace which the Holy Land should symbolize. As Latin Patriarch Michael Sabbah reminds us: 'This is a holy land, a land of faith and prayer. It is written nowhere that it should remain a land of hatred and blood. On the contrary, in the mercy of God, this land is determined to be a land of redemption and love'."*[462]

As the international community mobilized diplomatic initiatives, Egypt hosted a peace summit in Sharm Al Sheikh on October 17 attended by US President Bill Clinton, King Abdullah of Jordan, the UN Secretary General Kofi Annan, the EU High Representative Javier Solana, Yasser Arafat, and Israel's Ehud Barak. In his initial remarks, President Mubarak tried to define a path to end the stalemate by stating: *"The following days will witness redeployment of the Israeli forces, lift the blockade imposed on three million Palestinian people, reopening airports, ports, crossing points in order to pacify the Palestinian streets and bring matters back to normal."*[463]

President Clinton also tried to establish what could be defined as an initial road map, including the resumption of negotiations based on UNSC Resolutions 242 and 338, but the statement was void of more substantial demands. Arab diplomacy was mobilized and an Extraordinary Arab Summit Conference took place in Cairo on October 22 with a strong statement calling for a UN investigation: *"The Arab leaders affirm that the Al-Aqsa Intifada has broken out as a result of the maintenance and perpetuation of the occupation and because of Israel's encroachments on the Haram al-Sharif and on the other Islamic and Christian Holy Places in the occupied Palestinian territories."*[464] The statement also referred to the initiative led by Saudi Arabia to raise a sum of 800 million dollars for projects in Jerusalem, known as the Al Quds Intifada Fund. The idea had been presented to the Palestinians a few days earlier during a visit of FM Nabil Shaath to Riyad: *"I was received by the King who was very concerned about the situation in Palestine. He was interested to know how much money we needed to survive in a situation like this and claimed that he would be willing to fund half of it, hoping that other Arabs would fund the rest."*[465]

Diplomatic efforts by church leaders continued, with Episcopal Jerusalem Bishop Riah Abu El-Assal playing an increasingly prominent role alongside the efforts of Patriarch Michael Sabbah. At this stage they had been joined by Orthodox Archimendrite Atallah Hanna who became known for his strong statements calling for Arab and Muslim support for Palestinian independence. Upon the personal request of Yasser Arafat, Hanna addressed an Islamic Conference in Doha that was broadcast to the Arab world. The Holy See delegation to the UN made a statement on October 30 that, once again, expressed its concern about the situation in Jerusalem. By November the situation had escalated, including the killing of 13 Palestinian citizens of Israel by Israeli forces in October, and the effects of diplomacy had not been felt on the ground.

The heads of churches in Jerusalem issued an appeal on November 9 calling for respect of everyone's rights: *"As long as one people remains the subject of injustice, it will continue to be a constant source of fear and insecurity for its neighbor (...) Peace in justice remains the absolute and inviolable right of both peoples of this land. Peace should not be sacrificed for political pride. After all, peace can only be the fruit of justice."*[466] In the Vatican Pope John Paul II used of the presentation of credentials of the Lebanese Ambassador to state: *"The Holy Land, where God revealed himself and spoke to mankind, must become the place par excellence where peace and justice flourish. Jerusalem must be a particularly strong symbol of unity, peace and reconciliation for the whole human family!"*[467]

By November it had become clear that the much-awaited celebrations of Christmas 2000 would not take place. "Instead of 50 or 60 buses a day, we get a few taxis," minister Nabil Kassis told the *New York Times,*[468] amid reports that hotels were working at a mere 10% of their capacity. For first time since 1967, Palestinians opened fire against illegal Israeli settlements around Bethlehem, including Gilo, and Israel bombarded Beit Jala with tanks and helicopters. It was on one such night that Dr. Harald Fischer, a 68-year-old German doctor married to a Palestinian from Beit Jala, was killed by an Israeli missile fired from a helicopter as he was trying to assist an injured neighbor. Dr. Fischer received honors from the Palestinian government and became the first Lutheran to be considered a martyr of the Intifada. Parts of the city were reoccupied and a tight siege was established over Bethlehem.

The Israeli bombardment of a police station in Ramallah after the lynching of two Israeli soldiers who had entered the city became a symbol that this was a moment of no return. Groups that had opposed the peace process, particularly Hamas, gained more notoriety while Israeli forces were moving on the leaders of Fatah and the PFLP, including the destruction of the security infrastructure of the Palestinian government. By December the Christmas celebrations were significantly reduced; the globally marketed concerts were cancelled and there were almost no foreign tourists. One year earlier, Bethlehem had hosted massive celebrations that had included Algerian singers Cheb Chaled and Rachid Taha with their hit *Abdelkader,* as well as traditional Christmas carols by Fayrouz broadcast across the city.

In December 2000 Bethlehem was surrounded by Israeli forces. Hotels suffered a major blow after having reservations for over 90% of their capacity. Notably, no mass concerts took place. It was the last time that Yasser Arafat could attend a Christmas mass in Bethlehem, having arrived from Jordan in a military helicopter. This was the last time that he arrived to the heliport built on top of one of Bethlehem's highest mountains. When the Palestinian government had entered five years earlier, Arafat had enthusiastically endorsed the construction of a cultural center in Dheisheh refugee camp, an educational campus for the Lutheran Church (today's Dar Al Kalima University), and the heliport built to receive foreign authorities in the city, and which only a few months earlier, had welcomed Pope John Paul II in a different context.

That Christmas Eve, Patriarch Michael Sabbah had entered Bethlehem in the manner established in the Status Quo, including stops at Mar Elias monastery and a welcome at Nativity Square by Mayor Hanna Nasser. His words on that cold Sunday night of Christmas Eve were: *"Whether we live at war or in the Intifada, whether our houses are demolished, our brothers wounded or killed, it is here that God wants us to be Christians (...) This is our land, to claim our freedom among our demolished houses and in our besieged towns and villages."*[469] Arafat, who considered Christmas as a symbol for all Palestinians and who had adopted the tradition of moving all operations to Bethlehem between Western Christmas Eve (December 24) and Armenian Christmas (January 18), made use of the occasion to deliver a strong message to the international community. Only one year earlier, in the excitement of the previous celebrations, Arafat had declared: *"From the heart of this Holy City of Jesus, the city where it all began, in the name of God, in the name of Palestine, I declare open the celebrations of the third millennium."*[470] One year later, the situation was radically different.

In January 2001, right after the end of the Christmas season, a last effort was made to negotiate a peace agreement between Israelis and Palestinians. Negotiations took place in Taba, Egypt. The negotiating teams met, again in a different environment with elections in Israel rapidly approaching and polls suggesting the victory of Likud candidate Ariel Sharon. The substance of the discussions was summarized by European envoy Miguel Moratinos, who had briefly served as Spain's ambassador to Israel and who became one of the most enthusiastic promoters of the peace process and Palestinian statehood. In his summary, known as the Moratinos Non-Paper on Taba Negotiations, some of the positions were summarized as:[471]

- Territory: Negotiations based on the 1967 borders in accordance with UNSC Resolution 242.
- West Bank: For first time both sides presented maps, with Israel aiming to achieving exchanges of territory allowing them to keep around 80% of the settlers in Israeli territory, and a disagreement took place over the strategic Latroun area, most of it located in "no man's land" where the Trappist monastery is located.
- Jerusalem: There was a certain acceptance of the Clinton Parameters" (leaving most Israeli settlements in East Jerusalem under Israeli sovereignty while allowing a Palestinian capital in the Palestinian neighborhoods), and the Palestinian side *"understood that the Israeli side accepted to discuss Palestinian property claims in West Jerusalem."* The idea of Jerusalem being an "open city" was agreed between the parties without agreement on its borders.

- Refugees: Non-papers were exchanged between the parties and discussions took place on issues such as resettlement, compensation, and effective return. Israel agreed to discuss numbers of returnees.

The delegations left Taba on January 27 as Israel's PM Ehud Barak considered the negotiations overdue due to the Israeli elections in under 10 days. The election was won by Ariel Sharon, marking the end of the prospects for any sort of final status negotiations and the beginning of a new stage for the Palestinian national movement.

The Desperate Last Fight of Yasser Arafat

Sharon and Arafat knew each other well from the war in Lebanon. The general responsible for the massacre of Sabra and Shatila had developed a particular obsession against the Palestinian leader. Sharon's formula for ending the Intifada was not negotiations but a crushing military defeat of the Palestinian movement, including the policy of reoccupation of Palestinian cities that began with the Barak government. At the same time that Israeli troops were advancing, several groups of Zionist religious settlers began to impose their own facts on the ground with the construction of colonial-settlement outposts. At that stage the whole idea of security coordination had been abandoned and the pillars of the political process had collapsed, including violation of the time frames of the Oslo Agreement by Israel and the US.

The churches felt the impact of this new reality in a variety of forms. Claudette Habash, the iconic Jerusalemite refugee from Talbiya and the most prominent Palestinian woman in church circles, had taken control of CARITAS and had to run several emergency projects to deal with the injured and the economic devastation of the situation. Habash was a known nationalist who had consistently refused to recognize the facts imposed by the occupation. She was close to Patriarch Sabbah and together they formed an emergency front to deal with one of the biggest crises for the presence of Christians in Palestine: the growth in emigration. At that time there was speculation that Patriarch Sabbah himself had asked diplomats not to grant visas to Christians, although this claim could not be verified. According to other sources, the request was simply not to make things "too easy" for people to emigrate.[472] But the changing situation on the ground made it irrelevant for the efforts conducted by church officials to prevent the emigration of significant parts of their congregations.

On April 11, 2001, Elias Eid Samaan Eid, a member of National Security, the successor to the Palestine Liberation Army after the Oslo Agreement, was killed in Gaza. Eid had returned to Palestine as part of the agreements. Originally from the Galilee and raised in the refugee camps of Lebanon, he was one of few Palestinian Christians to join the National Security. Easter 2001 passed with a very limited number of tourists and with several Palestinian hotels in Jerusalem and Bethlehem simply shut down.

That spring and summer there continued to be a high number of casualties. A symbol of the new situation in Bethlehem was when Israeli forces surrounded the Lutheran Church in Beit Jala on August 17, including a boarding school for 45 orphans who were taken out of their bedrooms to be searched. Attempts by a group of Swedish peace activists to free the children went without response from the Israeli forces. Opposite the Lutheran Church was the local mosque whose minaret was used by Israeli snipers, including opening fire and damaging the Virgin Mary Orthodox Church.[473] The Israeli army declared that it was "clearing" the area of Palestinian snipers.[474]

At this stage, the Israeli army had already besieged Ramallah and imposed an increasing number of movement restrictions that critically affected all aspects of Palestinian life. On August 11 when the Episcopal priest of Birzeit, Fr. Samir Esaid, tried to reach his parish from Ramallah to conduct a baptism, Israeli soldiers stopped him at a flying checkpoint and prevented him from continuing his 12-kilometer journey to Birzeit. Not knowing when it would be possible for him to reach his parish, Fr. Esaid took an alternative step and called the Latin priest of Birzeit, Fr. Iyad Twal, who accepted to conduct the baptism. This created an unprecedented event in Palestine in which two children were baptized as Episcopal following a Latin rite in an Episcopal church.

The baptism was for twins Bassel and Layan Nasser. This was not the only time that the Israeli occupation would have an impact on their lives. Layan became a symbol for Palestinian students detained by Israeli forces when two decades later, the Israeli government pushed for the criminalization of Palestinian civil society and student organizations. Layan's "crime" was activism in a left-wing movement inside the campus of Birzeit University.[475]

In other cases, masses were simply not conducted. As Latin priest Fr. Akhtam Hijazeen was traveling to officiate mass for the first Sunday in the village of Aboud, he was stopped by a flying checkpoint and was not allowed to continue to the church. These were not isolated cases. On some occasions, priests served as human shields to protect their communities. In Bethlehem Fr. Faysal Hijazeen put a Vatican flag over his car to drive around the governorate during curfew and distribute humanitarian aid. Fr. Hijazeen's case was not unique and was effectively repeated in several other communities.

By the end of the month on August 27, there was a turning point when an Israeli missile executed Mustafa Zibri, known as Abu Ali Mustafa, the Secretary General of the PFLP. He had taken over from George Habash just one year earlier and had been allowed into the occupied territory by Israel. He was highly respected in Palestinian political circles and had managed to give the PFLP a prominent role in the Intifada. That night an emergency meeting took place at the residence of the UN Envoy, Norway's Terje Larsen. An experienced Norwegian diplomat who had been involved in the Oslo Agreements, Larsen's role was later heavily criticized by Palestinian officials. That meeting was attended by Israel's Army Chief of Staff Shaul Mofaz and by the Palestinian chief security official Mohammad Dahlan, accompanied by chief negotiator Saeb Erekat. That meeting ended with no results.

The PFLP responded on October 17 by killing Rehavam Zeevi at the Hyatt Jerusalem Hotel on Mount Scopus. Zeevi was the Israeli Tourism Minister and a prominent advocate of the "transfer" of the Palestinian people. He was ironically referred to by his Israeli colleagues as "Ghandi". His killing prompted a massive Israeli invasion of Palestinian cities, including a siege of the presidential compound in Ramallah. Soon the Statue of Virgin Mary located at the French Hospital in Bethlehem became a symbol of the Israeli re-occupation after it was hit by several bullets. On October 19, Musa George Abu Eid, a 19-year-old civilian from Beit Jala was killed by an Israeli sniper at his home. One day later, Rania Murrah, a 24-year-old mother of two children, was killed by Israeli fire while on her way to buy milk. Both funerals took place at the local Orthodox Church. A few kilometers away in Bethlehem that same day, Johnny Thalgieh, a 19-year-old Palestinian who wanted to become a priest, was killed while on his way to serve in the mass at the Nativity Church. On October 20, eight Palestinians were killed by Israeli forces.

Pope John Paul II said *"War and death arrived even on the square of the Basilica of the Nativity of Our Lord."*[476] As a response to the Israeli attacks in Bethlehem leaders from the 13 churches of

Jerusalem organized a demonstration at Bethlehem's Nativity Square where Episcopal Bishop Riah Abu El-Assal told reporters that *"there can be no justice without an end to the occupation."*[477] Archimendrite Atallah Hanna sent a message to the UN Human Rights Commission demanding *"immediate and rapid intervention to save the Palestinian people from the terrible massacres being carried out by the occupation forces"*[478].

Despite interventions by Christian leaders, things did not change in Bethlehem. That December, Israel did not allow Yasser Arafat to attend Christmas mass in Bethlehem. Fearing that Arafat would find a way to smuggle himself into the birthplace of Jesus, Israel forces checked the vehicles exiting Ramallah meticulously. The Latin Patriarchate agreed to keep Arafat's seat empty on the first row of Saint Catherine's Church, decorated with a kuffiyeh as a symbol of Arafat's presence. Instead, Arafat received a visit from the heads of churches in Ramallah. The decision to ban Arafat from Bethlehem was heavily criticized in Palestine and symbolized how Christmas had become not just a national holiday but a symbol of Palestinian presence and identity. There were few Christmas decorations in Bethlehem but the story of siege and occupation was headlined in the international media.

In March 2002 the Arab Summit of Beirut approved the Arab Peace Initiative". This represented the first time that all Arab countries had agreed on recognizing and normalizing relations with Israel in exchange for an Israeli withdrawal to the 1967 border, and the achievement of a *"just and agreed upon solution"* to the Palestinian refugee issue based on UNGA Resolution 194.[479] Arab League Secretary General Amr Mousa took the lead in promoting this historic initiative internationally, including the fact that it was closely linked to a Saudi diplomatic effort that could potentially give it greater relevance in Western and Israeli circles. Israel never responded to it.

One month later, Israel detained Marwan Barghouthi, Fatah's Secretary General and believed to be one of the main leaders of the Intifada. This did not stop Palestinian groups, including Fatah's Al Aqsa Martyrs Brigade, from continuing their operations against Israeli targets. A significant number of Palestinian Christians were part of the group and came to the fore when Israeli forces besieged the Nativity Church between April 2 and May 10 in what became one of the most fraught moments in Holy See-Israeli relations.

The Nativity Church was besieged when Israel reoccupied Bethlehem and a number of officials and activists sought protection. Among them was the governor of Bethlehem, Mohammad Madani, and his close confidant Anton Salman, who later became the mayor of Bethlehem. Members of various Palestinian factions, including Hamas and the Islamic Jihad, took refuge in the place where tradition marks the birthplace of Jesus. Among them was Chris Bandak, son of one of the most traditional Christian families of the city and a known operative of Fatah. A number of Arab clergy played a prominent role inside the church, including Fr. Ibrahim Faltas from Egypt and Fr. Amjad Sabbara from Palestine.

In addition to the involvement of Arab clergy, a statement was delivered by Latin Patriarch Michael Sabbah: *"The basilica, a church, is a place of refuge for everybody, even fighters, as long as they lay down their arms (...) In such a case, we have an obligation to give refuge to Palestinians and Israelis alike."*[480] This established a counter-narrative to Israeli claims that Palestinian militants were taking the clergy as hostages.[481] The news of the siege of the Naitivity Church was shocking for all the Arab world as it had never been anticipated that Israeli soldiers would besiege a church.

This event was a key moment for the recently launched Al Jazeera news channel and two young Palestinian correspondents became famous throughout the region: Shireen Abu Akleh was a Palestinian Christian, originally from Bethlehem but born and raised in Jerusalem. She covered the Israeli siege of Ramallah extensively and had worked with Al Jazeera since the opening of its Palestine bureau in 1997. Jivara al Budeiri was the daughter of a prominent Jerusalem family and a graduate of the Rosary School Sisters. *"Jevara Budeiri, Al Jazeera, from the Church of the Nativity, occupied Bethlehem"*, became a classic sign-off of that period, accompanied by images of smoke from the neighboring Syriac Orthodox Church of the Virgin Mary, which was hit on April 6 and became a symbol of the siege.

Two days into the siege, Israeli forces killed Samir Salman, a bell ringer for the Orthodox section of the church. This was a sign that Israeli forces would not tolerate any movement they could detect even if inside the complex. Yasser Arafat, besieged in the Ramallah presidential compound, was furious at the lack of international action to end the siege of the Nativity Church: *"I am asking you to ask the whole international world. This is a holy sacred place, not only for Christians, but for Christians and for Muslims. How are they keeping silent? About this death, this big criminal. Again, it's a holy sacred place, the Nativity Church (...) It's not important what is happening to me here, look at what happened in the Church... this is a crime! Silence on this is a crime! And all of you journalists that are silent about this are taking part in this crime! Go and show the world this crime! Don't call me!"*[482] said a visibly angry Arafat as he finished a press conference.

Negotiations to end the siege included official attempts led by Bethlehem's governor Salah Tamari, one of Bethlehem's most respected figures. The team included Minister Mitri Abu Aitah. The negotiations were mediated by EU Envoy Miguel Moratinos. At that stage an Armenian monk had been injured by Israeli fire and the bodies of Palestinians killed inside the church were being handed by monks to the ICRC. A second negotiating channel was opened in Jerusalem with the Americans. Mohammad Rashid, at that time an adviser to Yasser Arafat, was the main Palestinian representative. The Archbishop of Canterbury also intervened through his delegate Canon Andrew White, who enjoyed good relations with the Israelis. The tone of the statements from the Vatican and the Franciscans was clearly anger and Patriarch Sabbah stepped up his efforts. Britain's foreign minister Ben Bradshaw referred to the Israeli actions as *"totally unacceptable"*.[483]

The end of the siege came with an agreement that no Palestinians would be arrested but 26 Palestinians were to be sent to Gaza and another thirty were exiled to Europe.[484] The agreement was initially received as a victory for the Palestinians but the price paid by Bethlehem was huge. Yasser Arafat, surrounded by his Bethlehemite adviser Nabil Aburdeneh and his chief of staff Ramzi Khoury from an ancient Christian family in Gaza, understood the meaning of what had happened. Attacks on holy sites did not cease with the end of the siege and Israeli forces blew up the historic shrine of Saint Barbara in Aboud, northern Ramallah, where Palestinian tradition believes Saint Barbara hid from her father until found and killed. The event took place on May 31, 2002, with Israeli authorities claiming the church was destroyed *"by mistake"*.[485] It was yet another blow to what Arafat believed were signs of Palestinian identity and statehood. He asked for pictures of the destroyed shrine to show to visitors, provided funding immediately to rebuild the site, and even *"provided advice on how to rebuild it"* according to the local Orthodox priest.[486]

President Arafat's reaction to the siege was not simply based on the damage caused by Israeli forces to key archeological and historic sites in Bethlehem, but at how Israel had been allowed to attack a place as important as the Nativity Church without any concrete international response other than calls for a ceasefire. For Palestinians in Bethlehem, the Church represented a place of refugee, as was the case in 1967, and the Israeli siege highlighted that now nowhere was safe for them. An UN OCHA Report from 2004 stated that around 10% of the Christian population had left Bethlehem, Beit Jala and Beit Sahour during the Intifada.[487]

The Churches and Israel's Annexation Wall

On the rainy Sunday evening of March 23, 2003, the Saadeh family of Najwa and George, with their daughters Marian and Christine, was traveling on one of Bethlehem's main roads. Suddenly, the car was hit by a rain of 30 bullets from Israeli forces. The youngest daughter, Christine, aged 12 and a student at Saint Joseph School of Bethlehem, was killed and Marian was injured in her leg. Bassem Sabat, a neighbor who came to rescue the family from the car, also came under fire. For Israel, Christine represented "collateral damage". Despite an Israeli investigation, none of the killers served a single day in jail for this case. *"We are very sorry. We didn't mean to hit you,"* an Israeli soldier told Christine's mother.[488] George was the headmaster of the Orthodox School of Beit Sahour.

Only a week earlier, Israeli forces operating a bulldozer had killed Rachel Corrie, a 23-year-old American volunteer, when she tried to stop the demolition of Palestinian homes in Rafah. An Israeli statement expressed "regret" over the incident.[489] An Israeli court decided that the killing of Rachel Corrie was "an accident"[490] and impunity was granted yet again. US officials described the Israeli investigation as "not credible"[491] but no action was taken.

In May 2003 the Quartet (UN, US, EU, and Russia) presented a *"performance-based road map to a permanent two-state solution to the Israeli-Palestinian conflict"*. It included several phases and obligations for Israelis and Palestinians, from the full cessation of Israeli settlement activities, the dismantlement of settlement outposts, the reopening of Palestinian institutions in East Jerusalem, the disarmament of Palestinian groups, and security coordination.[492] While the parties met once again and committed to taking some steps, in reality Israel never implemented its obligations and the situation on the ground remain largely the same. Almost a year earlier, Israel approved the construction of a wall in the occupied West Bank on the grounds that it would prevent Palestinian attacks on its territory. The maps of the wall clearly showed that it was a tool for further annexation of occupied territory, with almost 90% of its construction inside occupied territory rather than on the 1967 border.

The wall particularly affected the areas where most Palestinian Christians resided in the occupied territory as it focused on Jerusalem and its surroundings. The churches immediately began to consider what action could be taken to protect some of the communities directly affected:

- All the northern areas of Bethlehem would be separated from the owners on the eastern side of the wall, effectively separating Bethlehem and Jerusalem for first time in centuries.

- Several Christian institutions, including schools, monasteries and housing complexes built in parts of Beit Hanina and Al Ram, northern Jerusalem, were to be separated from the city.

- The Cremisan and Makhour valleys of Beit Jala, plus all the rest of the western Bethlehem area, were to be de facto annexed.

- The village of Aboud would lose almost 70% of its land on the western of the wall.

Patriarch Sabbah released a document in December 2003, signed by the diocesan Theological Commission, expressing that: *"Legitimate self-defense is corroded by disproportionate and evil means, especially collective punishment or the support of the occupation under the guise of trying to ensure security or freedom."*[493]

Several Christian organizations and churches worldwide mobilized against the wall, including the WCC and the Lutheran World Federation. The very concept of the wall being built for "security reasons" or "self-defense" was challenged by Palestinian officials, with Ambassador Nasser Al Qudwa leading an offensive at the UN that led to the historic International Court of Justice Advisory Opinion of July 2004. In his introductory statement to the Court, Al Qudwa said: *"Suicide bombings have led to the death of 438 Israelis in Israel. Four hundred and ninety Israelis, mostly soldiers and settlers, have also been killed by other kinds of violence. In contrast, since September 2000 and as of 18 February 2004, the Israeli occupying forces have directly killed, including many by extrajudicial execution, a total of 2,770 Palestinian civilians, including children, women and men. Of those killed, more than 1,200 Palestinians have been killed by the Israeli occupying forces in the Gaza Strip, even though Israel has already built another kind of wall surrounding the Gaza Strip. The question that must be asked is: how then will this wall being built by Israel solve the security problem? If anything, its route and the illegal measures entailed in its construction ensure that it will actually exacerbate the security situation. It is more than obvious that when you deprive an entire people of their rights, expropriate their land (...) and property, and wall them into enclaves and ghettos, you are not solving the security problem but creating an untenable situation that will combust."*[494]

The Palestinian argument was accepted by the court, which ruled by 14 votes to one that the construction of the wall was illegal, that Israel was under an obligation to *"terminate its breaches of international law"*, including ceasing the wall construction, and that it should make reparations for the damages. For 13 votes to two the Court expressed that: *"All States are under an obligation not to recognize the illegal situation resulting from the construction of the wall and not to render aid or assistance in maintaining the situation created by such construction; all States parties to the Fourth Geneva Convention relative to the Protection of Civilian Persons in Time of War of 12 August 1949 have in addition the obligation, while respecting the United Nations Charter and international law, to ensure compliance by Israel with international humanitarian law as embodied in that Convention."*[495] This effectively set a framework for international action to protect the rights of the Palestinian people under Israeli occupation. Judge Nabil Al Arabi, a veteran Egyptian diplomat who years later served as Egypt's foreign minister, concluded his separate remarks by stating: *"The Advisory Opinion should herald a new era as the first concrete manifestation of a meaningful administration of justice related to Palestine. It is hoped that it will provide the impetus to steer and direct the long-dormant quest for a just peace."*[496]

Hopes to translate the ICJ opinion into concrete international measures remained unfulfilled and the wall continued to advance. The Palestinian leadership may have wanted Bethlehem to become a symbol of prosperity for the Palestinian state, but it became a symbol of the effects of the wall in thwarting the prospects of self-determination.

With Yasser Arafat still under siege, the prospects of a political solution were diminishing day by day. Many expressions of solidarity took place during those days, with the mobilization of churches worldwide being a pillar for the morale of the Palestinian President. One of the most moving moments was when foreign minister Nabil

Shaath visited the Coptic Cathedral of Saint Mark and was received by Pope Shenouda and thousands of Egyptian faithful. At that moment he communicated with Yasser Arafat via mobile phone, putting the Palestinian leader on speaker to receive the ovation of those present.

The relationship between President Arafat and Pope Shenouda was so close that the Palestinian leader gifted a piece of land to the Coptic Church in Ramallah, a city with less than five Coptic families living in it. Years later, a church was built on that land and it remains a symbol of the friendship between the two leaders. Yasser Arafat's "intimate diplomacy", as defined by his foreign minister Shaath, was full of such symbolisms, with the churches playing a fundamental role. *"Nabil, we're the Holy Land because of the churches and the mosques, not just the mosques. We represent all this tradition,"*[497] he would tell Shaath as he looked over the Old City of Jerusalem from a helicopter on the way from Gaza to Ramallah. This was the closest Abu Ammar could get to the city after returning from exile in 1994.

Ramallah – Amman – Paris – Cairo – Ramallah: End of an Era

Ambassador Laila Chahid was known to be close to Yasser Arafat and had established extensive relationships in Paris, where she was based. That last week of October, she was not in France but in Canada. It was in the office of the Speaker of the Quebec Parliament that she received a phone call from Palestinian PM Ahmad Qurea: *"Laila, the President's situation is very bad, is getting worse, and it is not just a cold. The only person who could convince him to leave for medical treatment is President Chirac. Could you please arrange for a phone call and a plane to take him from Amman to Paris?"* These instructions from Ramallah made Laila realize that she was at a determining moment. The head of the Quebec Parliament left her alone in his office to call Andre Parant, President Chirac's adviser for diplomatic affairs. The answer came within a few hours, with President Chirac personally requesting information on how to equip the plane that would be sent to Amman. *"It's a problem with his blood,"* Ramallah communicated.[498] Doctors from Egypt and Jordan had already arrived to help.

This phone call was the beginning of a marathon as Palestinian officials attempted to seek assurances that Arafat would be allowed to return to Palestine if he left the siege.[499] The journey began on October 29 with dozens of tearful security officers and close aides to the President bidding him farewell as he left via helicopter. With him was his wife Suha, who had been based in Paris during almost all the Intifada, and his chief of staff Ramzi Khoury. After landing in Amman, a French military falcon plane transported the President to Paris, where another helicopter took him to the Percy Army Teaching Hospital, France's top military hospital.

Soon Paris became the center for hundreds of reporters arriving at the French capital from various parts of the world. In the hospital, access was restricted and tensions grew as the mysterious disease affecting Yasser Arafat's blood could not be detected. Inside the hospital, Suha Tawil and Arafat's personal guard were given bedrooms nearby Arafat's room, while Ambassador Laila Chahid and Ramzi Khoury were given rooms in the nurses' area.[500] President Arafat's nephew Nasser Al Qudwa arrived 24 hours later from New York and was also given access to the hospital. During the early hours of November 8 they were informed: *"His situation has worsened and we are transferring him to the emergency room."* Phone calls were made to Ramallah and a plane brought a senior delegation including Ahmad Qurea and Mahmoud Abbas. *"We know what he doesn't have, but we don't know what he does have,"*[501] said one of the doctors to a group of Palestinian leaders. A few days later, on November 11, Yasser Arafat passed away at the age of 75. The cause of death was classified as *"unknown"* in the official certificate issued by the hospital.

In Palestine the news was received with sorrow and images of mourning soon appeared in the international media. Prayers for Yasser Arafat's soul were offered in mosques and churches all over the country, with his Christian friends Patriarch Sabbah, Bishop Abu El-Assal, Bishop Younan, and Archimendrite Hanna offering special prayers in their respective churches. In Beit Jala, at the Latin Patriarchate Seminary, an elderly, weak and retired Fr. Ibrahim Ayyad was following the news. Nobody saw him crying but he was deeply affected. Only a couple of years earlier, he had been seen encouraging the Palestinian fighters in the streets Bethlehem. Maybe he still saw himself as an envoy for Yasser Arafat. Maybe he recalled the siege of Beirut or that day in late 1964 when Arafat appeared in his Beirut Church to ask for his blessing to launch the armed struggle for the liberation of Palestine. That cold Palestinian winter, the Palestinian leader would return to the land and Fr. Ayyad wanted to take part in the funeral.

Statements were issued by the various factions and national leaders, including an emotional farewell from Arafat's political rival George Habash. The last wish of the Palestinian President was to be buried in Al Aqsa Mosque compound but this was denied by the Israeli authorities. A burial in Gaza close to his mother was also discussed, but eventually it was decided that Arafat would be buried in the closest point to Jerusalem, at the place where Israeli tanks had besieged him for the last years of his life: the Muqataa in Ramallah.

Arafat left France with the honors due to a head of state and preparations were made for two funerals. The first funeral was in

Cairo where leaders from all over the world gathered to say goodbye to a leader that some of them had even fought, yet they all respected. Delegates from the Arab world mixed with European envoys in Egypt, the country where Yasser Arafat studied engineering, formed the General Union of Palestinian Students, received military training and support from President Gamal Abdel Nasser for the revolution that would turn the Palestinian issue from being a "humanitarian concern" to a national liberation movement. Yasser Arafat's final destination was not Jerusalem, as he once stated confidently when leaving Beirut after 88 days of siege, but his funeral with all honors of a head of state proved that despite the efforts of the Israeli government, and particularly it's prime minister Ariel Sharon, Yasser Arafat's legacy remained intact with international recognition of the inalienable rights of the Palestinian people.

After the state funeral in Cairo, the final destination was Ramallah. Two military helicopters landed with difficulty due to the thousands of people who had taken over the streets of Ramallah to bid farewell to their leader. Arafat finally returned to the people to whom he had offered hope, people who in many cases disagreed with his tactics and positions, yet who overwhelmingly stood by him, especially after Camp David and the siege. He returned as one of them or as Mahmoud Darwish wrote: *"There is something of him in every one of us. He was the father and the son: the father of an entire phase of the history of the Palestinian people, and the son whose rhetoric and image they helped foster."*[502]

Diplomats and senior officials mixed with students and workers to bid farewell to the Palestinian leader. The Mufti of Jerusalem, the heads of churches, and there, somewhere around, was Fr. Ibrahim Ayyad. He had refused to listen to the warnings of the priests around him about the cold weather and the Ramallah winds. He wanted to be present to bury his comrade, the man who made him go around the world and organize an audience with the Pope to highlight the cause of his people.

Yasser Arafat was buried among his people with soil brought from Jerusalem. Later, a mausoleum was built and the tomb decorated with an olive tree. To signify that this was a temporary location, the tomb was surrounded by water, symbolizing a state of constant change, and a laser over a minaret points 12 kilometers away to the Old City of Jerusalem. Fr. Ayyad was there when Yasser Arafat was buried, but he was not strong enough to withstand the weather and returned to the seminary with a cold from which he did not recover. He passed away two months later, on January 8 and was buried in his hometown of Beit Sahour. This certainly marked the end of an era.

Conclusion

Just before 7:00 am on Wednesday 11 May 2022, breaking news from Jenin paralyzed Palestine: Shireen Abu Akleh, senior Al Jazeera correspondent in Palestine, had been assassinated as she was covering an Israeli raid. Israeli government officials changed their version of what had happened at least four times in less than 24 hours in a clear attempt to disseminate misinformation. For all the eyewitnesses, there was no doubt: Shireen had been killed by an Israeli bullet.

The images of priests praying around Shireen's body was the first indication for many that she was Christian. Shock about her assassination extended beyond the borders of historic Palestine and included countless demonstrations of mourning and solidarity throughout the Arab and Muslim world. She was bid farewell by thousands who managed to reach the Old City of Jerusalem despite all the obstacles imposed by the Israeli occupation, including the use of violence against mourners for raising the Palestinian flag. Israeli forces raided a Catholic hospital in occupied Jerusalem, broke the windows of the car that carried her coffin, and randomly attacked people. Their goal that Friday afternoon appeared to be to prevent the honors that the Palestinian people wished to bestow on one of their heroes, but the Israeli actions were unsuccessful. Thousands of people raised the flag of Palestine at Jaffa Gate during her funeral. One member of the crowd said, *"When the Israeli soldier shot her, he didn't ask whether she was Muslim or Christian. She was killed because she was Palestinian."*

Shireen's funeral demonstrated that Palestinian Christians as an integral part of Palestinian society is not a mere slogan but a reality.

Shireen was assassinated in a refugee camp, was honored in many towns and villages, and crossed Israeli checkpoints. She was laid to rest near to her parents in the Mount Zion Orthodox Cemetery where Palestinians from all over historic Palestine gathered to pray and mourn together.

It would be difficult to argue that the situation of the Jerusalem churches is the same today as it was during the Second Intifada. In 2005 a scandal over the alleged sale of church property to Israeli settlers at Jerusalem Old City's Jaffa Gate ended with Greek Orthodox Patriarch Irineos being deposed and replaced by Patriarch Theophilos. There have been other changes. The end of Patriarch Michael Sabbah's mandate in the Latin Patriarchate in 2008 marked a point of inflection that significantly weakened the role played previously by the heads of churches in Jerusalem in defending the rights of their congregations. Whether it be Christian Zionism, racist Israeli legislation or violations of rights in general, the lack of a strong Palestinian Christian voice has been clearly felt.

The role that Palestinians Christians have played historically continues to an extent that goes way beyond their numbers and includes through their institutions. It would be impossible to understand Palestinian nationalism without understanding the role played by Christians since the 19th century, and how intra-Christian issues such as the case of the Arab Orthodox in the Greek Orthodox Patriarchate have helped to shape events.

In this book I have also concluded a journey through my national identity. I felt compelled to put on paper the information I had been told about anonymous individuals and forgotten organizations that contributed to the Palestinian national liberation movement. I wanted to put these efforts into context to understand the historical perspective of Palestinian diplomacy.

My first inspiration was drawn from the library of the Latin Patriarchate Seminary of Beit Jala where Na'im Khader used to smuggle himself into the "forbidden" Marxist books section before he decided to become a diplomat instead of a priest. It concluded in the small Episcopal community of Birzeit with its beautiful stone church where Kamal Nasser used to play the organ occasionally before being exiled. Both men ended up giving their lives for Palestine.

In 1990 during the First Intifada, Patriarch Sabbah wrote words that could summarize the stories presented in this book: *"(Muslims) are our fellow compatriots. We share the same future, the same country, and the same heritage (...) My brothers and sisters, you yourselves must maintain this solidarity and this unity. You must love one another. Together we must share our suffering and our hope. Whatever we have at this time must be shared, be it much or little."*[503]

Endorsements

A gripping account of the Christian-Palestinian community completed with great documentary rigor, and an excellent historiographical piece on the development of Palestinian history from the Balfour Declaration to the present day. This book gives us the opportunity to discover thousands of anonymous protagonists who contributed to building the identity of the Palestinian people and helped defend their ideals as an independent nation. The book will undoubtedly enter the annals of the history of the Palestinian people.
Miguel Moratinos, former EU Special Representative for the Middle East Peace Process and Foreign Minister of Spain

This instructive, wide-ranging diplomatic history of Palestinian Christians, the product of years of research and extensive interviews conducted by a dedicated and well-informed member of that community, Xavier Abu Eid, highlights the important yet understudied role of the Christian community in the Palestinian national movement, explaining its organization, leadership, and internal divisions, and describing the tragic losses it has suffered during the past century in the Holy Land.
Nathan Thrall, author of The Only Language They Understand

This is not only an exceptional historical account and an outstanding scholarly publication of an under-researched topic. It is also a book that reflects Xavier Abu Eid's passion, dedication, and commitment to the struggle for national liberation, inspired by the history he discusses in this research. This is an informative, insightful, important, rich, and gripping research that is eloquently and articulately presented for readers to enjoy, learn from, engage with, and to inspire the process of national identity formation.

Dr. Alaa Tartir, Senior Researcher, The Graduate Institute of International and Development Studies, Geneva, Switzerland & Policy Advisor to Al-Shabaka: The Palestinian Policy Network

Xavier Abu Eid, born Chilean and baptized as Palestinian, has created a valuable book that fills the void about the role of Palestinian Christians in national liberation. Abu Eid dives deep into narrating the details with vibrant and analytical depth. He shares untold anecdotes and brilliantly introduces the reader to the historical Christian weight on individual and collective levels in the Middle East. The Palestinian library is now enriched with an authentic book that guides you through history to understand the role of Christian Palestinians not only in Palestine but also in regional politics. The book places Christians in their proper context and reminds the world of the inevitable mandate of the Church in ensuring peace and justice. The PLO and the Vatican must be gratified by this credible book that documents the Christian community struggle in Palestine.

Dr. Dalal Iriqat, Vice President for International Relations, Arab American University AAUP, Assistant Professor, Faculty of Graduate Studies, Arab American University Palestine AAUP, and columnist at AlQuds newspaper

Xavier Abu Eid offers a unique view into the essential role played by generations of Palestinian Christians in the national movement to liberate Palestine, and the resistance to attempts to push all Palestinians out of the Holy Land. This role ranges from diplomacy to armed struggle, challenging the predominant narrative that the Israeli-Palestinian conflict is a religious one between Muslims and Jews. The book reasserts the position of Palestinian Christians first and foremost as Palestinians and not just as a religious minority - a point disseminated by the Western narrative, including some church leaders who do not identify with the struggle of their parishioners. In this context, Abu Eid paints a picture of Palestinian Christians as active and leading members of the resistance infrastructure and not one of a helpless people. Abu Eid offers anecdotes from his experience in Palestine and Chile that help elucidate the evolution of the struggle for national liberation - both at home and in the Diaspora - from a Palestinian Christian prism. He sheds light on the key role played by Christian clergy, academics, writers and educators in the Palestinian national movement, and the struggle to Arabize some of the Western-led churches that do not always represent their communities in good faith and, among other things, have sold or leased church property to Zionist organizations. A must-read for policy-makers, academics and journalists as the Middle East continues to hemorrhage Christians, the indigenous population, once a prominent presence in the political, academic, cultural and resistance realms.
Dalia Hatouqa, journalist

Breaking with an international narrative where the Christian community's belonging to the national movement is too often erased, this rich thoroughly-researched book is a critical addition to Palestinian scholarship on the Palestinian political movement, and on the integral role of Palestinian Christian leaders and the churches in its development, successes, failures, and hopes in the 20st century.
Ines Abdel Razek, Advocacy Director, the Palestine Institute for Public Diplomacy

Endnotes

1. With over 800 years of presence in Palestine, the Franciscans were in charge of the holy sites for the Roman Catholics. In 1847 Pope Pius IX re-established the Latin Patriarchate of Jerusalem to work with the local communities.

2. The various churches included Greek Orthodox, Armenian Orthodox, Roman Catholic (Custodia and Latin Patriarchate), Greek Catholic, Armenian Catholic, Coptic, Maronite, Lutheran, Episcopal (Anglican), Syrian Orthodox, Syrian Catholic, and Ethiopian Orthodox.

3. Interview with Patriarch Emeritus Michael Sabbah, Taybeh, Palestine, April 3, 2017.

4. Morris, Benny (1999). *Righteous Victims*, p.83. Vintage Books: New York.

5. Sizer, Stephen. *The Road to Balfour: The History of Christian Zionism.* Available at http://www.balfourproject.org/the-road-to-balfour-the-history-of-christian-zionism-by-stephen-sizer/ last accessed on November 22, 2018.

6. Chomsky, Noam (1999). *Fateful Triangle: The United States, Israel & the Palestinians,* p.90. Pluto Press: London.

7. Sayegh, Selim (1971). *Le Statu Quo Des Lieux-Saints: Nature Juridique et Portee Internationale,* p.7. Libreria Della Pontificia Universita' Lateranense. Roma.

8. Farge, Elodie (2012). *The Vatican & Jerusalem*. PASSIA: Jerusalem.

9. Eordegian, Marlen. "British and Israeli Maintenance of the Status Quo in the Holy Places of Christendom" in *International Journal of Middle East Studies,* Vol. 35, No. 2 (May, 2003), p.308.

10. Odeh Issa, Anton (1977). *Les Minorites Chretiennes de Palestine: A Travers Les Siecles*, p.304. Franciscan Printing Press: Jerusalem.

11. Cardinal Acton Report in Kildani, Hanna (2010). *Modern Christianity in the Holy Land*, p.260. Authorhouse: Indiana.

12. Duvignau, Pierre (1979). *Una Vie Au Service De L'Eglise*: S. B. Mgr. Joseph Valerga. Latin Patriarchate: Jerusalem.

13. Ibid. p.310.

14. Library of the Latin Patriarchate Seminary, November 2018.

15.   Haiduc-Dale (2015), p.31.

16.   Various anonymous interviews in Ramallah, Beit Jala and Taybeh (Palestine) during 2017-2018.

17.   Archive of the Latin Patriarchate Seminary.

18.   Interview with Fr. Peter Madros, February 18, 2017. Ramallah, Palestine.

19.   Robson, Laura. "Communalism and Nationalism in the Mandate: The Greek Orthodox Controversy and the National Movement" in *Journal of Palestine Studies,* Vol. 41, No. 1 (Autumn 2011), p.9.

20.   Katz, Itamar & Ruth Kark. "The Greek Orthodox Patriarchate of Jerusalem and its Congregation: Dissent over Real Estate" in *International Journal of Middle East Studies,* Vol. 37, No. 4 (November 2005), p.519.

21.   Quoted in Palestine Mandate Debate, HL Deb 21 June 1922, Vol 50 cc994-1033 available at https://api.parliament.uk/historic-hansard/lords/1922/jun/21/palestine-mandate last accessed on May 3, 2020.

22.   Haiduc-Dale (2015), p.30.

23.   Tamari, Salim (2017). *The Great War and the Remaking of Palestine*, p.95. University of California Press: California.

24.   Tamari, Salim. "Issa al Issa's Unorthodoxy: Banned in Jerusalem, Permitted in Jaffa", in *Jerusalem Quarterly* Issue 59 (Summer 2014) p.29.

25.   Ibid, p.106.

26.   Ibid, p.97.

27.   Haiduc-Dale, p.38.

28.   Musallam, Adnan (2002) Development in Politics, Society, Press And Thought in Bethlehem In the British Era 1917 – 1948. Bethlehem: Wiam. p 22.

29.   Noha Tadros Khalaf. "Falastin versus the British Mandate and Zionism (1921-1931): Between a Rock and a Hard Place" in *Jerusalem Quarterly* Spring 2011 (45), p.12.

30.   Kimmerling. B & Migdal J (2003). *The Palestinian People,* p.86. Harvard University Press: Massachusetts.

31.   Klein, Menachem (2014). *Lives in Common: Arabs and Jews in Jerusalem, Jaffa and Hebron,* p.105. Hurst & Company: London.

32.   Ingrams, Doreen (1972). *Palestine Papers: 1917-1922 Seeds of Conflict,* p.34. Eland: London.

33.   Ibid, p.29.

34.   The quote that appeared in *Al Karmel* is available in Ayyad, Abdelazziz (1999). *Arab Nationalism and the Palestinians 1850-1939,* p.51. Passia: Jerusalem.

35.   Ibid, p.47.

36.   Farge, Elodie (2012). *The Vatican and Jerusalem*, p.9. Passia: Jerusalem.

37.   Ferrari, S. "The Vatican, the Palestine Question and the Internationalization of Jerusalem 1918-1948" in *Rivista di Studi Politici Internazionali* Vol 60, No 4 (240) (October-December 1993), p.554.

38.   There is also a smaller community of Armenian Catholics with their patriarchate located at the Third Station of the Via Dolorosa in the Muslim Quarter. Their presence in the city dates back to the 19th century.

39.   Der Matossian, Bedross. "The Armenians of Palestine: 1918- 48" in *Journal of Palestine Studies,* Vol. 41, No. 1 (Autinmn 2011), p.30. The author adds: "Britain conducted two censuses during the period, in 1922 and 1931. Both gave results by district and religious grouping, with the total number of Armenians (Gregorian and Catholic) in all Palestine put at 3,210 in 1922 and 3,524 in 1931. These figures cannot be verified."

40.   Ibid. p.31.

41.   During the 1948 Nakba, Armenians lost vast tracts of land and property in what became known as West Jerusalem, including a religious community and houses in Qatamon, Talbiya, Musrara, Mamilla, Baqaa, Greek Colony, Germany Colony, and Talpiyot.

42.   Goldman, Shalom. "The Rev. Herbert Danby (1889-1953): Hebrew Scholar, Zionist, Christian Missionary", in *Modern Judaism,* Vol. 27, No. 2 (May, 2007), p.219.

43.   Quoted in the Palestine Mandate Debate, HL Deb 21 June 1922, vol 50, cc994-1033 available at https://api.parliament.uk/historic-hansard/ lords/1922/jun/21/palestine-mandate last accessed on May 3, 2020.

44.   Ibid.

45.   Haiduc-Dale, p.185.

46.   Said, Edward (2000). *Out of Place: A Memoir,* p.6. Vintage Books: New York.

47.   There are several references to members of the Palestinian Orthodox elite having to seek Arab Orthodox education in Lebanon (dependent of the Arabized Patriarchate of Anthiokia).

48. Aghabekian, Varsen (2021). *A Palestinian Armenian: The Intertwine between the Social and the Political*. Diyar: Bethlehem.

49. Du College Saint Jean Baptiste De la Salle. *Souvenir du Cinquantenaire: 1878-1928*. Franciscan Press: Jerusalem.

50. Sir Marie Alphonsie Ghattas was canonized by the Holy See in 2015.

51. Khalidi, Rashid (2007). *The Iron Cage: The Story of the Palestinian Struggle for Statehood*, p.24. Beacon Press: Boston.

52. Kildani, Hanna (2010), p.582.

53. Unpublished memoirs of Ibrahim Mattar, a Lutheran pastor, under the title *Ibrahim Mattar 1905-1988*.

54. Haiduc-Dale (2015), p.61.

55. Ibid, p.133.

56. This had been confirmed by Fr. Ibrahim Ayyad to the Arab Higher Committee in an official correspondence from the Latin Patriarchate, February 12, 1947. (Archive of the Latin Patriarchate).

57. Interview with Patriarch Emeritus Michael Sabbah, November 16, 2018. Ramallah (via phone).

58. Khalidi, Rashid (2007), p.100.

59. Kildani, Hanna (2010), p.176.

60. Ibid, p.194.

61. Robson, Laura. "Communalism and Nationalism in the Mandate: The Greek Orthodox Controversy and the National Movement", in *Journal of Palestine Studies,* Vol. 41, No. 1 (Autumn 2011), p.12

62. Haiduc-Dale (2015), p.111.

63. Ibid, p.113.

64. Kayyali, Abdel Wahhab (2014). *Palestina: Una Historia Moderna*, p.218. Bosforo Libros: Madrid.

65. Robson, Laura (2011), p.13.

66. Interview with William Shaer, Beit Jala. 10 November 2021.

67. Fleishmann, Ellen "The Emergence of the Palestinian Women's Movement, 1929-39" available at The Emergence of the Palestinian Women›s Movement, 1929-39 | The Institute for Palestine Studies (palestine-studies.org) last accessed on 14 February 2022.

68. Ibid.

69. Ricks, Thomas (2009). *Turbulent Times in Palestine: The Diaries of Khalil Totah 1886-1955*, p.244. Institute of Palestine Studies: Ramallah.

70. Budeiri, Musa (2010). *The Palestine Communist Party 1919-1948*. Haymarket Books: Chicago.

71. Several interviews conducted in Ramallah, Beit Jala, and Bethlehem between December 2017 and November 2018.

72. Haiduc-Dale (2015), p.140.

73. Ibid, p.28.

74. Khalidi, R (2007), p.130.

75. Husseini, Serene (2000). *Jerusalem Memories*, p.180. Naufal: Beirut.

76. Segev, Tom (2000). *One Palestine, Complete: Jews and Arabs under the British Mandate*, p.440. Holt Paperbacks: New York.

77. Ricks, Thomas (2009). *Turbulent Times in Palestine: The Diaries of Khalil Totah 1886-1955*, p.262.

78. Khalidi (2006), p.125.

79. Sayigh, Rosemary (2007). *The Palestinians: From Peasants to Revolutionaries*, p.60. Zed Books: New York.

80. Farge, Elodie (2012), p.15.

81. Hadawi, Sami (1991). *Bitter Harvest: A Modern History of Palestine*, p.66. Olive Branch Press: New York.

82. The British promise of Palestine to the Zionist movement of November 2, 1917. Full text of the Balfour Declaration is available at https://www.independent.co.uk/news/uk/politics/balfour-declaration-read-full-text-israel-jewish-homeland-palestine-arthur-james-balfour-lord-a8033556.html last accessed on June 17, 2019.

83. Safty, Adel (2012). *Might over Right: How the Zionists took over Palestine*, p.167. Garnet: Reading.

84. Available at Press Release (NIGHT) SUMMARY of 24 November 1947, Press Release GA/PAL/85 of 24 November 1947 (un.org) last accessed on November 26, 2021.

85. UNGA Hundred and Twenty-Fourth Plenary Meeting, November 26 of 1947, available at https://unispal.un.org/DPA/DPR/unispal.nsf/0/1BCE87E6077A1A0685256CE70075D5BE last acccessed on June 9, 2019.

86.   Kattan, Victor (2009). *From Coexistence to Conquest: International Law and the Origins of the Arab-Israeli Conflict 1891-1949,* p.146. Pluto Press: New York.

87.   UN "The Origins and Evolution of the Question of Palestine: Part II (1947-1977) available at https://www.un.org/unispal/history/origins-and-evolution-of-the-palestine-problem/part-ii-1947-1977/#United_States last accessed on June 10, 2019.

88.   Pappe, Ilan (2006). *The Ethnic Cleansing of Palestine,* p.30. One World: Oxford.

89.   Farge, Elodie (2012). *The Vatican & Jerusalem,* p.16. Jerusalem: Passia.

90.   Greatly influenced by the Soviet Union and its support for partition, the Stalinist Palestinian party agreed to support the partition. Many Christians were part of this party.

91.   Pappe (2006), p.34.

92.   Morris, Benny (2001). *Righteous Victims,* p.184. Vintage Books: New York.

93.   Stevens, Richard. "The Vatican, the Catholic Church and Jerusalem" in *Journal of Palestine Studies,* Vol. 10, No. 3 (Spring 1981), p. 106.

94.   Haiduc-Dale (2015), p.185.

95.   Medebielle, Pierre (1963). *Le Diocese Patriarcal Latin de Jerusalem,* p.54. Latin Patriarchate of Jerusalem: Jerusalem.

96.   Interview with Fr. Peter Madros, February 18, 2017, Ramallah, Palestine.

97.   Order of the Knights of the Holy Sepulcher. *La Palestine,* February 1935.

98.   Interview with Fr. Julious Abdallah, February 5, 2017, Ramallah, Palestine.

99.   Odeh Issa, Anton (1977). *Les Minorites Chretiennes de Palestine: A Travers Les Siecles,* p.310. Franciscan Printing Press: Jerusalem.

100. Roberts, Nicholas. "Dividing Jerusalem: British Urban Planning in the Holy City", in *Journal of Palestine Studies,* Vol. 42, No. 4 (Summer 2013), p.7.

101. Tleel, John (2000). *I am Jerusalem,* p.31. Own publication: Jerusalem.

102. A plan of several military operations to take over strategic areas..

103. Khalidi, Walid (2010). *Before their Diaspora,* p.310. Washington: Institute of Palestine Studies.

104. Pappe (2006), p.39.

105. "The Fall of Jaffa" in *Journal of Palestine Studies,* Volume XXVII, Number 3, Spring 1998, p.105.

106. The Episcopal Church was reopened in 2022 to serve foreigners living in the Tel Aviv area.

107. Safti, Adel (2012). *Might over Right: How the Zionists Took Over Palestine.* Garnet Publishing: Reading.

108. Pappe (2006), p.90.

109. Begin, Menahem (2007). *The Revolt: Story of the Irgun*, p.163. Steimatzky House: Tel Aviv.

110. Chomsky, Noam (1999), p.96.

111. Begin (2007), p.165.

112. Hadawi (1991), p.88.

113. Mattar, Ibrahim (2018). *Jewish Migrant Forces Conquest*. The Commercial Press: Jerusalem. Introduction.

114. Kardahji, Nick. *The Palestine Police and the End of the British Mandate*, 2007. MPhil Thesis, p.75, Modern Middle East Studies, Oxford University. Available at Microsoft Word - Kardahji thesis.doc (ox.ac.uk) .

115. Jewish Telegraphic Agency, March 12, 1948 available at Jewish Agency Headquarters Wrecked by Explosion; 10 Reported Killed, 90 Wounded - Jewish Telegraphic Agency (jta.org) last accessed on January 22, 2021.

116. Saint Joseph School for Girls (2004). *Your stories are my stories,* p.111. SJS and WI'am. Bethlehem.

117. Interview with George Hinitilian, 3 June 2022.

118. Der Metossian, Bedros. "The Armenians of Palestine: 1918- 48" in *Journal of Palestine Studies,* Vol. 41, No 1 (Autumn 2011), p.39.

119. Ibid.

120. Begin (2007), p.165.

121. The most renowned such event took place in the village of Tantoura on May 22, 1948, in the area of Haifa following the fall of the city. A description of the context can be found in Pappe, Ilan (2007), p.133.

122. Interview with Rev. Naim Ateek, April 5, 2019. The number of 1200 Palestinian Anglicans in Haifa in 1948 is equivalent to the total number of Palestinian Anglicans in Jerusalem, Ramallah, Nablus and Zababdeh, the communities within the occupied West Bank under the Anglican Church in 2019.

123. Khalidi, Walid. "The Fall of Haifa Revisited" in *Journal of Palestine Studies,* Volume XXXVII, Number 3, Spring 2008, p.51.

124. Ibid, p.52.

125. Interview with Fr. Abdallah Julious.

126. Interview with Latin Patriarchate priest, Beit Jala.

127. Morris, Benny (2004). *The Birth of the Palestinian Refugee Problem Revisited.* Cambridge University Press.

128. Morris (2012), p.227.

129. Stevens, Richard (1981), p.106.

130. Available in https://www.akevot.org.il/en/article/intelligence-brief-from-1948-hidden-for-decades-indicates-jewish-fighters-actions-were-the-major-cause-of-arab-displacement-not-calls-from-arab-leadership/ last accessed on July 21, 2019.

131. Safty (2012), p.204.

132. Pappe (2006), p.40.

133. Khalidi, Walid (2012). *All That Remains: The Palestinian Villages Occupied and Depopulated by Israel in 1948,* p.273. Institute of Palestine Studies: Washington DC.

134. Interview with Nader Abuamsha, 19 February 2022.

135. Pappe (2006), p.142.

136. Ibid, p.9.

137. Interview with Professor Johnny Mansour, February 22, 2020.

138. UNGA Resolution 186 available at https://unispal.un.org/DPA/DPR/unispal.nsf/0/A9A8DA193BD46C54852560E50060C6FD last accessed on May 26, 2019.

139. FBA "History of Folke Bernadotte" available at https://fba.se/en/about-fba/history-of-folke-bernadotte/ last accessed on June 17, 2019.

140. Hadawi (1991), p.125.

141. Shlaim, Avi (2014). *The Iron Wall* p.39. Penguin Books: London.

142. UNGA Resolution 194 available at https://documents-dds-ny.un.org/doc/RESOLUTION/GEN/NR0/043/65/IMG/NR004365.pdf?OpenElement last accessed on June 11, 2019.

143. Quigley, John (2016). *The International Diplomacy of Israel's Founders,* p.109. Cambridge University Press.

144. UNGA Resolution 273 available at https://documents-dds-ny.un.org/doc/RESOLUTION/GEN/NR0/044/44/IMG/NR004444.pdf?OpenElement last accessed on June 11, 2019.

145 Morris (2004) p 429

146. Munayyer, Spiro. "The fall of Lydda" in *Journal of Palestine Studies,* Vol. 27, No. 4 (Summer, 1998), p.96.

147. Ibid.

148. Habash, George & Mahmoud Soueid. "Taking Stock. An Interview with George Habash" in *Journal of Palestine Studies,* Vol. 28, No.1 (Autumn, 1998), p.88.

149. Sayigh (2007), p.84.

150. Interview with Maher Barrouk, Ramallah, Palestine. July 24, 2019.

151. Morris (2004), p.418.

152. Khalidi (2012), p.349.

153. Masalha, Nur (2007). *The Bible and Zionism*, p.66. Zed Books: New York.

154. Pappe, Illan (20015) The Making of the Arab – Israeli Conflict 1947 – 1951. Taurus: London, p.97.

155. Interview with Bishop Atallah Hanna, August 2017, Birzeit, Palestine.

156. Medebielle, Pierre (1963). *Le Diocese Patriarcal de Jerusalem*, p.55. Jerusalem: Latin Patriarchate.

157. Mission Pontificale Pour La Palestine, (1950). *Le Pope et la Tragedie Palestinienne*, p.5. Published in Beirut, Lebanon.

158. Translation from French. Issa, Anton Odeh (1977). *Les Minorites Chretiennes de Palestine: A Travers Les Siecles*, p.311. Franciscan Printing Press: Jerusalem.

159. Stevens, Richard (1981), p.107.

160. UN General Assembly Resolution 303 "Palestine: The Question of an International Regime for the Jerusalem Area and the Protection of Holy Places" available at https://unispal.un.org/DPA/DPR/unispal.nsf/0/2669D6828A262EDB852560E50069738A last accessed on July 27, 2019.

161. One of her famous quotes of "there is no such a thing as a Palestinian people" was said to the *Sunday Times* in June 15, 1969. Her quote was also used by *The New York Times* in an interview with Golda Meir published on August

27, 1972. The interview is online in https://www.nytimes.com/1972/08/27/archives/a-talk-with-golda-meir.html last accessed on 28 July, 2019.

162. Beit Jala Parish Booklet, Latin Patriarchate.

163. Pontifical Mission Booklet, 1951.

164. Other bilateral armistice agreements had been signed in Rhodes between Israel and Egypt (February 24, 1949) and Israel and Lebanon (March 23, 1949). Jordan, then Syria signed the armistice agreement (July 20, 1949).

165. Aghabeakian (2021).

166. Morris, Benny (2004). *The Birth of the Palestinian Refugee Problem Revisited,* p.321. Cambridge University Press.

167. The Vatican "Redemptoris Nostri Cruciatus" available at http://www.vatican.va/content/pius-xii/en/encyclicals/documents/hf_p-xii_enc_15041949_redemptoris-nostri-cruciatus.html last accessed on March 20, 2020.

168. Quigley (2016), p.104.

169. Hagar Shezaf (Haaretz). *Burying the Nakba: How Israel Systematically Hides Evidence of 1948 Expulsion of Arabs*, July 5, 2019. https://www.haaretz.com/israel-news/.premium.MAGAZINE-how-israel-systematically-hides-evidence-of-1948-expulsion-of-arabs-1.7435103 last accessed on August 20, 2020.

170. Masalha, Nur (2003). *The Politics of Denial: Israel and the Palestinian Refugee Problem*, p.133. Pluto Press: London.

171. The full translation of the law can be found on the Adalah website available at https://www.adalah.org/uploads/oldfiles/Public/files/Discriminatory-Laws-Database/English/04-Absentees-Property-Law-1950.pdf last accessed on December 29, 2019.

172. Salibi, Kamal (2010). *The Modern History of Jordan*, p.165. I.B. Tauris: New York.

173. Shlaim (2007), p.33.

174. Shlaim, Avi (2007) Lion of Jordan: The Life of King Hussein in War and Peace". Pinguin Books. London: p 25.

175. Interview with Patriarch Michael Sabbah.

176. Church circles talk about a "compromise". There was no access to a written agreement.

177. Interview with an anonymous priest at the Latin Patriarchate Seminary of Beit Jala, 2018.

178. Shlaim (2007), p.49.

179. Interview with Archimendrite Atallah Hanna.

180. De Vialar, Emilie (1986). *Souvenirs and Documents*, p.313. Printifine Limited: Liverpool.

181. The church was built in 1880.

182. Interview with Fr. Manuel Musallam.

183. Kyle, Keith (2011). *Suez*, p.399. Ibtauris: London.

184. Hadawi (1991), p.150.

185. Ibid, p.152.

186. Chacour, Elias (1984). *Blood Brothers*, p.81. Chosen Books: New York.

187. Pappe (2006), p.187.

188. *Benny Morris (1997). Israel›s Border Wars, 1949-1956: Arab Infiltration, Israeli Retaliation, and the Countdown to the Suez War, p.432. Clarendon Press.*

189. Morris (2004).

190. Hadawi (1991), p.155.

191. The first visit to the cemetery was allowed in 2019 after an Israeli court ruling permitted it. More information in https://www.adalah.org/en/content/view/9750 last accessed in April 29, 2020.

192. De Vialar, Emilie (1986) Souvenirs and Documents, p.255. English edition published in 1986 by Printfine: Liverpool.

193. P.J. Vatikiotis (1994). "The Greek Orthodox Patriarchate of Jerusalem: Between Hellenism and Arabism" in *Middle Eastern Studies*, 30:4, 916.

194. New York Times, *Archbishop Gori of Jerusalem Is Dead*, November 26, 1970. Available at https://www.nytimes.com/1970/11/26/archives/archbishop-gori-of-jerusalem-is-dead.html last accessed on March 18, 2020.

195 Stocket, James. "The United States and the Struggle in the Armenian Patriarchate of Jerusalem, 1955-1960" in *Jerusalem Quarterly* Issue 71, Autumn 2017, p.19-29.

196. Ibid.

197. Interview with a relative of Archbishop Abu Saada, Ramallah, March 20, 2020.

198. The Church was reopened in 2011.

199.   Interview with Rev. Mitri Raheb, Ramallah, March 20, 2020.

200.   Until 1947 the Lutheran Church in Palestine was dependent on the Lutheran Church in Germany.

201.   Interview with Henry Khoury, March 1, 2020, Ramallah.

202.   Interview with Joe Mogannam, Ramallah, May 2019.

203.   Bandak served as a Jordanian diplomat, including as ambassador to Spain and to Chile. After 1967, Israel prevented him from returning to Bethlehem and he died in exile in 1984.

204.   From research by George Lama. Interview conducted in Ramallah in March 26, 2020.

205.   BBC News (March 21, 2000) "Flashback: 1964 Papal Visit" available at http://news.bbc.co.uk/2/hi/middle_east/685046.stm last accessed on June 14, 2020.

206.   Bethlehem University "Mission and History" available at https://www.bethlehem.edu/BBNC/www.bethlehem.edu/about/mission-history.html last accessed on June 14, 2020.

207.   In 1976 Dr. Sayegh, working as representative of Kuwait, was instrumental in efforts to pass Resolution 3379 referring to Zionism as a "Form of Racism and Racial Discrimination".

208.   His speech is available at https://ahmad-alshukairy.org/speeches/?lang=en last accessed on April 29, 2020.

209.   As it was an Arab/Jewish party, those who remained in the State of Israel retained the party as an Israeli/non-Zionist party. The merger with the Jordanian party took place by those factions in the West Bank and Gaza.

210.   Fouad Nassar became the first member of the Communist Party to become a member of the PNC. This happened only in 1973.

211.   The anecdote was repeated by Yasser Arafat at the Fifth Fatah Congress (Tunisia, August 1987) in the presence of Fr. Ibrahim Ayyad. The incident was recalled by Ambassador Husni Abdel Wahed, interviewed in July 2021.

212.   Anonymous interview in Ramallah, April 2020.

213.   English translation produced by the Egyptian branch of Fatah, available at http://fatehnews.org/ar/wp-content/uploads/2020/01/Fatah-Eg.pdf last accessed in July 2021.

214.   Interview with Patriarch Sabbah.

215.	Abdullah Schleifer "The Fall of Jerusalem, 1967" available at https://www.paljourneys.org/sites/default/files/The_Fall_of_Jerusalem_1967-S._Abdallah_Schleifer.pdf last accessed on 8 February 2022.

216.	Interview with Henry Khoury.

217.	Interview with Dr. Victor Batarseh, June 11, 2020, Bethlehem.

218.	Interview with Dr. Victor Batarseh, Bethlehem, June 11, 2020.

219.	PASSIA Documents on Jerusalem http://passia.org/media/filer_public/e7/d1/e7d1d05e-6c27-43f3-9ea4-384ad43c7746/vol-1-documents-on-jerusalem.pdf P 45. Last checked on July 5, 2020.

220.	Inteview with Victor Batarseh.

221.	Interview with Nakhleh Abu Eid.

222.	Quigley (2016), p.201.

223.	UN Security Council Resolution 242 (November 22, 1967) available at https://unispal.un.org/unispal.nsf/0/7D35E1F729DF491C85256EE700686136 last accessed on August 7, 2020.

224.	Israeli Ministry of Foreign Affairs, "Settlement in the Administered Territories" (18 September 1967) available at https://www.soas.ac.uk/lawpeacemideast/resources/file48485.pdf last accessed on April 19, 2020.

225.	Raz, Avi (2012). *The Bride and the Dowry: Israel, Jordan and the Palestinians in the Aftermath of the June 1967 War*, p.54. Yale University Press.

226.	Shtayyeh, Mohammad (2015). *Israeli Settlements and the Erosion of the Two-State Solution*, p.21. Shorok: Ramallah.

227.	Raz (2012), p.28.

228.	CIA Report including "Hebron Mayor Refutes Amman Charge of Treason" available at https://books.google.ps/books?id=Fgm7IYoW_7IC&pg=RA12-PP2&lpg=RA12-PP2&dq=sheikh+jaabari+hebron+mayor+1967&source=bl&ots=3hTax8CNyt&sig=ACfU3U3u0d2gqxfApRaUHiSZhkzuw0FyPg&hl=en&sa=X&ved=2ahUKEwj_yvukpIvrAhWRGBQKHSRDDBIQ6AEwEnoECAoQAQ#v=onepage&q=sheikh%20jaabari%20hebron%20mayor%201967&f=false last accessed on August 8, 2020.

229.	Raz (2012), p 239

230.	UN General Assembly "Resolution 2253 – Measures taken by Israel to change the status of the City of Jerusalem" 4 July 1967 available at https://unispal.un.org/DPA/DPR/unispal.nsf/0/A39A906C89D3E98685256C29006D4014 last accessed on July 19, 2020.

231.	Encyclopedia Britannica https://www.britannica.com/biography/David-Ben-Gurion last accessed on July 19, 2020.

232. PASSIA Documents on Jerusalem available at http://passia.org/media/filer_public/b4/c9/b4c92aea-22dc-462a-9860-6d44da796d82/vol-2-documents-on-jerusalem.pdf

233. The 1967 Census of the West Bank and Gaza Strip: A Digitalized Version http://www.levyinstitute.org/pubs/1967_census/dataset_doc.pdf last accessed on July 19, 2020.

234. Safieh, Afif (2010). *The Peace Process: From Breakthrough to Breakdown,* p.200. Saqi: London.

235. PASSIA Documents on Jerusalem, Vol. I, p.45. http://passia.org/media/filer_public/e7/d1/e7d1d05e-6c27-43f3-9ea4-384ad43c7746/vol-1-documents-on-jerusalem.pdf

236. Interview with Dr. Nabil Shaath.

237. https://unispal.un.org/DPA/DPR/unispal.nsf/0/7813B07830BDC77705256560006A7CB0

238. Jewish Telegraphic Agency "Israeli Police Arrest Minister, 2 Professionals in Market Bombing" available at https://www.jta.org/1969/03/05/archive/israeli-police-arrest-minister-2-professionals-in-market-bombing last accessed on 8 February 2022.

239. Raya, Arch. Joseph. *Basic Causes of Emigration*, p,15. Haifa, January 12, 1970.

240. King Abdullah II (2011) *Our Last Best Chance: The Pursuit of Peace in a Time of Peril,* p 28. Penguin Books: London.

241. Interview with Abdullah Abdullah, August 23, 2020.

242. Shlaim, Avi (2008). *Lion of Jordan: The Life of King Hussein in War and Peace,* p.321. Penguin Books: London.

243. Interview with Nicola, Amman, Jordan, September 20, 2016.

244. Interview with Fayez Saqqa, Bethlehem, August 15, 2020.

245. Pappe, Ilan (2013). *The Forgotten Palestinians: A History of the Palestinians in Israel,* p.67. Yale University Press.

246. Archbishop Raya, January 12, 1970.

247. The 961 "Meet The Lebanese Priest Who Stood Up To The Ku Klux Klan in the 1960s" avai"able at https://www.the961.com/lebanese-priest-stood-up-to-kkk/ last accessed on 8 May 2022.

248. Chacour, Elias (1992). *We belong to the land: The story of a Palestinian Israeli who lives for peace and reconciliation,* p.88. Harper San Francisco: New York.

249. Ateek, Naim (1989). *Justice, and only Justice: A Palestinian Theology of Liberation,* p.58. Orbis Books: New York.

250. Archbishop Joseph Raya, (1970), p.14.

251. Bishop Giovanni Marcuzzo (2007) in *The Forgotten Faithful: A window into the life and witness of Christians in the Holy Land,* p.134. Sabeel Ecumenical Liberation Theology Center: Jerusalem.

252. Ghandour, Hind (2017). *Naturalised Palestinians in Lebanon: Experiences of belonging, identity and citizenship.* Swinburne University. Doctoral Thesis available at https://pdfs.semanticscholar.org/b8ab/a5bc9188c8ff3317d5404fd2c4f2538c9512.pdf p.66.

253. Interview with Zahi Khoury, August 2020.

254. Learn Palestine. *Therese Halasa: Crossing the Border from 1948 Palestine to Lebanon and Joining the Revolution* available at https://www.youtube.com/watch?v=Yo-ssnV676Y last accessed on September 20, 2020.

255. PLO. *Palestinian Political Prisoners: Struggle Behind Iron Walls* available at https://samidoun.net/2020/03/remembering-therese-halasa-palestinian-revolutionary-rima-tannous-prison-story/ last accessed on September 20, 2020.

256. Anonymous interview. Ramallah, June 20, 2020.

257. His full name is omitted at the request of those who provided their testimony.

258. Anonymous interview, Ramallah, September 24, 2020.

259. Al Assifa ("the storm") was the military branch of Fatah.

260. Interview with Fr. Manuel Musallam.

261. ARIJ Atlas of Palestine, available at https://www.arij.org/atlas40/chapter2.2.html last accessed on September 27, 2020.

262. The first time was in 1948 for Abdel Qader Husseini; the second time was for Gamal Abdel Nasser (1970); the third time for Faysal Husseini (2001); and the fourth time for Shireen Abu Akleh (2022).

263. Shlaim (2008), p.359.

264. The Syrian Army did mobilize Palestinian units in the Golan, but no actions were planned for Gaza or the West Bank.

265. New York Times "Israelis Arrest Greek Catholic Archbishop on Weapons Charges", 19 August 1974, available at https://www.nytimes.com/1974/08/19/archives/israelis-arrest-greek-catholic-archbishop-on-weapons-charges-linked.html last accessed on 2 February 2022.

266. La Documentation Catholique 1975, No. 1668, pp. 98–99

267. New York Times "Arab Cleric Defies Jerusalem Court" 30 October 1974 available at https://www.nytimes.com/1974/10/30/archives/arab-cleric-defies-jerusalem-court.html last accessed on 2 February 2022.

268. New York Times "Israelis Sentence Archbishop to 12 Years for Smuggling Arms" 10 December 1974 available at https://www.nytimes.com/1974/12/10/archives/israelis-sentence-archbishop-to-12-years-for-smuggling-arms-greek.html last accessed on 2 February 2022.

269. Resolution available at A/RES/3210 (XXIX) of 14 October 1974 (un.org) last accessed on November 21, 2021.

270. Address available at https://unispal.un.org/DPA/DPR/unispal.nsf/0/A238EC7A3E13EED18525624A007697EC last accessed on 22 June 2022.

271. Ibid.

272. While officially in charge of the Palestinian intelligence services, Salah Khalaf (known as Abu Iyad) had established relations with several revolutionary movements worldwide. Unlike the PFLP's Wadie' Haddad, he did not focus operations outside the Mediterranean Levant. Fatah's collaboration with international groups, from the Uruguayan Tupamaros to the Cypriot resistance, forms part of the organization's history.

273. Al-Hout, Shafik (2011). "My Life in the PLO: The Inside Story of the Palestinian Struggle". New York: Pluto Press. p 104

274. PLO Political Program adopted on June 9, 1974. Available at PLO political programme/ "10-point programme" - 12th Palestine National Council (1-9 June 1974, Cairo) - Text/Non-UN document - Question of Palestine last accessed on December 12, 2020.

275. Separated from the PFLP, it became a member of the PLO in 1974.

276. CIA. *Individual and Group Influences on the Decision-making of Key Palestinian Organizations: A Research Paper* (February 1979). Available at 1979-02-01.pdf (cia.gov) last accessed on December 12, 2020.

277. Interview with Mahmoud Al Aloul.

278. Interview with Fr. Abdallah Joulious.

279. Interview with Mahmoud Al Aloul.

280. Interview with Fr. Abdallah Joulius, Ramallah.

281. Interview with Mahmoud Al Aloul.

282. Chomsky (1999), p.186.

283. Ibid.

284. Fisk, Robert (2001) Pity the Nation: Lebanon at War. Oxford University Press: London, p.99.

285. Interview with Mahmoud Al-Aloul.

286. Interview with Amb. Ibrahim Khraisheh.

287. Interview with Dr. Nabil Shaath.

288. Interview with Abdul Jawad Saleh, Al Bireh, Palestine, December 30, 2020.

289. A/8089 of 5 October 1970 (un.org) last accessed on January 1, 2020.

290. Ibid.

291. Interview with Abdul Jawad Saleh.

292. Gordon, Neve (2008). *Israel's Occupation*, p.105. University of California Press: Los Angeles.

293. MILITANTS SCORE SWEEPING VICTORY IN WEST BANK VOTE - The New York Times (nytimes.com) last accessed on January 2, 2021.

294. 40 Years Of Israeli Occupation (arij.org) last accessed on January 2, 2021.

295. MILITANTS SCORE SWEEPING VICTORY IN WEST BANK VOTE - The New York Times (nytimes.com) last accessed on January 2, 2021.

296. Woolfson, Marion (1981). *Bassam Shakaa: Portrait of a Palestinian*, p.47. Third World Centre: Beirut.

297. Interview in Beit Jala.

298. Archbishop Joseph Raya (1970), p.8-9.

299. The village ended up being demolished in 1981.

300. Pappe (2013), p.130.

301. Interview (anonymous) with former PFLP – EO operative on January 3, 2021.

302. Capucci Released from Jail - Jewish Telegraphic Agency (jta.org) last accessed on January 4, 2021.

303. Israel Deports Prelate Jailed for Gunrunning - The Washington Post last accessed on January 4, 2021.

304. Interview with Dr. Nasser Al Qudwa.

305. Palestine Leader At Vatican For Talks - from the Catholic Herald Archive last accessed on January 5, 2021.

306. Argentina and Chile Accept Papal Effort in Dispute - The New York Times (nytimes.com) last accessed on January 8, 2020.

307. Strange Bedfellows: The Pope and the PLO - The Washington Post Washington Post, January 24, 1982.

308. "Treaty of Peace Between the Arab Republic of Egypt and the State of Israel" available at https://www.mfa.gov.eg/Lists/Treaties/Attachments/2278/Peace%20Treaty_en.pdf last accessed on June 14, 2019.

309. Interview with Dr. Nabeel Shaath.

310. Washington Post, June 3, 1980 Terrorist Bombs Maim 2 Mayors On West Bank - The Washington Post last accessed on January 9, 2020.

311. Pedahzur, Ami & Perliger, Arie (2009). *Jewish Terrorism in Israel*, p.39-53. New York: Columbia University Press.

312. Chicago Tribune, July 11, 1985 ISRAELI COURT CONVICTS 3 JEWS IN TERRORIST KILLING OF ARABS - Chicago Tribune last accessed on January 9, 2020.

313. Haaretz March 5, 2018 Terrorist sponsorship for a night - Opinion - Haaretz. com last accessed on January 9, 2020.

314. Washington Post, March 26, 1982 Israel Fires 2 Mayors in West Bank - The Washington Post last accessed on January 9, 2020.

315. Ibid.

316. Basic Law: Jerusalem, Capital of Israel (knesset.gov.il) last accessed on January 8, 2020.

317. S/RES/478 (1980) of 20 August 1980 (un.org) last accessed on January 8, 2020.

318. PASSIA Documents. Vol II, p.219-220.

319. S/RES/465 (1980) of 1 March 1980 (un.org) last accessed on January 8, 2020.

320. Jerusalem/Holy places - Position of the Holy See - Letter from the Holy See - Question of Palestine (un.org) last accessed on January 8, 2020.

321. Ibid.

322. PASSIA Documents on Jerusalem. Vol II, p.25.

323. New York Times Egypt Calls Begin Remarks 'Inappropriate' - The New York Times (nytimes.com) March 21, 1979. Last accessed on January 8, 2020.

324. PASSIA Documents on Jerusalem. Vol II, p.217.

325. Haaretz, 14 May 2005, available at PART 2: The unseen village - Israel News - Haaretz.com last accessed on 23 June 2022.

326. One Magazine, Fall 1976. Jerusalem's Latin Patriarch | CNEWA last accessed on January 8, 2021.

327. PASSIA Documents on Jerusalem. Vol I, p.51.

328. Ibid.

329. PASSIA Documents on Jerusalem. Vol I, p.52.

330. Fatah has a revolutionary council that serves as its parliament. This is not the same "revolutionary council" as that of Abu Nidal's organization.

331. *Al Fajr* newspaper, Vol II No. 58 June 7-13, 1981, p.6.

332. Sayigh, Yezid (1997). *Armed Struggle and the Search for State: The Palestinian National Movement 1949-1993,* p.518. Oxford University Press.

333. *The Guardian*, February 24, 2003. Shlomo Argov | Israel | The Guardian last accessed on January 10, 2020.

334. Hadawi (1991), p.280.

335. Chomsky (1999), p.213.

336. *Time Magazine.* "Cover Story: The Holy Alliance" June 24, 2001. Available at Cover Story: The Holy Alliance - TIME

337. Shlaim (2014), p.96.

338. Pope John Paul II met privately with PLO chief... - UPI Archives Last accessed on April 16, 2021.

339. Ibid.

340. ARAFAT SEES POPE AND ITALY'S LEADER - The New York Times (nytimes.com) last accessed on April 16, 2021.

341. The Sabra and Shatila Massacre: New Evidence | Institute for Palestine Studies (palestine-studies.org) last accessed on April 16, 2021.

342. Shultz, George P. (1993). *Turmoil and Triumph: My Years as Secretary of State*, p.105. Maxwell Macmillan International: New York.

343. Interview with Johnny Abu Eid, April 24, 2021.

344. Ibid.

345. World Council of Churches, Sixth Assembly Statement on the Middle East, Vancouber, Canada, July/August 1983. Available at PASSIA (2007) Documents on Palestine – Vol III 1974-1987, p.378. PASSIA: Jerusalem.

346. AP "Today's Topic: Elia Khoury, Anglican Bishop, PLO Activist", January 16, 1985, available at TODAY'S TOPIC:Elia Khoury, Anglican Bishop, PLO Activist (apnews.com) last accessed on April 30, 2021.

347. Interview with former Baathist member, Beit Jala, November 2021.

348 *Journal of Palestine Studies*, Vol. 14, No. 2, Winter 1985.

349. Jordanian Prime Minister Zaid Ar-Rifai, Statement Regarding an International Middle East Conference, Amman, May 3, 1987.

350. Gordon (2008) p.148.

351. Anonymous interview, Bethlehem, 2020.

352. Interview with Fr. Faysal Hijazeen, Ramallah, August 2011.

353. A few years later, no longer under the leadership of Bishop Marcuzzo, the name of the map ended up being changed to "Holy Land".

354. Interview with Patriarch Michael Sabbah.

355. Ibid.

356. Settlers in West Bank Kill a Palestinian - The New York Times (nytimes.com) last accessed on May 7, 2021.

357. Sketches Of Nine Palestinians Ordered Deported With PM-Israel-Violence (apnews.com) last accessed on May 7, 2021.

358. Patriarch Michael Sabbah (2005). *Pastoral Letters – Latin Patriarch of Jerusalem,* p.17. Latin Patriarchate Printing Press: Jerusalem.

359. The story is told in the Canadian/Palestinian documentary *The Wanted 18* by directors Amer Shomali and Paul Cowan, released in 2014.

360. Draft resolution S/20945/Rev.1 available at United Nations Official Document Last accessed on May 7, 2021.

361. Interview with Patriarch Michael Sabbah.

362. Declaration of Independence as submitted by Palestine to the United Nations on November 18, 1988 available at A/43/827-S/20278 of 18 November 1988 (un.org) last accessed on May 7, 2021.

363. *The Guardian* November 16, 1988 available at From the archive, 16 November 1988: Troops stifle West Bank rejoicing | Palestinian territories | The Guardian last accessed on May 7, 2021.

364. Address by President Yasser Arafat to the UN General Assembly, December 13, 1988 A/43/PV.78 of 3 January 1989 (un.org)

365. *Los Angeles Times*, December 24, 1988 available at Pope Meets Arafat, Urges Negotiations to Settle Mideast Crisis - Los Angeles Times (latimes.com) last accessed on May 7, 2021.

366. Al Haq (1989). *A Nation Under Siege*, p.22. Ramallah.

367. Ibid, p.327.

368. *New York Times* June 14, 1988 available at Over Protests, Israel Expels Palestinian-American - The New York Times (nytimes.com) last accessed on May 7, 2021.

369. New York Times, 24 December 1989, available at Tutu, Visiting Jerusalem, Backs Palestinian Statehood - The New York Times (nytimes.com) last accessed on 7 February 2022.

370. Passia Documents on Jerusalem, Vol. 1, p.53.

371. BEATING VICTIMS' ANGER FESTERS - The Washington Post Last checked on May 7, 2021.

372. S/RES/611(1988) - E - S/RES/611(1988) -Desktop (undocs.org)

373. Al Haq (1989). *A Nation Under Siege*. Turbo: Ramallah.

374. Interview with Fr. Peter Madros.

375. PASSIA Documents on Palestine – Vol. IV, p.31.

376. PASSIA Documents on Jerusalem – Vol. I, p.53.

377. The Episcopal Church in Jerusalem and the Middle East, Diocesan Council Report 1987/1988. P 90.

378. PASSIA Documents on Jerusalem - Vol 1, p.54.

379. News report from 23 April 1990 (New York Times and Los Angeles Times) available at Israel admits financing Jerusalem settlement (tampabay.com) last accessed on 23 June 2022.

380. In Old Jerusalem, Christians and Muslims Protest Settlement - The New York Times (nytimes.com)

381. PASSIA Documents on Jerusalem – Vol 1, p.57.

382. Al Haq (1989). *Punishing a Nation: Human Rights Violations During the Palestinian Uprising: December 1987-December 1988,* p.134. Ramallah.

383. Israeli practices - SpCttee annual report - Question of Palestine (un.org) last accessed on 14 February 2022.

384. Interview with Nader Abuamsha, 14 February 2022.

385. A/43/694 of 24 October 1988 (un.org) last accessed on 1 August 2021.

386. A/43/694 of 24 October 1988 (un.org) last accessed on 1 August 2021.

387. Sabbah (2005), p.46.

388. *Los Angeles Times*, 22 June 1990 Colonel Says Rabin Ordered Breaking of Palestinians' Bones - Los Angeles Times (latimes.com) last accessed on August 21, 2021.

389. New York Times, 20 January 1993, available at Israeli Parliament Lifts a Ban on P.L.O. Contacts - The New York Times (nytimes.com) last accessed on 4 May 2022.

390. Shamir, Yitzhak (1994). *Summing Up: An Autobiography*, p.197. Weidenfeld and Nicolson: London.

391. PASSIA Documents on Palestine -Vol IV, p.137-138.

392. Interview with member of the Palestinian delegation, Ramallah, August 2020.

393. Ibid.

394. Shlaim (2014), p 506.

395. Shlaim (2010), p 210

396. PASSIA Documents on Palestine – Vol. IV, p.213.

397. Safieh, Afif (1999). *Children of a Lesser God?* Palestinian General Delegation to the UK and the Office of Representation of the PLO to the Holy See: London.

398. *New York Times* June 27, 1992 Shamir Is Said to Admit Plan To Stall Talks 'for 10 Years' - The New York Times (nytimes.com) last accessed on September 4, 2021.

399. Interview with Nabil Shaath.

400. Interview with member of the delegation to the Washington talks.

401. Edward Said in the *London Review of Books*, Vol. 15 No 20, October 21, 1993, available at Edward Said · The Morning After · LRB 21 October 1993 last accessed on September 11, 2021.

402. Interview with Dr. Nabil Shaath, Ramallah, 2020.

403. Btselem (1991 March). *Interrogation of Palestinians During the Intifada: Ill-Treatment, 'Moderate Physical Pressure' or Torture?* Available at Interrogation of Palestinians During the Intifada: Ill-Treatment, "Moderate Physical Pressure" or Torture? | [site:name (btselem.org) last accessed on September 12, 2021.

404. Interview with an official of the Latin Patriarchate, August 2021..

405. Interview with Dr. Mai Kaila, 19 February 2022.

406. Interview with Armenian leader (Jerusalem), June 2022.

407. Interview with Abbas Zaki, June 2021.

408. Interview with Jonathan Kuttab, October 3, 2021.

409. Ibid.

410. Jerusalem letter – FM Peres available at Jerusalem letter- FM Peres - Text/Non UN-document - Question of Palestine last accessed on October 4, 2021.

411. New York Times 23 December 1994 available at Bethlehem Journal; On Manger Square, Joyful Tidings Are Delayed - The New York Times (nytimes.com) last accessed on October 4, 2021.

412. PASSIA Documents on Palestine – Vol. IV: 8. Middle East Peace Negotiations, p.447.

413. PASSIA Documents on Jerusalem - Vol. I,p.66.

414. Interview (anonymous), Bethlehem. December 2018.

415. Interview with Fayez Saqqa, Bethlehem. December 2018.

416. BADIL Resource Center for Palestinian Residency and Refugee Rights - The Palestinian Crisis in Libya 1994-1996 (Interview with Professor Bassem Sirhan) last accessed on October 5, 2021.

417. Akiva Eldar available at Israel admits it revoked residency rights of a quarter million Palestinians - Haaretz Com - Haaretz.com last accessed on October 10, 2021.

418. The *Achille Lauro* was a ship hijacked by members of the Palestine Liberation Front (PLF), headed by Mohammad Abu Abbas, on its way from Alexandria (Egypt) to Ashdod (Israel). The incident ended with the killing of a disabled Jewish-American citizen called Leon Klinghoffer. The PLO always denied its participation in the attack.

419. *Los Angeles Times*, 14 October 1985, available at Britain Drops Talks With PLO Leaders : Pledge to Renounce Violence Not Kept, Foreign Office Says - Los Angeles Times (latimes.com) last accessed on September 12, 2021.

420. Palestinian General Delegation in the United Kingdom and the Office of Representation of the PLO to the Holy See (1998). *On the eve of the new Millennium,* p.40. Self-publication. London.

421. Ibid.

422. Full text available at IL JO_941026_PeaceTreatyIsraelJordan.pdf (un.org) last accessed on October 6, 2021.

423. Ibid.

424. Muasher, Marwan (2008). *The Arab Center,* p.36. Yale University Press: New Haven.

425. Ibid, p.40.

426. Full agreement available at Fundamental Agreement-Israel-Holy See (mfa. gov.il) last accessed on October 6, 2021.

427. PASSIA Documents on Jerusalem, Volume I p.72.

428. Interview with Dr. Saeb Erekat, December 2017.

429. Palestinian Central Elections Commission. *The 1996 Presidential and Legislative Elections*, available at Microsoft Word - Document7 (elections.ps) last accessed on October 8, 2021.

430. Interview with Dr. Saeb Erekat.

431. *Washington Post* available at SUMMIT CONCLUDES WITH LITTLE PROGRESS - The Washington Post last accessed on October 6, 2021.

432. PASSIA Documents on Jerusalem – Vol. I, p.79.

433. Ibid, p.81.

434. Michael Dumper. "The Christian Churches of Jerusalem in the Post-Oslo Period" in *Journal of Palestine Studies*, Vol. 31, No. 2 (Winter 2002), p.56.

435. Bishop Kafity also served as part of the Advisory Committee to the Orient House in Jerusalem and was decorated by President Yasser Arafat in 1997 being the first recipient of the "Star of Jerusalem".

436. United Nations SPEAKERS REAFFIRM SUPPORT FOR BETHLEHEM 2000 PROJECT AND JUST PEACE IN MIDDLE EAST REGION | Meetings Coverage and Press Releases (un.org) last accessed on October 6, 2021.

437. UN Resolution 53/27 available at Bethlehem 2000 - GA resolution - Question of Palestine (un.org) last accessed on October 6, 2021.

438. UN Website S/PV.3747 of 7 March 1997 (un.org) last accessed on October 8, 2021.

439. UN Security Council 3756 meeting, March 21, 1997, available at pdf (undocs. org) last accessed on October 8, 2021.

440. PASSIA Documents on Jerusalem - Vol.1, p.91.

441. Ibid, p.92.

442. PASSIA Documents on Palestine Vol.V, p.432.

443. Ibid, p.436.

444. Anonymous interview with Latin Patriarchate priest, Ramallah, June 2021.

445. Speech by Pope Francis at Al Maghtas, March 22, 2000, available at Jubilee Pilgrimage to the Holy Land: Visit to Al-Maghtas, place of Christ's Baptism (March 22, 2000) | John Paul II (vatican.va) last accessed on October 14, 2021.

446. Basic Agreement Between the Holy See and the Palestine Liberation Organization available at Basic Agreement between the Holy See and the Palestine Liberation Organization (vatican.va) last accessed on October 14, 2021.

447. Ibid.

448. Speech of Pope John Paul II at Dheisheh Refugee Camp, March 22, 2000, available at Jubilee Pilgrimage to the Holy Land: Visit to the Refugee Deheisheh Camp (March 22, 2000) | John Paul II (vatican.va) last accessed on October 14, 2021.

449. *The Guardian* "Pope's passionate plea for Palestinian homeland" March 22, 2000, available at Pope's passionate plea for Palestinian homeland | Israel | The Guardian last accessed on October 14, 2021.

450. Speech of Pope John Paul II at welcoming ceremony in Bethlehem March 22, 2000, available at Jubilee Pilgrimage to the Holy Land: Welcome Ceremony in the Palestinian Autonomous Territories (Bethlehem Airport) (March 22, 2000) | John Paul II (vatican.va) last accessed on October 14, 2021.

451. Interview with Dr. Nabil Shaath, Ramallah, June 2020.

452. Haniyeh, Akram (2001). *Camp David Papers*, p.53. Available at «Ë—«,†«„— Â†ÁÊÍ…†»«‰«ÊÃ‰Í"Í… (miftah.org)

453. PASSIA Documents on Jerusalem - Vol.1, p.108.

454. Haniyeh (2001), p.53.

455. Interview with Dr. Nabil Shaath.

456. Interview with Dr. Saeb Erekat.

457. Trilateral Statement on the Middle East Peace Summit at Camp David, July 25, 2000. Available at Mideast peace process/Camp David Summit (July 2000) - Trilateral statement/Non-UN document - Question of Palestine last accessed on October 10, 2021.

458. Interview with Dr. Nabil Shaath.

459. UNSC Resolution 1322, October 7, 2000, available at S/RES/1322 (2000) of 7 October 2000 (un.org) last accessed on October 15, 2021.

460. PASSIA Documents on Palestine - Vol.VI, p.79.

461. Ibid, p.84.

462. Ibid, p.85.

463. Ibid, p.86.

464. Ibid, p.92.

465. Interview with Dr. Nabil Shaath.

466. PASSIA Documents on Jerusalem - Vol.I, p.119.

467. Address of Pope John Paul II to the new Ambassador of the Republic of Lebanon to the Holy See, October 26, 2021, available at To the Ambassador of Lebanon accredited to the Holy See on the occasion of the presentation of Credentials (October 26, 2000) | John Paul II (vatican.va) last accessed on October 14, 2021.

468. The New York Times, 11 November 2000, available at Fighting in Mideast Blocks Wave of Christian Tourism - The New York Times (nytimes.com) last accessed on 23 June 2022.

469. AP, December 25, 2000, available at Gloomy Christmas in Bethlehem (apnews.com) last accessed on October 15, 2021.

470. *New York Times*, December 5, 1999, available at Arafat Opens Bethlehem 2000 Festivities (nytimes.com) last accessed on October 15, 2021.

471. Moratinos' non-paper available at Moratinos' "Non-Paper" on Taba negotiations - Non-UN document - Question of Palestine last accessed on October 15, 2021.

472. Interview with Latin Patriarchate official, 2018.

473. POICA Israeli Forces Re-Occupy Beit Jala – POICA last accessed October 17, 2021.

474. Ibid.

475. Rev. Fadi Diab available at West Bank church stands with unjustly incarcerated parishioner Layan Nasir – Mondoweiss last accessed on 3 May 2022.

476. Washington Post, 22 October 2021, available at In Bethlehem, Altar Boy›s Death Brings Conflict Home - The Washington Post last accessed on 7 May 2022.

477. The Guardian, 24 October 2021, available at Sharon defies US demand to retreat | World news | The Guardian last accessed on 7 May 2022.

478. Available at Chronological Review of Events/October 2001 - DPR review - Question of Palestine (un.org) last accessed on 7 May 2022.

479. Arab Peace Initiative available at Arab Peace Initiative - LAS Summit - Letter from Lebanon (excerpts) - Question of Palestine (un.org) last accessed on October 17, 2021.

480. *New York Times* available at MIDEAST TURMOIL: HOLY PLACES; A Church and a Site Revered by 3 Faiths - The New York Times (nytimes.com) last accessed on November 21, 2021.

481. *Haaretz* "Palestinians Deny Hostages Held in Nativity Church" available at Palestinians deny hostages held in Nativity Church - Haaretz Com - Haaretz.com last accessed on November 21, 2021.

482. AP, May 2, 2002 available at WRAP Ramallah pullout, prisoners, Arafat, Bethlehem, Israeli reax - YouTube last accessed on October 17, 2021.

483. BBC BBC News | MIDDLE EAST | Vatican outrage over church siege last accessed on October 17, 2021.

484. *New York Times* MIDEAST TURMOIL: THE OVERVIEW; EXILE AGREEMENT APPEARS TO SETTLE BETHLEHEM SIEGE - The New York Times (nytimes.com) last accessed on October 17, 2021.

485. POICA Uprooting of Olive trees in Aboud Village – POICA last accessed on October 17, 2021.

486. Interview with Fr. Emmanuel Awwad, Aboud, December 2020.

487. UN OCHA. *Costs of Conflict: The Changing Face of Bethlehem*, December 1, 2004. Available at Costs of conflict: the changing face of Bethlehem - OCHA report - Question of Palestine (un.org) last accessed on October 17, 2021.

488. Chicago Tribune, 27 March 2003, available at Parents mourn daughter killed in West Bank gunfight – Chicago Tribune last accessed on 7 May 2022.

489. Haaretz, 17 March 2003, available at Parents mourn daughter killed in West Bank gunfight – Chicago Tribune last accessed on 7 May 2022.

490. The Guardian, 28 August 2012, available at Rachel Corrie›s death was an accident, Israeli judge rules | Rachel Corrie | The Guardian last accessed on 7 May 2022.

491. Haaretz, 23 August 2012, available at U.S.: Israeli probe into Rachel Corrie›s death wasn't 'credible' - Haaretz Com - Haaretz.com last accessed on 7 May 2022.

492. Road Map available at IL PS_030430_PerformanceBasedRoadmapTwo-StateSolution.pdf (un.org) last accessed on October 17, 2021.

493. Sabbah (2005), p.153.

494. PASSIA Documents on Palestine – Vol.VII, p.199.

495. ICJ Opinion available at 131-20040709-ADV-01-00-EN.pdf (icj-cij.org) last accessed on October 17, 2021.

496. Separate Opinion by Judge Elaraby available at 131-20040709-ADV-01-06-EN.pdf (icj-cij.org) last accessed on October 17, 2021.

497. Interview with Dr. Nabil Shaath.

498. Interview with Laila Chahid, October 18, 2021.

499. *Irish Times*, October 29, 2004 available at Arafat to fly to Paris for care (irishtimes.com) last accessed on October 18, 2021.

500. Interview with Laila Chahid.

501. Interview with Nabil Shaath.

502. Available at Mahmoud Darwish - Yasser Arafat Foundation (yaf.ps) last accessed on October 19, 2021.

503. Sabbah (2005), p.50.

Index

I

Y

Z